Battles for Delhi

-Dilli Kareeb Ast

Battles for Delhi

-Dilli Kareeb Ast

Rajeev Katyal

Foreword by David Frawley (Pandit Vamadeva)

Indus Source Books

Indian Spirit, Universal Wisdom

Indus Source Books
PO Box 6194
Malabar Hill PO
Mumbai 400 006
INDIA
Email: info@indussource.com
www.indussource.com

Battles for Delhi: Dilli Kareeb Ast

Published in India by
Indus Source Books, Mumbai

First published in 2016

ISBN: 978-81-88569-87-8

Printed at Thomson Press (I) Ltd.

Contents

To the memory of my parents

Late Dr. M.L. Katyal and Late Mrs. Krishna Katyal

Author's Note

When I got down to writing this book, the motive was twofold. First was the need to contribute more to the understanding of Indian history among Indians by writing about it. Relatively little writing has been done by Indians on their own history resulting in a lack of knowledge of our history among our own people. Secondly, we live in an increasingly volatile world, in a very dangerous neighbourhood. Without being unduly paranoid, security of the nation cannot be taken for granted.

I thought the best way to present history is to string together a series of momentous events that present moments of truth where India's security as a nation was either strengthened or jeopardised, all thanks to its own people. The objective was to increase knowledge of such events in the minds of Indians and help the nation learn from its past. I was much motivated by a play I read in my school St. Columba's called *Dhruvswamini* by Jaishankar Prasad. He said history should be written for people to learn for the present. The book encapsulates knowledge of all I have read in history in my life and hopefully is the harbinger of more to come.

I think what we are we owe to our elders. I have dedicated this book to my late parents Dr. M.L. Katyal and Smt. Krishna Katyal, an educationist. I cannot forget my grandfather Shri Sewa Ram Julka who laid the foundation of my education, my grandmother Smt. Dhanwanti Julka who read so much on history, most of which I read too, and my aunt Tripta Julka who brought me most of the books to read.

A special thanks to my wife Preeti, who I believe is potentially a much better writer than me. My sons Arjun and Shiva, the first an IT professional and the second a student of history in Delhi University. A silent tribute to my father-in-law Col. H.S. Ahluwalia and a thank you to my mother-in-law Santosh Ahluwalia, and my sister Meenakshi.

A huge thanks to Indus Source Books and its owner Ms. Sonavi Desai who had the guts to take up the work of a first time author. A big thanks to Mr. R.P. Jain, owner of Motilal Banarsidass who has been friend, philosopher, and guide in this entire process; Naveen Pandey, my colleague who took me into the publishing industry; my colleague Ms. Aditi Chakaraborty who has been a pillar of support in guiding me on how to launch this book; and Rajesh, for all the pictures.

My friends GK, Rajnish Virmani and Uday Mathur who went through the text to help me. National Museum, Delhi, for kindly consenting to provide pictures for the book. The museum staff of Ms. Joyoti Roy and Surichika Chawla and others were professionalism exemplified. To mentors like Dr. MGK Menon, Prof. Aftab Seth, Prof. Ashvini Agrawal, Lt. General Sudhir Sharma who provided the quotes to a new author's book. And to my organisation, Global Indian International School for encouraging me all the way through.

I hope the book provides relevant reading material and that too to a critical mass. That is every author's hope. If this hope sees culmination in success, I would want to write more, just to contribute to increasing knowledge of Indian history. To me, India is the most fascinating country in the world.

Foreword

India has possessed a powerful culture and a great civilisation over the last five thousand years that has dominated South and East Asia, as well as influenced Central and West Asia, and Europe. Yet India's affluence has also made it vulnerable to attacks by outside forces seeking to benefit from the fabled wealth of the country.

The history of Delhi is to a great extent the history of India, particularly in recent centuries. Delhi has been the throne of the country that each faction has hoped to occupy and rule by its sanction. This struggle for Delhi has not just been with outside invaders but also with the different groups within India itself, striving for supremacy—sometimes making alliances with invaders for their own benefit but to the detriment of the country as a whole.

Delhi became a great city at the end of the Vedic era when it was the Indraprastha of the Mahabharata. People had moved from the Sarasvati River that was drying up to the more reliable waters of the Yamuna. This shift of the rivers occurred around four thousand years ago according to the Geological Survey of India. Delhi remained important historically throughout the following centuries and became the dominant city, if not capital, of India over the last thousand years.

This means that studying and understanding Delhi's history provides many secrets and much insight into the history of India. Delhi's tragedies have often been the tragedies of the country as a whole and of the entire region.

The current book, *Battles for Delhi*, offers much important insight and information. This covers first of all the outer facts of Delhi's history and the many intrigues around it that have followed one after the other through various dynasties across the centuries. But the book also extends to the national and spiritual implications of these crucial events in Delhi, which have deeply affected the culture of India on various levels. The book is worthy of extensive examination by all those deeply concerned not only about the past but also about the future of India.

Though having a broad cultural unity extending to Southeast Asia, India has seldom sustained a political unity as a country overall. It has witnessed the rise and fall of several large empires, but few of these have ruled the region as a whole. For such a large subcontinent, however, political unity is naturally very difficult to achieve.

China has been the only country of India's size that has been able to maintain a strong unitary rule throughout its history. This rested upon an enduring military tradition that often ruthlessly crushed any opposition to the emperors, and on a strong sense of national unity in the common people, which India was rarely able to create.

We should note that Europe has failed at political unity even more so than India—though it had a common culture, and its nation states themselves had vast empires on several continents during the colonial era. Even today, the future of the European Union, which is primarily an economic union, remains in doubt. Like Europe, India has often been fragmented by strong regional interests and a greater political loyalty to a particularly section of the country or local culture in the subcontinent that did not extend to the country as a whole.

This lack of political unity made India vulnerable to outside forces, even though it had extensive human and economic resources that were often much greater than those of the conquering invaders. India fell according to a divide and conquer strategy from the outside, that was able to benefit by the deep-seated divisions within the country.

This battle for India, as the author notes, is not over, but is simply in a new phase. Yet today the battle for Delhi is a media battle more than it is a physical battle, a scripted clash of political and economic policies and ideologies, East and West, ancient and modern.

Delhi is the home of the political, cultural, intellectual and media elite of modern India, which often thinks its can rule or guide the country as a whole. The curious thing is that though Delhi is the capital of India, we find significant anti-nationalistic sentiments in Delhi itself, including the prevalence of the views that do not seem to honour or follow the dharmic ethos of the region. Delhi intellectuals seem more at home copying the latest trends in Western thought. Marxism remains a formidable ideological force in the Delhi intelligentsia, though not a single truly Marxist country in the world remains.

For this new battle of Delhi, a new group of defenders of India are necessary at a cultural level. Such individuals must understand the greater culture of India but also have the tools to express that to the modern world and debate any opponents in a skilful manner. Otherwise the same divide and conquer strategy that has so often worked at a military level can be successful at a cultural level, with India losing its historical culture to outside trends.

The current book provides a thorough, interesting and thought-provoking analysis of the history of Delhi from ancient times to the present day. It brings alive the fascinating dramas and intrigues that have occurred over the centuries, and the notable personalities involved in these. It examines with depth and clarity the factors that have prevented India from being united, and from responding with a united front to foreign invasions since the time the Greeks first assaulted India over two thousand years ago to the British a few centuries ago.

Battles for Delhi documents what has often been a great political and cultural failure of India, based upon placing local, regional and family interests over any national concern. The book provides both helpful guidance and a clear warning for the future that Indians overall should carefully regard when they consider the future of their nation. Delhi remains a battle on many levels and will likely continue to be so for the foreseeable future. Let us hope that a higher Dharma prevails, but that requires both a special effort and a special insight!

~ David Frawley (Pandit Vamadeva)
July 2015

CHAPTER I

Centrality and Inclusiveness of Governance

INDIA HAS BEEN A LAND THAT HAS ATTRACTED CONQUERORS through the ages. Semiramis, Darius, Alexander, the Mongols, Huns, Arabs, Turks and the British are some of the people who have attacked India over centuries. Some have had the desire to plunder India's fabulous riches while others have had the desire to establish an empire here. Whenever these forces have succeeded, India has seen capitulation to foreign invaders followed by massacres, ruin and loot, as well as the destruction of cultural and architectural symbols dear to it. Whenever these invading forces have been defeated, the ruling dynasty has succeeded in preserving the people, culture and wealth of India.

A lot of attention has been paid to those battles that have been decisive in terms of the defeat of the forces ruling India and where the invaders have been successful. These battles have resulted in unwanted destruction in India and the emergence of new empires. The three battles of Panipat, and the battles of Delhi and Tarain to name a few, have become well-known. But in the continuum of history, that is not the only way things happened. The battles that led to the defeats of India have happened not one after another but after considerable intervals. In between these battles, there have been numerous instances where existing Indian empires and kingdoms have triumphed over the foreign invaders, be it the defeat of Seleucus by Chandragupta Maurya, of the Arabs by the Rajput kingdoms, of the Mongols by Allaudin Khilji or of the British by the Marathas and the Mysoreans. The war history of India has not just been one of defeats and subjugation of India by foreign invaders. In between these defeats, strong Indian kingdoms have, time and again, inflicted defeats on invaders and preserved the unity and integrity of India.

However, so incessant has been the influx of invading forces into India, that at critical points of time the invading forces have succeeded and this has led to a change in the ruling dynasty or the governing entity. Whenever India has been strong, these invaders have been defeated.

History has shown that whenever India had a strong empire or kingdom, ruled by emperors or kings who were capable military commanders, governing from a capital city but ruling over a large area of India under a strong hand, the invaders have been defeated. The defeat of Seleucus the Greek by the Mauryas; the defeat of the Huns by Skandagupta; the defeat of invading Arabs by Rajputs and Pratiharas; the defeat of the Mongols by the Khiljis; the Mughals defeating the Afghans; and the defeats inflicted on the British by Hyder Ali and Mahadji Scindia are cases in point.

However, history has also shown that whenever the strength of the ruling kingdom waned on account of the passage of time, and there was a debilitation of economic and military resources with successor kings being weak, India has lost to invaders. So the Greeks overcame a weaker Maurya empire; the Huns overran the Gupta domains in the later stages of the Gupta empire; the Turks defeated the Rajputs; Taimur defeated a weak Tughlaq kingdom; the Mughals defeated the Lodhis; the Persians under Nadir Shah defeated the Mughals under Mohammed Shah Rangila; and the British defeated the Mysoreans and the Marathas.

The Greeks could not defeat the Mauryas as long as strong emperors like Chandragupta and Bindusara ruled. They overcame weaker Maurya rulers later. The Huns were defeated by a strong Gupta emperor in Skandagupta but they defeated the later Guptas. Arabs and Turks tried hard but could not defeat the strong Pratiharas and the Rajput confederacy. It was an internecine struggle between Rajputs that resulted in Ghori emerging triumphant and planting Islamic rule in India. The invaders from the northwest could not have dared enter India as long as strong kings like Allaudin Khilji and Ghiyasuddin Tughlaq were in place. They succeeded via Taimur when a weak kingdom of Mahmud Shah Tughlaq existed. The Mughals would have found Sikander Lodhi a hard nut to crack. They succeeded against a weak Ibrahim Lodhi whose rule was racked by internal rebellions. The Persians would not have dared touch India under a Shah Jahan or an Aurangzeb, who were formidable emperors and generals. They defeated a weak Mughal empire under a debauched Mohammed Shah Rangila. The British, for all their bluster, did not dare raise their voice against a Jahangir or Shah Jahan or Aurangzeb. Even Nawab Alivardi Khan was left alone by them in Bengal. They tasted defeat against strong generals like Hyder Ali of Mysore and Mahadji Scindia near Pune. They succeeded against Siraj ud-Daulah, a weak ruler, in Bengal; Tipu Sultan who fought them alone; and against Daulat Rao Scindia who was a weak successor to Mahadji Scindia.

The history of India, therefore, has not been about a string of defeats by foreign invaders alone. We remember these defeats because they represent milestones that saw new empires take over. The periods between these defeats also include sagas of heroic and successful defence against invading forces and substantial defeats handed out to them by Indians. King Dahir defeated the Arabs on a few occasions before succumbing to Mohammed Bin Qasim. The Guptas resisted foreign invasions for a long period before weakening and losing.

When we look at these successful defences, certain things stand out. First and foremost, a strong and large kingdom existed that could lead such a defence against a foreign invasion. The Maurya, Gupta, Khilji, Pratihara and Mughal empires are some of the prime examples. So are the Mysore kingdom and the Maratha Confederacy. Secondly, the kingdom or empire that was successful in the defence of India was economically strong and administratively well-managed through a network of provincial governors, the fountainhead of which was a centrally led government with a well established ruling infrastructure. Akbar, Chandragupta Maurya, and Chandragupta Vikramaditya, among others, ensured the emergence of strong centrally led governance in India. Thirdly, the rulers who led such empires or kingdoms were not only strong rulers but also militarily very capable. They were capable of leading large armies in battle and of taking the enemy head on. Chandragupta Maurya defeated Seleucus, Chandragupta Vikramaditya defeated the Sakas, Nagabhatta Pratihara defeated the Arabs, Allaudin Khilji defeated the Mongols, Hyder Ali and Mahadji defeated the British, and Akbar pushed back the Afghans and Persians.

These emperors and kings ensured economic prosperity through efficient governance that enabled them to field large, well-equipped armies in the field. Moreover, by leading personally and using capable commanders, they led armies in a state of forward defence and also of defence in depth, ensuring the defeat of enemy forces. Chandragupta defeated Seleucus by aggressively moving forward and challenging his mighty Greek army. Allaudin Khilji routed the Mongols and then sent his best general, Ghiyasuddin Tughlaq, to pound them into submission in Afghanistan. Mahadji Scindia forced an abject surrender of British forces in the Western Ghats. Hyder Ali dictated terms at Madras, now called Chennai, to the British.

These empires or large kingdoms always operated from a central or capital city from where the power of the ruler emanated to all corners of his domain. The ruling polity operated from this central place of governance and the administrative as well as military infrastructure was controlled from there. Large armies were placed to secure the central citadels, and military governors were equipped with strong forces in *suba*s and forward areas to deter and defeat oncoming forces.

The Mughals always kept the Persians engaged in Kabul and Kandahar. This forward defence policy, coupled with large forces positioned in districts and the centre, deterred the Persians from even remotely contemplating coming into India. Allaudin Khilji did the same against the Mongols. After defeating the British in the First Anglo-Maratha War near Pune, Mahadji Scindia spiritedly engaged them in Central India. The imperial capital, be it Delhi or Pataliputra or Pune, was removed from threat as the enemy was pressed into submission and fear near or in its own territories. Thereby the core centre of the empire, existing in the imperial capital, was always safe to govern and strengthen the empire further.

A weak ruler resulted in the empire becoming weaker economically and militarily. The capacity for proactive forward defence was lost along with a corresponding loss of strength of the military at the centre. Defeat became inevitable against a strong invader. A peace-oriented Emperor Ashoka may have led to a militarily less aggressive Mauryan empire and the pincering of its defences by the Greeks. Weak Gupta rulers after Skandagupta would have led to capitulation to the Huns. After Aurangzeb, a succession of feeble rulers led to a lack of defence of the Northwest, incapable armies and the sack of Delhi by Nadir Shah. A weak Daulat Rao Scindia meant the decimation of the Maratha Confederacy at the hands of the British.

Every empire or kingdom has had its zenith and fall. The highs saw strong rulers who were also strong generals, and strong armies ready to provide defence in depth as also proactive defence against enemies.

The ruin came when strong rulers ceased to exist, kings did not have the military sagacity or capability, and governance started becoming weak. This happened when the empire was riddled with corruption, or when weak rulers, dependent upon strong nobles, came to the throne. An air of decadence started prevailing and soon pervaded the realms of the kingdom. The enemy outside was incessantly knocking at the doors. And sooner or later, a persistent enemy found an entry, then created a bigger gap and surged through to overwhelm what had hitherto been an impregnable kingdom.

The British succeeded in ruling India as they conquered a divided India in stages. Under the Grand Mughals, they were subservient traders. The Persians kept knocking on the doors of India's Northwest only to sweep in against a lethargic Mohammed Shah Rangila. The Huns did the same to the Guptas and the Turks to the Rajputs.

Large kingdoms and empires are symbolised by, and derive their source of power from, the imperial capital. That is where the rulers govern from. The rise and fall of kingdoms and empires of India have been defined by what happens inside those imperial capitals. The Nandas fell as they were a decaying empire in Pataliputra and could not withstand the onslaught of Chandragupta Maurya. The Mauryas fell to the Greeks and the Guptas were defeated by the Huns. The story of a united ancient India governed from the imperial heart was the story of Pataliputra.

Kanauj became the most important city in North India after Pataliputra lost its pre-eminence. The Palas, Pratiharas and Rashtrakutas struggled for it. Harsha ruled from there. The Rajputs too ruled from there until the Turks defeated them. The rise and fall of Kanauj was the rise and fall of India.

The Muslim Sultanates made Delhi the most important city of India and it has been that way almost continuously since then. The Mamluks, Khiljis, Tughlaqs, Sayyids, Lodhis and Mughals have come and gone and the saga of India for the last eight hundred years has been the saga of Delhi. The story of a strong India under capable governance is interspersed with periods of internal decadence and dissension rendering it weak and making it capitulate to foreign invasions and rule.

We need to examine how the fortunes of India rose and fell in the light of what happened in the imperial capital of Delhi. It was for this city that battles for India were fought since the end of the twelfth century AD. Victory or defeat for the ruling dynasty and the consequent prosperity and ruin for India depended mainly on how the ruling dynasty preserved its economic strength, military might, and political sagacity. The change of fortunes of Delhi, and therefore of India, was decided in critical battles for Delhi but the seeds of success or failure for the kingdom at Delhi were sown beforehand by the character of its rulers. In this book we examine what happened so that we can learn from the past so as not to repeat the same in the future.

India has remained strong and unconquerable throughout history when it has had strong central rule. This central rule was seen under the Mauryas, Guptas, some of the Islamic Sultanates, as well as the Mughals. No foreign invader could come in and conquer India as long as a strong central empire existed. The moment this central control weakened and India became fragmented, it fell prey to these foreign invaders and became enslaved. That was not the only end result. Its people were massacred or treated as second class citizens, its religious places were destroyed, and its wealth looted.

India today is again centrally governed. The central governance is under a parliamentary democracy. It is also a federal structure with constituent state units and within these states reside people of various communities and religions. This diverse entity called India has had a history of fissiparous tendencies where some parts fancy they would be better off being independent, little realising that such struggles, whether they fail or succeed, weaken national unity.

We have had a history of such movements in the Northeast, Jammu & Kashmir and other areas. It has given foreign powers that are not happy to see a strong India, the opportunity to intervene. We have as a people little realised that history always has a habit of repeating itself. It was such internal dissensions that led to the weakening of India under the Mauryas, Guptas, Rajputs, Tughlaqs, Lodhis, Mughals and the Marathas. It paved the way for external aggressors to come in and enslave India. One hundred and forty four years of British rule is a comparatively recent memory.

Moreover, India has never lacked enemies. Whether it was the Greeks, Persians, Arabs, Turks, Afghans or Huns poised on its northwestern borders or the British coming in from the sea, the enemies always existed. Today we have Pakistan and China on our northwestern and northern borders, and even Bangladesh and Myanmar laying claim to our territories. The external threat has persisted for centuries and does so even more strongly today.

Are we prepared for it? How strong are we? How prepared are we? How well-fortified is our national unity and purpose to defeat such internal and external enemies? How well-focused is our continuous attention to strengthen ourselves economically as well as to make our national growth inclusive in character? How rich is our effort at national integration? How ruthless are we in tackling our internal enemies and deterring our external ones? How strong is the rigour and aggression of our external diplomacy?

Efforts are required in the above areas continuously in much the same way as the Americans and Chinese exhibit. A continuously evolving, strong and centrally governed India with an all-inclusive federal character is a prerequisite for preserving our national unity and integrity. India has to emerge again as one of the richest and most powerful nations on earth. It has just restarted its journey. Let it not flounder. History shows that the past has not been kind to us whenever we have floundered.

CHAPTER II

Delhi Through the Ages

WHEN DID DELHI BECOME THE CENTRE OF POLITICAL governance for India? Go back to antiquity and the epic *Mahabharata* comes to mind. The Mahabharata war was fought for the city of Indraprastha, said to have been situated approximately where the Purana Qila stands now. There was a village there called Indrapat. Some say that Humayun created the city of Din Panah at that location because he was told that the locals held the place in high esteem, deeming it to be the site of ancient Indraprastha.

The Battle of Mahabharata, a struggle of gigantic proportions, involving kings from the length and breadth of India, with numerous *akshauhini*s on both sides put together, was fought for the control of Indraprastha, a city kingdom at the site of Delhi. It led to the defeat of a kingdom at Hastinapur led by King Dhritarashtra, and of his army in battle led by his son Duryodhana with the help of army commanders such as Bhishma, Drona, Shalya and Karna. It led to the establishment of the kingdom of the Pandavas under the Chakravarthin rulership of Yudhisthira. Yudhisthira ultimately performed the *Ashwamedha Yagya*, a sign of imperial overlordship. Thus, the Mahabharata war involved a struggle for the control of political supremacy over a kingdom of considerable importance in India, situated around present day Delhi. After a period of time, Indraprastha disappeared as a centrally important city.

We find Delhi emerging from historical insignificance thanks to the efforts of the Tomara dynasty. The areas around Anangpur, Suraj Kund and Mehrauli were the ones where Delhi got re-established by Tomara kings. It was Anangpal who set up the first formidable citadel of Delhi—Lal Kot—which is at Mehrauli. The walls of this citadel are still visible in parts. Lal Kot grew into Qila Rai Pithora, named after the legendary Rajput king, Prithviraj Chauhan, a brave warrior king who laid down his life for the defence of India against the invading Turks.

However, Delhi had still not reclaimed the centrality that it once occupied during the Mahabharata era. Ancient India had Pataliputra as its capital for centuries. From the time of Emperor Ajatshatru to the Nandas, from the Mauryas to the Guptas, India, or more specifically northern, eastern and northwestern India were ruled centrally from Magadha. Pataliputra grew to be the capital of Magadha. Whenever a large empire arose that combined major portions of India into a centrally controlled entity, Pataliputra was the epicentre of that movement.

It was the decline of the Guptas that later paved the way for the location of central control to move to Kanauj, in modern day UP, from what is modern day Bihar. It is called the Age of Imperial Kanauj by historians. Involving the Rashtrakutas, Palas, and Pratiharas, the eighth to tenth centuries saw a tripartite struggle in which sometimes one and sometimes the other party emerged victorious. It was an unending struggle but the result was always changing.

Kanauj, however, remained central to the affairs of India. Mahmud Ghazni made his seventeen raids into India starting with the decimation of the Hindushahi Kingdom of Punjab and Northwest India. Ghazni ruptured the heartland of India, getting in as far as Mathura and Central India and going up northwards to the borders of Kashmir. Recognising the threat of this vicious conqueror, the various kingdoms of India united under the age old banner of Kanauj and went to battle against Ghazni in what is modern day Afghanistan. A battle that could have resulted in victory ended in the defeat of Indian forces and the day ultimately belonged to Ghazni.

The eleventh and twelfth centuries saw Delhi consolidate its status first under the Tomaras and then the Chauhans or Chahmanas. However, even when Prithviraj Chauhan ruled as king of both Delhi and Ajmer and possessed tremendous military strength, a more formidable army lay with King Jaichand of Kanauj. Kanauj still claimed supremacy as the centre of gravity.

However, the time for change had come. The centre of political and imperial importance had inexorably started moving in the western direction, as it had from Pataliputra to Kanauj. Perhaps it was due to the fact that India was facing increasing invasions from the Northwest across the Hindu Kush and the centre of gravity had to shift more to the West to meet such threats. It was the Pratiharas that first donned this mantle and transferred significance to Kanauj. It was the Rajputs, their successors who further created a westward movement, distributing this power between Kanauj and Delhi. However, there were to follow a chain of events that would make Delhi and its twin city Agra the new centres of power.

These were the Muslim invasions not of Ghazni but of Shahabuddin Ghori. Ghazni came to plunder and kill. Ghori came to conquer and establish a Muslim Sultanate. He first met defeat and, very strangely for a successful empire builder, is called by historians as the hero of three defeats. In fact, he tasted defeat twice in India, in Gujarat and then at the hands of Prithviraj at Tarain. It is said he also lost to the Persians at Andhkhud. But it was his sheer persistence that ultimately saw him defeat Prithviraj at the Second Battle of Tarain. He did not commit the mistake Prithviraj did when he defeated Ghori but failed to chase and kill him. Ghori went ahead and captured Prithviraj. And then he conquered Delhi from Prithviraj's chief Govindraj's son Chandraraj. Govindraj is said to have grievously injured Ghori in personal combat in the First Battle of Tarain. Ghori triumphantly rode into Delhi. He did not stay back to assume kingship in Delhi. It was his slave, Qutubuddin Aibak, who became the Sultan and established what came to be known as the Mamluk or Slave Dynasty.

From here onwards Indian history is centred around Delhi and it is Delhi that assumes importance as Northern India's, if not India's, political capital, destined to grow later into India's most important city politically. This happened most probably because the Muslim Sultanates had come from the west. They may have realised that the route they took to conquer the Indo-Gangetic plains was the one that future invading armies could follow and that is what eventually happened. At the same time, the Gangetic Doab was perpetually in contest as also was Central India. The Muslim Sultanates required a central location, a seat of power that enabled them to foray deeper into the Indian plains as well as turn back and repel invading armies from the Northwest.

Delhi, with the Aravali Hills and desert into the South, and rising hills into the North, was a gateway from the West to the fertile East and also a point from where invading armies could be denied ingress into the heartland of India. It emerged as a centre of power because of its fulcrum position. Therein lay the reason for successive Muslim Sultanates from Mamluks to Khiljis, Tughlaqs, Sayyids and Mughals and then of course the British, to create Delhi as the capital of India. There were occasional moves to Agra and Kolkata, but not long enough and the centre of power always returned to Delhi.

This is why the first and second battles of Tarain can be regarded as the first battles to be called the battles for Delhi. These battles that first swung one way and then the other, led to the establishment of a formidable imperial power that claimed Delhi as a central seat. This was the power of the Islamic Mamluk dynasty. The first battle or series of battles described in this book are the battles between Prithviraj Chauhan and Mohammed Ghori.

The Mamluks gave way to the Khiljis, and Allaudin Khilji became the first Muslim Sultan who sent his armies far down south to subjugate the Indian subcontinent. It was his Muslim convert General Malik Kafur who destroyed the rich kingdom of Devagiri and looted its tremendous riches for the Khiljis to create the formidable military power to subjugate the rest of India.

Allaudin Khilji created the city of Siri, located near Hauz Khas. It was here that a dominant power that was the scourge of the world threatened India with massive destruction. The fate of India could have been the same as that of many kingdoms destroyed by the Mongols but Allaudin Khilji had outstanding generals, a strong army and was himself a great general. This struggle can be called another important battle or series of battles for Delhi, a struggle that took place between the Khiljis and the Mongols. It led to the ultimate defeat of the Mongols and may have saved India from horrendous ruin. This book explores this battle series too. Unlike the battle between Prithviraj Chauhan and Ghori that led to the defeat of the power defending India, the battles fought between Allaudin Khilji and the Mongols saw an Indian ruler defeat invading forces and preserve India from the terrible onslaught of a brutal Mongol race.

The Khiljis gave way to the Tughlaqs—Ghiyasuddin, Mohammad Bin and then Firozshah. It was during the reign of the Tughlaqs that an invader appeared who rendered to Delhi the worst treatment it had received until then. This was Taimur Lang or Taimur the Lame, a Central Asian Turkic conqueror, a precursor to the famed Mughals. He defeated Mahmud Shah Tughlaq on the battlefields of Delhi. The battle was fought for Delhi inside Delhi and led to the defeat of the Tughlaq army. What followed was a horrendous massacre, the kind not seen until then. This battle, an important landmark that helps us realise what the destruction of a strong central authority can do to a kingdom, is dealt with in this book. This battle again shows a weak India capitulating to a rapacious invader.

More Sultanates followed, finally leading to the establishment of the Lodhi dynasty by Bahlol Lodhi. The seat of power under the Lodhi Sultans shifted to Agra or Akbarabad, as established by Sikander Lodhi. His son Ibrahim Lodhi was defeated by Babar, the first Mughal emperor of India, who assumed the imperial throne at Agra. This was at the First Battle of Panipat, fought for control of the seat of power in imperial North India. It also led to the establishment of a dynasty, the Mughals, whose name and fame stands alongside the Mauryas and Guptas in terms of splendour and military prowess when it comes to naming India's leading ruling dynasties.

It was, however, Humayun, Babar's son, who established his capital Din Panah at the site of the legendary Indraprastha. He lost to Sher Shah Suri in what is now central UP and fled India only to come back when circumstances were more favourable, and then recapture Delhi. He died on the steps of Sher Mandal in the present day Purana Qila. His young son, Akbar, was in Punjab. The legendary Hemu, one of the most fascinating characters of Indian history and a commander of the Afghan army of the Surs, realised the importance of Delhi as the central seat of power. Led by a powerful elephant corps and a formidable army, he vanquished one Mughal garrison after another in North and Central India. He reached Delhi and defeated the Mughal general, Tardi Beg, in the Battle of Delhi only to lose his kingdom through a tragic stroke of bad luck in the Second Battle of Panipat to the Mughal commander, Ali Quli Khan. It is this battle combination that Hemu fought, first at Delhi and then at Panipat, that are also written about here as battles for Delhi. These battles led to the long term re-establishment of the Mughal dynasty as the rulers of India from 1556 to the middle of the eighteenth century until they became the puppets of the Afghans, Marathas and ultimately the British. These battles show the emergence of a strong empire to fill a power vacuum and the beginning of the consolidation of India as a major economic and military power.

What followed after Humayun was a long reign of powerful Mughal monarchs who ensured stability and strength to the core of India while trying to continuously expand the frontiers of the empire. The seat of Mughal governance alternated between Agra and Delhi. However, the centrality and power of Mughal emperors was never questioned and the bulk of India had a stable rule under the overlordship of a strong, central Mughal empire. However, increasingly the succession to the Mughal throne came to be decided by the force of arms where brother fought brother, until all but the ultimate ruler were vanquished. This struggle was the most bitter and intense for the successor to Shah Jahan, the builder of the Taj Mahal. This resulted in the famous Battle of Samugarh between Aurangzeb and Dara Shikoh with the control of the imperial throne as the ultimate objective. Aurangzeb was the victor and chose Delhi as his seat of governance and continued thereon.

After Aurangzeb, the Mughal throne came under contest between his sons Muazzam and Azam Tara. This led to a particularly sanguinary battle at Jajua. The defeat of Azam Tara or Azam Shah placed his brother Muazzam as Bahadur Shah I on the throne. Bahadur Shah had come to power at a very late age and died after five years in power. This led to another battle between the future king Muizuddin or Jahandar Shah and his brother Azimushshan. Jahandar Shah won the Battle of Lahore. However, his debased monarchy was the first real nail into what was to become the coffin of the Mughal empire. His debauched ways led to another battle for Delhi where his nephew Farrukh Siyar defeated him and became the emperor.

These were major battles that can broadly be clubbed as battles of succession among later Mughals, emperors who were not fit enough to be even the shadows of the six great monarchs who strode India like giants and made it economically the world's most powerful nation and militarily a power no other country dared cross. These battles were for the control of Delhi, the seat of the Mughal empire and are significant more for the instability they caused. They led to India ultimately succumbing to foreign invasions.

These battles resulted in the decimation of the power of Mughal military leadership. It was a decimation that would cause the Mughals dear as they crossed swords with the Sikhs, Afghans, Persians, Jats and Marathas in future years. After these battles, barring an odd exception of Nizam ul Mulk or Mirza Najaf Khan, no significant Mughal commanders like Man Singh, Mahabat Khan or Mirza Raja Jai Singh surfaced. This was coupled with an effeminate Mughal emperorship leading to the fall and decline of the Mughal empire. It led to battles for Delhi that went more in favour of forces meant to weaken the core of India rather than those which could preserve it.

A succession of short-term imperial rulers among the Mughals finally gave way to a longer term emperorship of Mohammad Shah Rangila, who earned his title well. His weakness paved the way for the Persian king, Nadir Shah, to invade India. The Mughal armies went in to face him with the majority of knights who were derisively referred to in that era as Carpet Knights with little prowess in leading armies in battle. A botched battle, a peace plan sabotaged by a jealous courtier, Saadat Khan, and the ultimate humiliation of a Mughal emperor captured by an invading force tell their own story. This battle for Delhi was fought at Karnal and led to a major defeat for the Mughals. Delhi, the seat of the Mughal throne was captured by the Persians. It led to the massacre by Nadir Shah's soldiers of Delhi citizenry, a massacre Mughal forces were incapable of preventing. Even today, whenever demonstrations take place in Delhi, that massacre is remembered by slogans such as "*Nadir Shahi nahin chalegi*" (Nadir Shah's ways cannot be allowed).

The defeat by Nadir Shah is said to have been a major cause of dismemberment of the Mughal empire and the start of a palpable weakening of central imperial authority. This weakening, which successive generations have learnt little from, led to the subjugation of India by the British 64 years later and 144 years of rule of India by a European power. The British were yet to come in when the events concerning Nadir Shah described above occurred. In the intervening time there was a Maratha thrust to create a Hindu *pad padshahi*. This aggressive action was initiated by the ambitious and far sighted Peshwas—Balaji Vishwanath and later his son Baji Rao I. The initial thrusts were more in Central and West India but gradually inched their way to Delhi and what followed was a lightning strike by Baji Rao to the capital, a short successful action and a quick withdrawal. However, the Maratha armies soon found able contenders in the Afghans. Ahmad Shah Abdali also started counter-forays into India aiming for Delhi, more as actions to generate revenue rather than to acquire kingship.

Sooner or later there had to be a major contest between the Marathas and the Afghans. Things came to a head in 1760 and this spilled into early 1761. The Battle of Burari Ghat saw Afghan forces defeat the

Marathas led by Dattaji Scindia. This was a battle that led to a quick response from the Marathas who sent a formidable force to Delhi led by Sadashiv Rao Bhao. After a skirmish that led to the capture of Delhi and then Kunjpura, the Marathas soon found themselves hemmed in at Panipat and saw their retreat to the safer environs of Delhi and Gwalior cut off by combined forces of Afghans, Rohillas and the army of the Awadh King Shujauddaulah. What followed was the most sanguinary battle fought for Delhi on 14 January 1761, famously called the Third Battle of Panipat. Fought by a soldier strength that reached 150,000 on both sides put together, the fortunes initially favoured the Marathas but the presence of significant reserves and more determined generalship by Abdali against a starving Maratha host led to Maratha reverses and later on a complete rout. The Marathas fought bravely but hopelessly against unfavourable circumstances and a determined enemy. They lost the most significant battle for Delhi. Abdali came to Delhi, reinstalled the Mughals on the throne and went away, decimating however the ability of the Marathas to present a threat to Delhi for a decade.

Delhi saw swinging fortunes until the Marathas, this time under the able leadership of the Maratha general, Mahadji Scindia, captured Delhi, placed Shah Alam on the throne and became rulers in all but name. The Marathas henceforth controlled Delhi and the Indo-Gangetic Doab. While Marathas do remember the Third Battle of Panipat with lots of regret, this achievement of Mahadji Scindia in controlling Delhi and the affairs of North India should get much more credit than is given by historians. The Marathas also controlled West India, Central India, parts of East India and large parts of Deccan. They were the most powerful entity in India, loosely described as the Maratha Confederacy. This confederacy ultimately clashed with a well-organised European power, the British. The British, by winning the Battle of Plassey against the Nawab of Bengal, Siraj ud-Daulah, and the Battle of Buxar against the Nawab of Awadh, Shujauddaulah, had gained control of East India and also penetrated into the Gangetic heartland until Awadh. The British and Marathas ultimately had to contest for the control of India as the Afghans and Marathas had done earlier.

The first Anglo-Maratha war, largely confined to West India and also later to Central and North India, saw the Marathas gain at the expense of the British. The Marathas can be said to have won the first Anglo-Maratha war and fearing the military might of Mahadji Scindia and the political sagacity of Nana Phadnavis, the British confined themselves to East India and thence until Awadh. It was the death of Mahadji Scindia and then Nana Phadnavis that led to the British deciding to interfere and try and wrest India from the Maratha confederacy. This led to a series of battles in South, Central and North India. One very important battle was the Battle of Delhi fought approximately where the Noida golf course stands today, resulting in the defeat of Maratha forces led by Louis Burquoin by the British forces led by Lord Lake. Lord Lake won more such battles against Maratha armies in the North at Aligarh and Laswari while Arthur Wellesley did the same at Argaum and Assaye in the South. Thereafte, the British were the masters of India and significantly, the masters of Delhi, holding a captive, pensioner Mughal emperor. The loss of Delhi meant the end of Maratha aspirations to Indian imperial supremacy.

Things reached a status quo except for a brief interlude where a determined Yashwant Rao Holkar attacked Delhi, which was under the British, to win it back for the Marathas but alas in vain.

The last battle for Delhi was the War of Independence in 1857. Delhi was captured from the British by Indian sepoys from Meerut. A massacre of British and Europeans and the proclamation of Bahadur Shah Zafar as King Emperor by the sepoys led to dreams of the restoration of the grand Mughal empire. Soon the ranks of these sepoys were increased manifold by other sepoys from Neemuch, Bareilly and other parts of India as well as by Jehadis and other forces. Delhi rose up in arms. So did many other parts of India through combined armies of sepoys and local forces led by Indian rulers. Indians fought in a disjointed but determined manner to end British rule in India. The British were expelled from Delhi but almost immediately came back to surround Delhi and regain control. They considered the recapture of Delhi as critical to the control of India. However, initially they had neither the military strength nor the guns to attack the imperial capital. They were rather busy fending off Indian attacks from Delhi forces led by Bakht Khan, a man whose contribution to the 1857 war of independence is highly underrated in history. He deserves to be rated a much bigger hero on the lines of the Rani of Jhansi and Tatya Tope.

However, the British soon gathered strength, got their siege guns and, bolstered by traitors inside Delhi, attacked the capital. What followed was a week of a bitter contest for Delhi, a battle for Delhi fought hand to hand for days inside the houses and by lanes of Delhi. It led to the defeat of Bahadur Shah Zafar's forces by the British, his abject capitulation and another massacre of Delhi citizenry. But finally Delhi, and therefore India, belonged to the British until 1947. This was indeed the final military battle for Delhi.

Delhi has long been the symbol and seat of the Indian government. It stands for more than being just a city. It stands testimony to the fact that as long as there is a strong central government in India, and there is economic and military strength in this country, it is difficult for foreign powers to harm India. Weakening of this strength leads to enslavement, massacres and slavery of India. The battles for Delhi have been for long battles for the control of India. Delhi stands for a strong unitary India.

Chapter III

Dilli Kareeb Ast

Delhi has been pronounced in different ways through the ages and has also had different names. It was called Yoginipur, possibly because it was considered to be a city of yoginis. It was also called Indraprastha in the times of Mahabharata.

It acquired the name Dhillika most probably because of a legend that the Tomara king of Delhi had an obsession with the Iron Pillar or *Killi* that he was trying to stabilise on its foundations in his capital and it became loose (*dhilli*), not stabilising. Or it was fixed stable into the ground and curiosity got the better of him to understand what held it so firm—was it the Lord Sheshnag? In the process he may have dug it out and found its bottom coloured with the blood of the serpent.

Be that as it may, the saying became famous: "*Killi jo Dhilli bhayi, Tomara nrip Bhaiya hoye matiheen*" meaning that "*The iron pillar became loose and would not firmly establish itself in the ground, driving the Tomara king to despair*".

From then on the city could have acquired the name Dhillika which over time was pronounced differently as Dhilli, Dilli, Delhi or Dehli. It became the centre of the Islamic Sultanates that went on to rule India from the late twelfth century AD to the early sixteenth century. These Sultanates remained Islamic under the Mughals too but in a more secular manner from AD 1526, when Babar defeated Ibrahim Lodhi in the First Battle of Panipat and things remained so until the advent of the British.

The capture of Delhi, the imperial capital, became the objective of all conquerors from the thirteenth century onwards after the Battle of Tarain. It did not matter whether they came from the Northwest over the Hindu Kush mountains or from the sea as the British did.

It was in the thirteenth century that a famous Sultan came to rule Delhi. His name was Ghiyasuddin Tughlaq. Of all the Islamic Sultans, the Tughlaqs have been the most notorious for their religious zeal and fanaticism. At the same time there lived in a village called Ghiyaspur a Sufi saint called Hazrat Nizamuddin. The saint was accepted by both Hindus and Muslims for his piety, acts of kindliness, holiness, goodness and the widely perceived ability to deliver miracles and miraculous cures to his disciples and believers.

For some reason, one of them being his secular credentials, the saint fell afoul of Ghiyasuddin Tughlaq who tried to harass, threaten and browbeat him. The saint in all his holiness resisted these pressures until things came to a boil.

It was at this time that Sultan Ghiyasuddin Tughlaq was called to Bengal to suppress a rebellion. He issued instructions that upon his return, he would not like to see Hazrat Nizamuddin still staying at Delhi. The saint's worried disciples urged him to leave but he refused.

Sultan Ghiyasuddin successfully accomplished his mission of suppressing the rebellion and decided to return to the imperial capital of Delhi. He enquired if Hazrat Nizamuddin was still staying in Delhi. On being told that it was indeed the case, the Sultan issued a warning to the saint to depart else calamity would befall him upon the Sultan's return.

The saint's disciples hurried back to him and pleaded with him to clear the capital to avoid the terrible consequences. The saint was unperturbed and replied in a mysterious manner, "*Hunooz, Dilli dur ast*"—Delhi is still far off for the Sultan. As the Sultan approached Delhi, he again enquired about the saint and was met with the same reply that Hazrat Nizamuddin was still present in Delhi. Again he issued dire warnings which were duly conveyed to him by the saint's disciples. Again came the mysterious reply, "*Hunooz, Dilli dur ast*".

The disciples got extremely worried for the safety of their holy master and kept pleading with him to leave. They received the same reply—"*Hunooz, Dilli dur ast*". They were aghast at the nonchalant attitude of their master to the powerful threat issued by a man at whose name the whole of India trembled.

At last Sultan Ghiyasuddin reached the outskirts of Delhi. By now the presence of Hazrat Nizamuddin in Delhi was a major eyesore for him and a prestige issue. Again the query was raised as to Hazrat Nizamuddin's whereabouts and the same reply was received. The disciples, by now demented with worry, again repaired to Hazrat and pleaded with him to leave. "*Hunooz, Dilli dur ast*" was the reply.

The day before his entry into Delhi, the Sultan was to be welcomed by his son, Jauna Khan, later to become famous as Sultan Mohammed bin Tughlaq. For this purpose a royal enclosure with a roof was erected where the Sultan would sit and be welcomed. The royal enclosure collapsed and fell over the hapless Sultan inside. Upon its removal, Sultan Ghiyasuddin Tughlaq, the conqueror of India was found dead. Jauna Khan was suspected of assassinating his father but the death is also widely attributed to the curse of Hazrat Nizamuddin. Possibly the divine personage had foreseen what others could not. Dilli was *dur,* or Delhi proved to be far, for the Sultan.

Delhi has been the imperial target for all conquerors— Ghurs, Taimur, Mughals, Persians, Afghans and British. The capture of Delhi has been only possible when the ruling entities and the empires that controlled Delhi were weak and incapable of defending it. When the central empire and the rulers have been strong Delhi has been defended well—whether it was the Khiljis, Tughlaqs, Mughals or Balban.

Delhi is *dur* or far for the invaders if people ruling Delhi have built a strong empire based on economic growth, secular and inclusive practices, military strength and preparedness, proactive defence and a just and industrious method of rule or when many of such conditions existed. The Khiljis defeated the Mongols, the Mughals did not let the Persians even dream of crossing Kandahar or Kabul, and Mahadji Scindia fought the British to a standstill in Central and North India.

However, Delhi is *kareeb* or near for the invaders whenever the central ruling entity has withered due to weak successor rulers, indolence in military preparedness, inability to handle inclusive growth, religious intolerance, lack of proactive defence to defend the country's borders and economic and administrative mismanagement.

The Mauryas could handle the external aggression of the Greeks as long as they were a strong central empire way back in history when Pataliputra was the centre of an Indian empire. The moment they got weak kings, internal dissensions could not be handled and the frontiers became out of control. The same Mauryan empire that decisively moved forward and defeated a world conquering Greek host under Seleucus Nikator, became helpless to stem the internal rise of rebellions and the depredations of the Greeks.

The Guptas defeated foreign invaders under the Sakas and extended their empire to modern day Afghanistan. Samudragupta was invincible and expanded the empire further. Skandagupta defeated the Huns decisively. The central capital of the empire was Pataliputra. But the later Gupta kings were weak and were defeated.

The Arabs made inroads into Sindh until Multan. However, they found formidable opponents in the strong Pratihara empire and were defeated and repelled. A united Rajput confederacy defeated the Arabs in the battles of Rajasthan. A disunited Rajput race lost to Shahabuddin Mohammed Ghori one by one, firstly Prithviraj Chauhan, then Jaichand and then the others.

A strong Islamic Sultanate under the Mamluk king Balban, then the Khiljis and then the earlier Tughlaqs was equal to the task of defending India's external borders against invading tribes, especially the Mongols. The moment weak kings came to power and internal dissensions arose, in came the Mongols and Turkic tribes. Mahmud Shah lost to Taimur. The Lodhis were strong under Bahlol and Sikander. Ibrahim was a weak ruler and provinces broke away while formidable kingdoms emerged in Rajasthan, Bengal and Gujarat. The Mughals were able to overcome the Lodhis at the first sanguinary battle of Panipat.

Babar, Akbar, Jahangir, Shah Jahan and Aurangzeb were formidable monarchs, the Great Mughals, the envy of the Western world. They maintained a large empire in India, had massive armies capable of taking on any one, and rich economic resources. Europeans came and begged for trade. Persians, Turks, Uzbegs and Afghans rushed to India to sell their administrative, artistic and, most of all, military talent to the Mughal empire. India was strong and powerful under the Mughals. However, once the Mughals lost their way under a succession of weak rulers like Jahandar Shah, Farrukh Siyar and Mohammed Shah Rangila, it led to a military weakness. Economic mismanagement led to a depleted treasury. Religious intolerance led to revolts from Jats, Sikhs, Marathas and Rajputs. The result was a declining Mughal empire with Nadir Shah's invasion brutally exposing its weaknesses.

The Marathas, when united, proved more than a match for the British. In separate and united engagements, the Scindia and Holkar armies under Mahadji and Tukoji and the Peshwa army under Nana Phadnavis defeated the British in the first Anglo-Maratha war. However, the moment it became Holkars versus Scindia and Peshwa, the British moved in and in less than a year conquered India almost from tip to toe, decimating the hold of the Maratha confederacy.

The weakness began from within, mostly when the ruling entity was weak and indecisive, possessing lower levels of military, administrative and political skills than their predecessors. Mismanagement led to fights inside the kingdoms between contending factions. Rulers got overthrown and courtiers became all powerful. The central ruling entity or the emperor ceased to have any substantial say in the run of things. It happened to Ibrahim Lodhi, to the later Mughal emperors and to the Marathas trying to control Delhi. This led to military weakening as economic resources were too weak to manage a large army and there was a downgradation of military skills and readiness.

There was additional pressure from provinces or sub-national entities that saw their chance and had mistaken notions that they needed to become independent, little realising that it was a strong India that preserved them and once split from the national entity, they were sooner or later likely to fall prey to a rapacious invader.

The Rajputs found it to their cost with the Turks when their belief that infighting and personal independence were more important than national unity made way for disaster at Tarain and Chandrawar. The Afghans and Rajputs learnt the same against Babar. The Mughals realised it too late and lost territories to Sikhs, Jats, Rajputs, Afghans and mostly the Marathas. Their policy of infighting led to disaster when the power of their military leadership got decimated, their treasury became bankrupt and the army came to be led by carpet knights.

The same Mughal army that forced the Persians to a standstill in Kabul and Kandahar under Akbar, Shah Jahan and Aurangzeb, capitulated like a pack of cards at the field of Karnal to a Persian host under Nadir Shah. They neglected the defence of the Northwest Frontier, so busy were the Hindustani and Turani parties scoring brownie points against each other. Nadir Shah came in until Ambala and when a Mughal host twice its size went out to fight, it was terrorised with fear. The amusing part is that there was hardly a battle, more of a skirmish. On one hand we had Nadir Shah, even after the first round going to him, staying put and not daring to attack a formidably entrenched Mughal army. On the other we had this same large Mughal army with non-combative generals scared to fight and begging for terms. Without giving battle a Mughal emperor and his leading nobles allowed themselves to be captured. It led to the loot of Delhi, the loss by Mughals of wealth garnered through generations, the lowering of prestige of the emperor and the breakaway of the provinces of Bengal, Awadh and Hyderabad.

The weakness first manifested itself in the frontier provinces that got rebellious and out of control. It then showed itself in the inability to defend the frontier against an invader. This led to border provinces becoming either independent or coming under the control of the invader. Internal dissensions then arose and weakened the empire further from within. The empire became militarily and administratively weak as well as economically impoverished. The border districts were already lost. Independent or semi-independent kingdoms emerged within the empire in its hinterlands. These semi-independent kingdoms mistakenly perceived the foreign invader as a welcome intervention as it helped weaken the central authority against which these sub-national semi-independent kingdoms were fighting. It is then that this invader came in and smashed the weak empire out of existence. He became the new ruler. These so called independent and semi-independent kingdoms rejoiced for awhile but were also apprehensive of this new master. Their apprehensions were well founded and all the hard work they put in to become independent ultimately came to naught as they fell one by one to this new master.

It happened to the Rajputs and Afghan chiefs against Babar when initially they had rejoiced seeing Ibrahim Lodhi getting discomfited by him. It happened to Awadh, Rajputs, Sikhs, Jats and Nizam as they lost their kingdoms to the British. Dilli was then no longer *dur*. It was *kareeb* or near for the invader.

National unity or integrity cannot be taken for granted. It has to be preserved carefully and diligently through a conscious, continuous and ever evolving national effort without a moment of relaxation against both external and internal enemies.

China covets our land in Arunachal and in Jammu and Kashmir. Pakistan covets Jammu and Kashmir. Naxalites menace and eat into our internals. A few insurgent outfits mushroom in the Northeast, each desperately demanding a small portion of land as an independent kingdom. Terror outfits like Indian Mujahideen or SIMI plant bombs all over India.

What is our response? It is not that nothing is done to counter such forces but it is insufficient and at times weakened by internal dissensions.

Our border roads on the China frontier are not made while the Chinese have a fine network of rail and roads and warn us not to do anything in Arunachal. We find ourselves facing a repeat of 1962 after fifty years of having faced a military disaster on the same border. China is supposed to possess a 3:1 men and material advantage, decisive in a conflict if push comes to shove.

Racked by scams, our defence procurement suffers. In spite of having no problems with foreign exchange, our air force squadron strength is down to abysmal levels. We can neither develop our own aircraft nor buy new ones. Defence contracts take years as if we have all the time in the world. We do not have artillery guns as we cannot procure them without stirring a hornet's nest post-Bofors.

When it comes to fighting Naxalites (the battle has to be both on the development as well as armed front), each state has its own theory and method. Our security forces, driven by poor training, poor arms and lack of coordination, keep losing men. **An almost entire political leadership of a state gets wiped out, which we soon forget and get on with our daily tasks.**

A national party as well as regional state satraps oppose a National Bill to tackle terrorism saying it infringes upon the federal character of our country. Of what use is this federal character, if an internal terrorist movement eats up the innards of our country? Where will this federal character lead us when this terror outfit spreads its tentacles far and wide into India as we had no national unity to tackle them?

And where is economic growth? We are frittering away a demographic dividend of a youthful population. The national character is mired in corruption. Politicians merrily and shamelessly continue to get involved in scams. This impacts economic decision making and lowers economic growth.

The battle for Delhi is the battle that is continuous. It is a battle to drive economic growth, preserve national character, make national growth inclusive and secular, bring in strong administration, improve military preparedness, practise strong diplomacy and engage in proactive defence against external and internal enemies.

The USA that lectures to the world on human rights, does not hesitate to bomb and pulverise into submission countries tens of thousands of miles away if it feels even remotely threatened by terrorists from such countries. Britain did not hesitate to send a heavily armed flountila to win back Falkland Islands, and defeated Argentina in a costly war to preserve that part of its territory. China ruthlessly claims and preserves its territories and fights running battles with India, Japan, Philippines and

Vietnam over lands and waters it considers its own. Pakistan, a country carved out of India, demands more territory as its god given right and finds people from inside India backing that claim.

The world has always been dominated by nations that are strong by themselves economically, administratively and militarily. National frontiers are preserved and defined by such countries. India has to become stronger and remain so for Dilli to be *dur* and not *kareeb.*

The fact that we have not learnt from history has been demonstrated time and again. The subsequent chapters deal with important milestones or battles for Delhi, in the hope we will learn from history.

Chapter IV

Battles of Tarain

Mahmud of Ghazni is notorious in India for his seventeen invasions in which he plundered India of its wealth, desecrated its temples and massacred its people. His death led to his sons succeeding him, and then their progeny. The Ghaznavi kingdom was beset with internecine struggles for power. However, in this period, the Ghazni kings continued to conduct raids into India, at times capturing kingdoms, sacking cities and attempting to go into India beyond the Punjab. They were in this process resisted by the Rajput kingdoms and there were numerous struggles with the Chaulukyas of Gujarat and Rajput kingdoms. However, by the second half of the twelfth century, the situation seemed to have settled where Kanauj, Delhi, Ajmer and other cities in the North were ruled by Rajput kings with a sufficient degree of stability until Sirhind against the Ghaznavi kingdoms. The Chaulukyas ruled Gujarat area and the Chandelas ruled Central India.

While the marauding Ghazni kings were thus entrenched until the middle of Punjab and faced a strong resistance from Hindu Kings in the North, a threat developed in their own backyard. They came into conflict with the kingdom of Ghur and came off worse in the conflict. Ghazni was destroyed by the kingdom of Ghur and went up in flames. The Ghaznavi princes fled to Lahore and ruled from there. Ghiyasuddin of Ghur proclaimed Shahabuddin Ghori, his brother, as the ruler of Ghazni. Shahabuddin Ghori, also known as Muizuddin, became a ruler of a kingdom far from Delhi. However, in time to come, he would be the person most responsible for changing the history of India and in some ways leave an impact on India even more profound than the British did.

India is a country bounded by the Himalayas in the north, hilly forests in the northeast, deserts and forbidding mountains in the northwest and the seas to its west, south and east. It had until then an existence where it had hardly ventured on conquests abroad and had been invaded only after large intervals. There is a reference to the invasion of Semiramis in ancient Greek texts, the invasion of India by the Assyrian queen with a large army and her defeat by an Indian king, Stabrobates, with an army led by elephants. Her retreat in a badly wounded state across the Indus has been documented in certain texts and the battle described in some detail.

Darius invaded northwestern India and ruled parts of Punjab. Alexander came, conquered territories, ran into the stiff resistance posed by Porus and his army including two hundred elephants across a swollen Jhelum. Dissuaded by this experience, his army refused to advance further. Then came more Greek and Hun invasions over centuries, threatening to engulf India. These invaders either got assimilated in the Indian system or were beaten back. Even if they succeeded in making ingress into India, ultimately India with its huge resilience wrested back its territories.

However, the Indian ability to handle sustained invasions would be severely tested by the advent of Islam. As Islamic power rapidly overwhelmed and became predominant in the countries of the Gulf, West Asia and Central Asia, it came into contact with India. The Arab power conquered Sindh and moved forward, only to be beaten back and confined to Sindh. Then it was the invasion of Mahmud of Ghazni who encountered an India composed of distributed kingdoms. India was incapable of taking him on and also not in a position to defeat him as a cohesively governed country could have done. He was stoutly opposed and probably checked by King Vidyadhar in Central India and decided not to go any further. But a strong, centrally administered Indian empire was just not there to handle this rapacious invader.

Luckily, Mahmud of Ghazni was interested more in plunder, not conquest. However, there emerged the Ghoris who had different ideas. But what was more important was that along with the Ghoris emerged an idea that India could be repeatedly invaded, subjugated and ruled. This aspect assumed a certain inexorable feature and since the late twelfth century, this idea has seen realisation through a number of invasions—Turks, Afghans, Mongols, Mughals, Persians and more Afghans. They battered the Indian state again and again. Whenever there was a strong central military force or the Indian system had sufficient economic and military might, invasions were repulsed—Arabs and Turks by Pratiharas and Rajputs; Mongols by Khiljis; Persians by Mughals; Afghans by

Marathas. However, whenever the central Indian power has waned or there has been lack of military prowess in a cohesive central form, these invasions have succeeded thereby either altering the political landscape or causing severe damage. Witness what Ghazni, Nadir Shah and Abdali did as damage. Understand what Ghoris and Mughals achieved through setting up permanent empires. And this idea continues to this day that it is possible for these invasions to carry on until there is a central weakening. Ultimately the opportunity to alter the basic ruling scenario of India is presented and permanent damage is caused.

The Ghoris came as invaders, like Ghazni, but their intentions were to stay. The territorial sanctity of India had been preserved by the Pratiharas and the Rajput clans. All this was to wane later against a determined enemy willing to repeatedly attack the fortress of Hind, come back despite defeats, learning from the defeats to create a change that was to completely alter India. A force that continues to repeatedly knock its head against India even today with similar intentions, single minded focus, sure of its ultimate victory, history having taught it no other lesson, convinced of what it considers the ultimate weakness of India.

Ghori initially decided to do a repeat of Ghazni, and conquer the rich Gujarat. Shahabuddin marched and captured Uch and Multan in AD 1175. In AD 1178 he was up against the Chaulukya Rajputs. Knowing that a powerful Rajput kingdom ruled from Ajmer and Delhi and led by the Chauhans existed in his flank, he sought to protect his left flank and asked Prithviraj for friendship and assistance against Chaulukyas, Prithviraj's old enemies. Prithviraj, to his credit, refused. However, Prithviraj did not realise the ultimate danger of the Ghoris and their ability to move against him once they had dealt with the Chaulukyas. Advised by his minister Kadambavasa, he sat back to let the Chaulukyas and Ghoris finish off each other. There was no strategic Indian mindset or power that realised that there was an inexhaustible supply of manpower to create armies that could keep invading India from the Northwest. The march of Islam, both as a proselytising religion and as a conquering force had begun thanks to an energy which was to prove inexhaustible, albeit in different forms.

Ghori's plans were, however, dealt a severe blow by the Chaulukyas. He was met with an army led nominally by child-king Mularaja but in the field by the queen Naikidevi. The Chaulukyas fought determinedly and

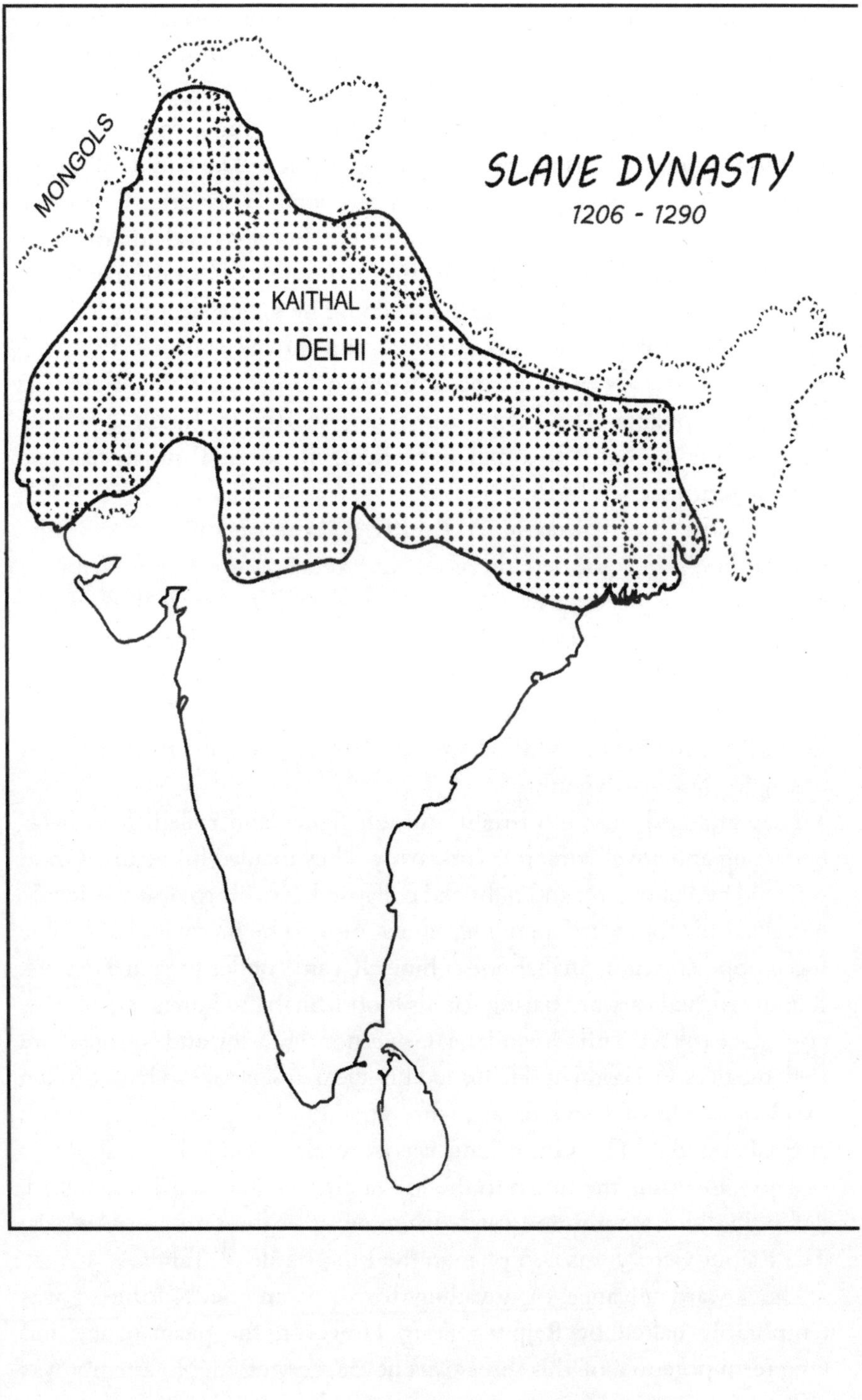
SLAVE DYNASTY
1206 - 1290
MONGOLS
KAITHAL
DELHI

routed the invading army of Turks, once again proving that determined Indian armies, well led and powerfully equipped, were capable of defeating invading forces. Ghori fled for dear life.

However, the idea of invading and conquering India had taken firm root in his mind. In his hearts of hearts, he believed he could ultimately defeat Indian kingdoms and conquer the land. This time he moved into Punjab. He followed on the lines of Sabuktigin and Mahmud of Ghazni because history had taught him that just as the Ghaznavis had defeated Jayapala and Anangapala, so could he also defeat the Rajputs. He captured Tabarindah Fort (Sirhind) and moved forward. Prithviraj realised the danger and advanced with an army of 200,000 soldiers and 300 elephants. The armies came face to face at Tarain, south of Thaneshwar. Perhaps no other battlefield, not even Panipat, has had such significance for India.

The battle took place in AD 1191. Ghori organised his armies into central, right and left divisions and attacked the Rajput army of Prithviraj through his central force, hoping to rip it apart through the sheer force of his attack. He had confidence in the hardy mountaineers of his region. Much to his surprise, he again faced a very powerful and determined army, highly skilled in the art of fighting, having soldiers with great prowess in hand to hand combat. The Rajputs made him pay dearly for his misadventure.

They attacked the Ghori right and left flanks and rolled them back, encircling and enveloping the Turk army. They mauled his centre. Ghori was told his centre, left and right had collapsed. Unable to bear this insult, he rallied his forces for a counter attack only to be met with irresistible force opposing him. Shahabuddin himself came under personal danger. Rajputs rushed forward baying for his blood. Shahabuddin is said to have come face to face with Govindraja, Governor of Delhi, and engaged him in fierce personal combat. He hurled his spear and is said to have broken two front teeth of Govindaraja, who replied in kind, hurling his javelin at Shahabuddin. The Ghori king was severely wounded and about to collapse. Realising the threat to the life of their Sultan, the Turks rallied, defending him stoutly, and carried him away to the safety of Ambala. The Rajput victory was complete in the First Battle of Tarain.

The inward advance of invading forces from the Northwest was temporarily halted by Rajput valour. However, the permanency and long term potential of this threat was never recognised. No attempt was made to chase the Sultan and finish him off. The Rajputs never realised that Shahabuddin Ghori was a determined, long-term foe of India, with a potential to cause lasting damage. Ghori was allowed to escape. A thirteen-month long siege of Tabarindah was conducted with success but there was no attempt made to secure the Northwest routes through strengthening forts, garrisons and trying to proactively prevent ingress through such passes. India would pay dearly for this lapse.

Shahabuddin Ghori did not take his defeat lightly. His eyes were set irrevocably on India and he seemed to have a single-minded intention of subduing the country. It is said that after the defeat in the First Battle of Tarain, "he never slumbered in ease nor waked but in sorrow and anxiety". The net result, however, was a renewed effort to create a new army with a new strategy. There was no lack of recruits willing to join a force to harass and invade India, a reality that continued throughout the second millennia and continues to this day. A force of 120,000 Central Asian warriors was assembled under Ghori and rode back to defeat and conquer India. India's riches and careless kingdoms beckoned the rapacious invaders.

Shahabuddin conquered Peshawar, then Lahore, and finally he made himself master of Sirhind again. He wrote to Prithviraj asking him to surrender and embrace Islam. The Chauhan rejected the letter and moved forward to thwart Ghori. There was a crucial difference this time. Ghori had learnt his lesson and come better prepared. Prithviraj seemed to have underestimated the threat and was complacent. His general, Skanda, said to have been responsible for victory in the First Battle of Tarain, was not a part of his army. Many chiefs and generals did not join although at 300,000 soldiers and 300 elephants, the Chauhan army was still formidable.

Prithviraj wrote to Ghori offering that the latter could remain master of Punjab until Sirhind and the two sides could retain stable borders there. Shahabuddin artfully replied saying that he had to get his brother Ghiyasuddin's consent but would observe truce until then. The Rajputs got lulled into a sense of complacency while Ghori plotted. He gave the appearance of a normal army camp not intending to give battle but at a chosen time, did a night march and attacked the Rajput camp at dawn in the rear. The Rajputs were completely taken by surprise but to their credit kept their senses and reformed to counter attack. The result was something Shahabuddin had not intended and his army was again beaten back. The first attack of the Turks failed.

However, Ghori was determined and he regrouped his forces to attack again. He kept a strong reserve of heavy mailed cavalry and formed up the rest of the army into light cavalry units. These units were instructed to charge the Rajputs, induce them to charge back and then withdraw. This became the pattern of battle for quite some time. The Rajputs could make little sense of what was happening while Ghori was playing his cards well as per a pre-set plan. This game of cat and mouse continued until the Rajputs became totally frustrated and disorganised. Their army, led by this game of attack and withdrawal, became a tired and dishevelled lot losing its organisation. By the afternoon, Ghori sensed his time had come and charged forward with his heavy central reserve into a bedraggled Rajput host, tearing through its mass. Another part of his army followed. The charge was repeated, throwing the Rajputs into turmoil. The light cavalry of the Turks reappeared and closed in from the flanks. The Rajputs were in a mess. They became a disorganised lot, thrown into leaderless confusion, broken into small groups surrounded by Turks. It became a massacre of Rajputs and they had lost the battle. Prithviraj tried to escape but was overtaken and captured near Sirsauti. The Second Battle of Tarain was lost by Indians to a determined adversary who learnt from his defeats while the Indians did not.

What followed was inevitable. Shahabuddin captured towns like Hansi, Samana and Sirsauti. Ajmer was attacked, captured, temples destroyed and replaced by mosques, palaces ground to dust and a general massacre conducted. Prithviraj was put to death. Delhi was besieged and conquered.

Shahabuddin Ghori returned to Afghanistan but Qutubuddin Aibak made Delhi his base. He captured Meerut, Bulandshahar and entrenched Islamic rule in the heartland of India. The next year Shahabuddin returned and defeated Jaichand Gahadvala of Kanauj at Chandawar. This was the same Jaichand who had sat back complacently, content to see a fellow Indian being destroyed by an external foe. He little realised that this same foe would come back and be a menace to him as well. A lesson many Indians have not learnt even today.

Ghori had to fight a very determined foe in the Gahadvala and nearly lost the battle. However, Jaichand, the king of Gahadvalas, was struck and wounded badly in his elephant and collapsed. The Rajput army thought they had lost their king and they lost heart, thereby losing a winning battle. Ghori then tore into Varanasi and other cities. Shahabuddin

Ghori had to fight two very tough battles, one at Tarain and the other at Chandawar. He could have lost either of these battles. If Prithviraj and Jaichand had not been sworn enemies of each other, but had united against Ghori, the result would have been different. But it was not to be. A strong central empire or a cohesive coalition was not to be found and Indian kingdoms fell one after another to the advancing Turks who established a sway from the Northwest to East India as well as to Central India.

A new Muslim empire was formed in another part of the world, this time India. The landscape of India was altered forever thanks to the lack of foresight and proactive aggression of Indian rulers. A battle of Tarain was fought for capturing North India and ended up creating an Islamic Sultanate with its capital at Delhi. The Battle of Tarain became a battle for Delhi as it established Delhi at the centre of a new empire, ruled by a foreign power. Qutubuddin Aibak, who eventually became the first Muslim Sultan of India, chose Delhi as his base. Henceforth, battles for Delhi decided the fate of India as Delhi became central to the control of North, East and Central India.

The Battle of Tarain is an event possibly of the greatest significance in the history of India as it changed forever the political and military landscape of India. Hitherto India had been invaded by the Greeks and Persians but they had mostly been conquerors who came as far as Punjab, mainly contested the Northwest Frontier regions and then left. The Arabs were the first to conquer Sindh and stay there, converting a Buddhist and Brahmanical society into a partially Islamic one. However, their presence was confined to that region due to the energy and fortitude displayed by the Pratiharas and Rajputs.

Mahmud Ghazni pierced the Northwest Frontier and came well into India's heartland seventeen times but always to loot and never to stay and rule. His long-term impact was to destroy the Hindushahi kingdom of Jaipal and bring the Islamic foothold into the plains bordering the Indian heartland, ripping open the defences of India's Northwest Frontier forever. Few Indians realise that Kabul was once considered a part of India or of its componential ruling kingdoms. Punjab partially went to the Ghaznavaids. However, a resilient India came up again and powerful Rajput kingdoms arose in Central and North India to defend the nation.

The Ghur invasion was completely different in character. The Islamic armies were now at the doorstep of the Indian heartland as Punjab had already been lost to them. Mohammed Ghori came with entirely different ideas. He planned to plant an Islamic empire in India. He defeated Prithviraj Chauhan at Tarain and then defeated Jaichand of Kanauj, ripping open the Gangetic heartland. Bengal, Rajputana and Central India were to follow in terms of capitulation.

For the first time an alien invader now ruled India, establishing a foreign empire on a land mass that had until now been under the control of Indians. This invasion destroyed kingdoms and uprooted people. Massacres and loot were conducted, grand buildings were razed to the ground and new architecture came up. India's culture, religions, political set up, internal and external boundaries were changed forever.

Then it was a matter of time before the Khiljis and Tughlaqs tore into South India and changed the landscape there also. The net result was that for six hundred years from the twelfth to the eighteenth centuries, India was largely ruled by Islamic Sultanates.

As time passed, these Islamic rulers and people came to be recognised as Indians. They regarded Hindustan as their land. They may not have been religiously and politically well inclined towards the Hindu population but they adopted this country as their own and fought against further invasions either successfully or unsuccessfully, often laying down their lives in the process. They regarded Hindustan as their country.

They brought in new food, new cultural traditions, literary works, music, costumes and architecture into India. They brought in new methods of warfare with their emphasis on mobile cavalry, mounted archers, army hosts split into more effectively functional parts like harawal, iltutmish, chandawal, kul, baranghar and jaranghar. They brought in a different and possibly more effective military system.

India became a mix of Hindu and Islamic cultures and religions. A birthplace of the Jain and Buddhist religions as well as the great Sikh religion, it also welcomed Jews, Christians and Parsis. It continues to be that way today.

It is in many ways the richest country in the world in terms of the sheer diversity of talent that it holds: people with different looks and features, different religions, languages and dialects running into thousands, myriad music and dance forms, different forms of architecture and art, customs and mores, and a rich literary tradition. And this admixture is the essential strength of India and the holding together of all this is the only way it can progress.

CHAPTER V

Allaudin Khilji Against the Mongols

THE FIRST ISLAMIC SULTANATE WAS KNOWN AS THE MAMLUK OR the Slave dynasty. This is because a person who had previously been a slave succeeded another—Iltutmish succeeded Qutubuddin Aibak and Balban succeeded the successors of Iltutmish. Qutubuddin had been the slave of Mohammed Ghori. Iltutmish had been the slave of Qutubuddin. Balban had been a slave of Iltutmish.

The Mamluk Sultanates survived internal dissensions and power struggles as well as wars with indigenous ruling Indian kingdoms. The Slave dynasty ultimately collapsed. Towards the end of the thirteenth century the Khiljis came to power. The first Khilji, Sultan Jalaluddin, was murdered by his nephew and son-in-law Allaudin Khilji who embarked on a determined conquest of India, focusing his attention on the hitherto unpenetrated but fabulously rich South as well as the defiant Rajput kingdoms in Rajasthan.

However, the greatest challenge the Khilji Sultanate faced was not from existing Indian kingdoms that mainly fought it in defensive battles. Its greatest challenge came from the Mongols, the descendants of Genghis Khan. Genghis Khan had reached India as far as the Indus and destroyed the Khwarizm empire of Persia. But thankfully, this ruthless and irresistible conqueror decided to spare India. This was in turn aided by the wise policy of the Delhi Sultanate not to extend aid to the fleeing Khwarizm Prince Jalaluddin, denying Genghis Khan an excuse to attack the Delhi Sultanate.

However, the Mongol kingdoms were thirsty for fresh conquests. The defeat of the Rajputs, who guarded the approaches to India for four hundred years and had fought the battles of Rajasthan and Tarain against Islamic invaders, had opened the floodgates to India. It was now thought feasible to attack India from the Northwest and from around the late twelfth century onwards, this was the route of attack, a threat that still exists. The strategy was to keep attacking. As long as there was a strong kingdom under an able ruler to defend the Indo-Gangetic plain, this threat was confined to India's borders and repulsed. However, the invaders from the Northwest were a persistent lot who knew that they had to find one chink in the defending army, break through to destroy this defensive force once and then the route would be open into the heart of North India. The Mongols followed this strategy and kept attacking ferociously from 1297 to 1306. Unfortunately, they more than met their match in Allaudin Khilji, a determined and obdurate Sultan and a military genius.

The determination with which he repeatedly met the invading Mongols, never lost heart even in the most adverse of circumstances, employing strong forces to go out and meet the invaders, proactively strengthening the defences of the Northwest and even leading forces beyond the Indus to deter invasions, is a lesson very few succeeding ruling dynasties and governing powers have learnt, save the Mughals and the British. His policy and tactics are worth studying in detail by current strategists. They show the superiority of forward defence and strong defensive preparations in depth that eliminates threats from the most ferocious of invading armies and keeps internal dissensions under control. A lesson which hopefully is not lost on whoever governs India.

Amir Daud of Mawa un Nehr captured Ghazni. However, his ambitions were not restricted to Afghanistan. He wanted to capture the Turkish Kingdom of India. His determination was equal to that of Shahabuddin Ghori. He launched six raids into India between 1297 and 1306, each time sending a strong cavalry force, determined to wrest the kingdom of India from the hands of the Turks. Unfortunately for him, he met a very accomplished and proactive ruler, Allaudin Khilji, equally determined to protect his kingdom from ruin; something, alas, that the Chauhans and Gahadvalas should have exhibited earlier against invading Turks.

A Mongol force under Kadar with 100,000 Mongols crossed the Indus and attacked to capture Lahore, Multan and Sindh. The Mongols reached Lahore and from there would have attacked Delhi. However, much to their chagrin, Allaudin showed what he was capable of. He did not sit back and wait until the last moment to meet the enemy when it was at the gates of Delhi, where one defeat meant the key city was now at the mercy of the victor. He decided to proactively engage the enemy while it was some distance away, employing a strong force under capable generals. He sent an army under Ulugh Khan and Zafar Khan to repulse the invasion. The battle took place in February 1298, and the Mongols were defeated near Jalandhar, suffering tremendous casualties. Mongol officers were captured and killed and women and children sold as slaves. The immediate threat was turned back. And even if the Mongols had broken through, the tough battle would have taken its toll on them and the reserve forces of the Delhi Sultanate would have been there as the second line of defence. This policy of taking the enemy head on some distance from the seat of government proved to be very sound.

However, the enemy was determined as it never lost sight of the opportunity, something even Ghori never did. The difference was in the quality of the opposition it met, an opposition which was ever ready and waiting to meet the threat. The defensive preparedness never went down. In 1298, the Mongols under Saldi attacked Punjab and captured Sehwan. Again the Delhi Sultan realised the nature of the menace and decided on proactive defence. His most capable and daring general, Zafar Khan, was dispatched by the Delhi Sultanate to handle them. Zafar Khan proved equal to the task, defeated Saldi and captured him and his brother. Another round of invasion was defeated. The difference is stark with the Second Battle of Tarain which was lost due to complacency by the Delhi Rajput kingdom.

This difference of mentality has to be studied in great detail. On one hand was the mentality of the Rajputs, skilled and courageous warriors, unbeatable in hand to hand combat and sword fights but showing a complete neglect of strategic foresight and tactical acumen. The mentality bordered on indolence when it came to realising that the threat from the Northwest would always continue. The threat would come back with increased vigour and better tactics each time. It would keep coming until it found the weak chink. It would finally find that weakness, break through and destroy what existed.

India was economically stronger and richer than the lands beyond the Indus. Those lands contained hardy men who coveted the fertile and rich plains of India. This threat could not have been met by holding defensive positions, meeting the enemy in Indian territory but away from the capital. The battle, in every way, had to be fought to deter and weaken the enemy proactively, anticipating what it would do next and nipping

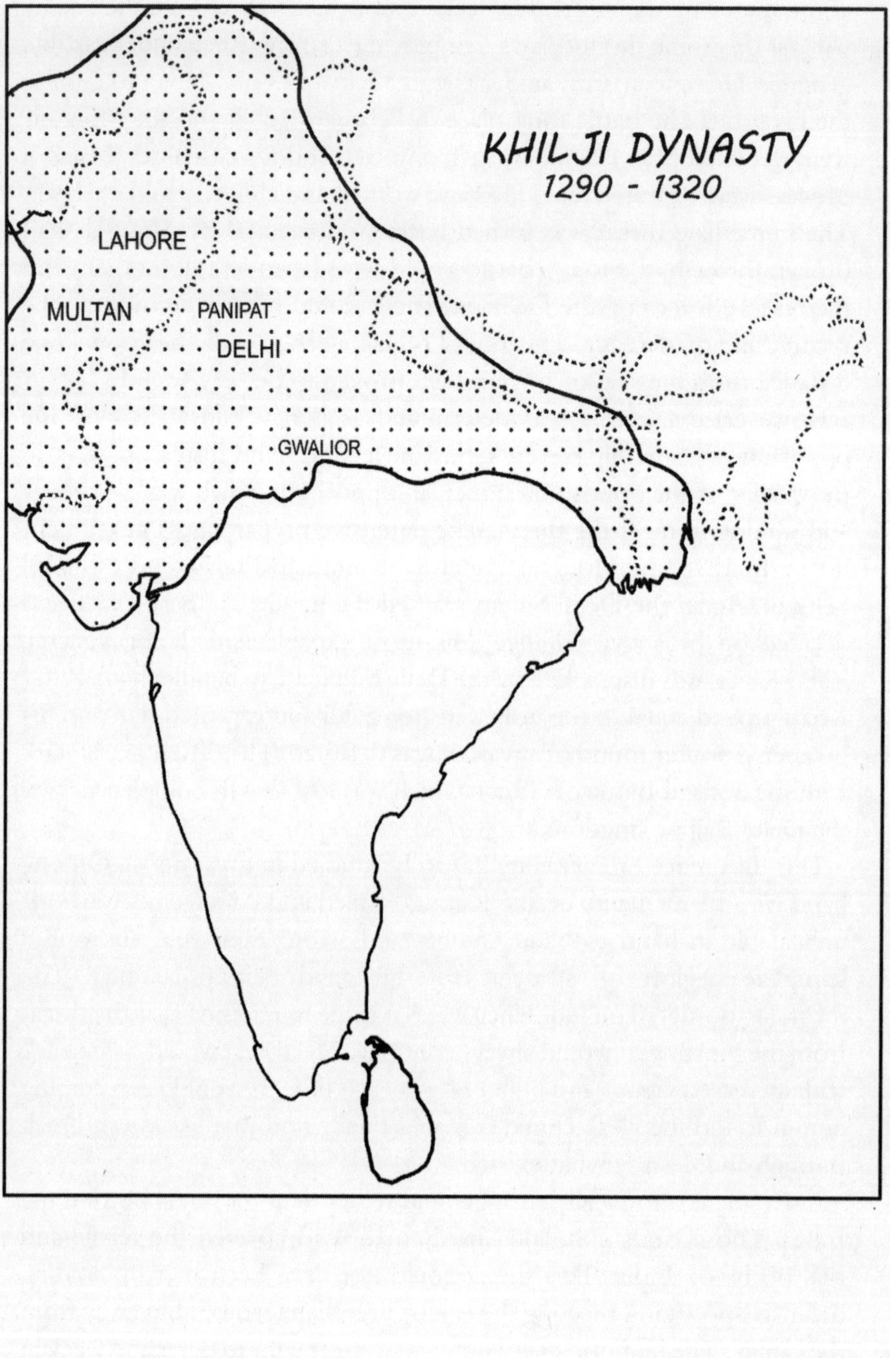
KHILJI DYNASTY
1290 - 1320
LAHORE
MULTAN
PANIPAT
DELHI
GWALIOR

the threat before it landed up unheralded at the imperial capital. Many historians rightly call it the Panipat Syndrome. The Khilji Turks, having come from those very lands the next invaders came from, realised the threat and were equal to the task.

The Mongol thirst to conquer India's rich territories was unquenched and continued unabated. In 1299, to avenge Saldi's death, Amir Daud launched another Mongol invasion with 200,000 horses under the command of his son Qutlugh Khwaja. Mongols did not fight deliberately but reached the environs of Delhi. This was the most serious threat and caught even an astute and ruthless king like Allaudin Khilji unprepared. The Turks were afraid to take this Mongol force head on. Allaudin's counsels advised him to avoid battle against this heavy force. However, the Sultan had other ideas. He decided to fight the enemy instead of sitting in a defensive position behind fortifications. Allaudin Khilji marched out of Badayun Gate with a formidable force of 3,00,000 horses and 2700 elephants. The battle with the Mongols took place at Kili, north of Delhi.

Allaudin Khilji commanded the centre, Zafar Khan the right wing. The left wing was under Ulugh Khan. Groups of elephants were placed in front of each Turkic division to absorb the fierce Mongol charge. In the rear was a body of reserve under the Wazir of the Delhi Sultanate.

The Mongols formed with Qutlugh Khwaja at the centre. Hajlik commanded the left wing and Bugha the right wing. Zafar Khan on the Turk right attacked Hajlik on the Mongol left. He broke through the Mongol left and even damaged the Mongol centre. The Khilji centre withstood the assault of the attack from the Mongol centre. Ulugh Khan went on the offensive from the Turk left and attacked the Mongol right wing but did not achieve the kind of success that the Turk right did. Hajlik counter-attacked Zafar and pressed him hard. Zafar expected reinforcements which never materialised. Zafar, in desperation, counter -attacked, defeated Hajlik and pursued him quite a few miles. He continued to pursue the Mongols and reached far but received no reinforcements and camped at night for the next day. The Mongols learnt of Zafar Khan's perilous position and surrounded to attack him under Qutlugh Khwaja and Targhi. Zafar Khan was killed but the Mongols had seen enough determined resistance and withdrew from India.

A hard pressed Sultan, thrown into a weaker position by a large army appearing at his gates, had kept a strong and stable army under capable generals with the capacity to meet such a large threat and fought a very determined battle to successfully defend his kingdom. The Mongol threat abated for a while. They had suffered a crushing defeat and did not attack India for four years. This gave the Sultan reasons to focus inward into India and try and conquer the South and the brave and defiant Rajputs in the West.

This policy was to have its own repercussions as the threat from the Northwest reappeared again. And this time even Allaudin Khilji was completely unprepared. The threat to the unity and integrity of a nation never dies down, can come from multiple directions, especially from the most obvious ones where the enemy is indefatigable and consumed with a continuous desire to conquer you. It may be economically and resources-wise weaker but it makes up for it with its determination, ferocity and total concentration of its strength for the purpose of war, nothing else. A lesson that should never be forgotten.

In 1303 Allaudin had attacked Chittor. Mongols decided to take advantage of this and attacked the Delhi Sultanate. 120,000 horse under Targhi attacked Delhi exploiting the absence of the Sultan's main army. Allaudin's main armies had either been away or were depleted. The main army had gone to attack Telengana and the other part of the army was weak after the war at Chittor. The Sultan was therefore forced on the defensive and had to fight a defensive battle of attrition. In the meantime he sent out instructions for his armies dispersed in various provinces to return.

Allaudin deployed his armies in the plain of Siri. His army had Siri Fort on the west, Yamuna in the east and dense forests in the south. The Mongol army was camped in the north opposite it. A ditch was dug around the Delhi Army, obstacles constructed behind it and detachments posted at intervals to monitor army movement. These detachments had elephants, cavalry and infantry. Every effort by Mongols to penetrate was thwarted. The Mongols could not go through the Turk army's defences. It looted the areas around and tried to starve the Delhi srmy into submission. Delhi suffered immensely. The Mongols were able to prevent reinforcements from reaching for the relief of Allaudin's army. They could not however carry on this effort for long. Being inexperienced in the art of siege warfare, the Mongols withdrew. Allaudin's determined defence of Delhi was successful.

Now we can see a real difference between the attitude and mind set of Prithviraj Chauhan and Allaudin Khilji. Prithviraj defeated Ghori and then retired into a complacent stupor. For him the continuity of the threat from the Northwest had ceased to exist like a bad dream. Allaudin was the exact opposite. He realised that the real threat came from renewed invasions from the Northwest and decided to take proactive action. He strengthened weak outposts, increased the infrastructural and armed strength of existing forts, constructed new forts and outposts and posted guarding armies at main approaches. The seat of government moved inside Siri Fort. A wall was constructed around the capital with battlements and ditches. A large central reserve cavalry force of almost half a million was created, always stationed at the capital to prevent the threat to Delhi. A governor was appointed for the Northwest with a large army to handle the first enemy offensive, deter it and weaken it. This was the real difference. A proactive and aggressive posture was adopted against a perennial source of invasion. Allaudin did not wait to be informed of the invasion and then wake up and rush to meet it in an ill-prepared manner at his doorstep. It was a policy that was to reap rich dividends when it came to preserving the security of the Khilji Sultanate.

In 1305, 50,000 Mongols under Ali Beg Gurgan and Tartaq crossed the Indus and made their way to Rohilkhand, bypassing Delhi. Targhi, eager to avenge his earlier defeat, accompanied this force. Malik Kafur with 40,000 cavalry was deputed by Allaudin to engage the enemy. Malik Kafur, who became famous for conquering South India for the Sultan, moved forward with purpose and daring. He made a surprise night attack and destroyed the enemy forces. This is a great example of how a defensive formation takes the offensive and surprises an invading army instead of being surprised by them. Unfortunately, succeeding governments to this day have suffered from the ignominy of being taken for surprise, as if they relish the prospect. 1962 and Kargil are clear examples.

Targhi was killed. Ali Beg and Tartaq were captured and later executed. This happened on 30/31 December 1305. Prisoners were brought to Delhi and beheaded. Their heads were built into the walls of Siri fort. The captured commanders were trampled to death under the feet of elephants.

It has to be said of the Mongols that they were never prepared to give up. It was a different issue that the calibre of the Sultan they faced as a military commander was far superior to their own. To avenge the defeat of 1305, Amir Daud attacked again in 1306.The invading Mongol army split into two, one coming towards Lahore and the other towards Nagaur.

Allaudin sent Malik Kafur and Ghazi Malik to defeat the Mongols. Malik Kafur kept his force as one and his advance army under Ghazi Malik engaged the Mongols under Kabak on the banks of River Ravi. The Mongols were defeated and Kabak was captured and brought to Delhi. The other Mongol force was engaged near Nagaur, its right flank destroyed and it fled for safety. About 50,000 to 60,000 captives were brought to Delhi. Male prisoners were trampled under the feet of elephants, and women and children sold as slaves. A tower of their skulls was made in front of Badayun gate.

Then the Delhi Sultan followed a policy that showed a military foresight that was only shown by Mughal Emperor Akbar and a few of his successors a few hundred years later. To prevent further Mongol raids, the Delhi army under Ghazi Malik crossed the Indus annually to attack Mongols, even going as far as Kabul, Ghazni and Kandahar. The Mongols, already preoccupied with troubles in Central Asia, did not bother the Khilji Sultanate anymore.

Because of his policy of attacking Hindu kingdoms, looting their wealth, destroying temples and building mosques, forcing women to resort to *jauhar*, and massacring inhabitants of captured cities, Allaudin Khilji comes across as a despicable conqueror in the history of India. And rightly so.

However, if one were to look at the offensive and defensive mechanisms undertaken by him to counter the threat from the Northwest, then possibly he has no equal save Chandragupta Maurya earlier and Emperor Akbar later. Allaudin Khilji faced a determined enemy, an enemy that had no cultural or economic ambitions but only military ones, those of conquest. Economically it would be a poor enemy compared to kingdoms in India but militarily always ready and armed. Its single-minded focus was the weakening and conquest of India.

It never gave up but kept coming back for eight years repeatedly in great and vigorous strength. A lesser military personality than Allaudin might have crumbled. The Sultan not only realised the gravity of the threat but was ever ready. First of all was the mindset and attitude. Instead of adopting a feeble and indolent attitude, his military readiness was first class. He realised that this threat existed and would continue to do so. He always had capable generals and ready armies. He foresaw the advance of the Mongols and sent strong armies to intercept the invaders far from his capital and repulse them at a distance from the imperial city. He built fortifications, kept standing armies oriented towards the Northwest and was always ready to meet the threat. Even if taken by surprise, he had a strong army ready for a last ditch defence. And he neither forgot nor spared the defeated army. He meted out terrible punishment to the captured invaders. Even if the Mongols withdrew to the Northwest of India, he sent his capable general, Ghazi Malik, to ravage their lands and destroy them in their home territory, further nullifying the threat.

Current governments of India need to study this. A strong defence is half the battle won. Hopes that the threats from across borders will subside are foolhardy. In this day and age, proactive weapons like diplomacy, intelligence, counter insurgent action, depletion of enemy strength and splitting his concentration are something they may need to learn from this Sultan.

Chapter VI

Taimur Lang

Taimur Lang was possibly the most bloodthirsty conqueror to visit India. The history of how he invaded India, defeated a weakening central emperor and then ransacked and massacred people in thousands should serve as a lesson to those who forget that unity and strength are not perennial in nature and need to be carefully and diligently preserved. Weakening of central authority exposes everyone who played a part in the process to ultimately suffer at the hands of a conqueror, whose threat was underplayed and invasion facilitated. It also opens one's eyes to what can happen once this country comes under the rule of a bloodthirsty conqueror who is a religious zealot. Such a conqueror is destructive with little or no regard for human life. And events in the neighbourhood show it can happen again and again even in modern times.

The Tughlaq dynasty that succeeded the Khiljis had three powerful rulers—Ghiyasuddin Tughlaq, Mohammed Bin Tughlaq and Firoz Shah Tughlaq. They were, in terms of religious bigotry, avowedly Islamic fanatics. But they succeeded in keeping a strong central empire with Delhi as the seat of the capital. They invaded the South and brought about the death knell of Hindu kingdoms there while Allaudin Khilji had only promoted the concept of suzerainty. In the process they looted, massacred, pillaged and indulged in religious bigotry. The Tughlaqs created a more permanent Islamic presence in the Deccan than did the Khiljis.

Ghiyasuddin Tughlaq built Tughlaqabad and was probably done to death in an accident engineered by his son on the outskirts of Delhi. His son, Mohammed Bin Tughlaq, built Jahanpanah. He tried to shift the capital to Daulatabad and one of the reasons could have been to set up a capital in Central India as he had to keep control of North India while trying to subjugate the South. That experiment ended in disaster and forced a return to Delhi.

After him came Firoz Shah Tughlaq, a bloodthirsty religious zealot, known for his cruelty in conversions and atrocities on Hindus. He was more of a builder than a conqueror. He can also be credited with being one of the longest serving monarchs in Delhi. His death and last years of life trace the decline of the Tughlaqs, which was a rather rapid decline. Firoz Shah built the city of Firozshah Kotla or Firozabad. He lost his most beloved son, who could have been a worthy successor, in 1374. This death affected Firoz Shah Tughlaq very badly. A rebellion happened in Gujarat and was suppressed. Another happened at Katehar and was suppressed with the highest of brutality and the massacre of the Hindu population.

Firoz Shah had unworthy successors when it came to building and preserving empires. He abdicated in favour of his son Mohammed Khan but had to return as the son proved to be an unworthy ruler. Firoz Shah died in 1388. He had been a long serving, successful monarch credited with having preserved the Tughlaq dynasty's hold on North India. But his activities, unlike that of another monarch Akbar who also ruled for a long period, were in favour of his own religion and decidedly against other religions.

The last decade of the fourteenth century was a particularly tumultuous one for the Tughlaq dynasty. Many successors came from the Tughlaq lineage but lost their lives and the throne. Outposts and outlying provinces declared independence. There were rival claimants for the throne. Firoz Shah had created an elite palace guard that played its own role in the overthrow and replacement of Sultans. There was anarchy everywhere, the kingdom fell prey to civil wars and there was general confusion.

Ghiyasuddin, Mohammed Bin and Firoz Shah Tughlaq had their faults but they ran strong central empires. Conquering India when they were in power would not have been easy for a foreign invader. But the moment Firoz Shah died, there was tumult in the empire. Strong central governance was replaced by chaos.

Firoz Shah was succeeded by his grandson Tughlaq Shah. Firoz Shah's third son tried to overthrow him but failed. However, Tughlaq Shah was given to a life of pleasure and misrule. Abu Bakr, another grandson of Firoz Shah, overthrew him to claim the throne. Firoz Shah's son,

Prince Mohammed, challenged him and overthrew him. More deaths and struggles followed and ultimately we come to the reign of Sultan Nasiruddin Mahmud Shah, the last of the Tughlaqs.

In the process, the Tughlaq empire disintegrated. Bengal, Central India, South India, Gujarat, Rajasthan, Jaunpur and Punjab became independent. Another son of Firoz Shah, Nusrat Shah, challenged him and set up a rival kingdom at Firozabad. So there were two Sultans ruling a dynasty from different power centres and a disintegrated empire with a host of rival kingdoms, a situation tailor-made for an invader to come in and take advantage of. This is what internecine struggles as well as pretensions to establish independent kingdoms out of a united India achieve. Ultimately it means death and destruction for all those who have such notions.

Into this chaotic space stepped in Taimur Lang. Taimur was born in AD 1336 in a town near Samarkand. He was from the branch of Chagatai Turks owning a small kingdom near Samarkand. However, this intrepid conqueror created an empire across Central Asia and the Middle East. His empire extended from Syria to Afghanistan. In one of his battles, his leg was wounded, giving him a limp, and hence his name Taimur Lang. His decision to invade India came from the zeal to plunder wealth, convert and crush the so called infidels. The unsteady state of the Delhi Sultanate was another factor that propelled him to attack India. An unsteady government with a weak centre always attracts conquerors. Conquerors beyond the Hindu Kush have always waited for signs of weakening before attacking to conquer. History has shown that this threat never ceased from AD 700 onwards and whenever the strength of ruling monarchs and dynasties withered, the attacker became successful.

An initial force was sent by him under his grandson, Peer Mohammed, that occupied Uch and Multan. Taimur left Samarkand in AD 1398 and reached Afghanistan with 100,000 horse at the age of 62. He conducted his first bloodthirsty massacre in Kator either killing people or converting them. He fought against the Khokhars who defended resolutely but ultimately lost the battle. He then crossed the Jhelum and Chenab.

He proceeded to attack the Rajput Raja of Bhatner, faced stiff resistance, overcame it and conducted his usual massacre. The battle raged for a few days and Taimur faced a very tough battle. Raja Duli Chand of Bhatner fought valiantly with his army throwing all kinds of

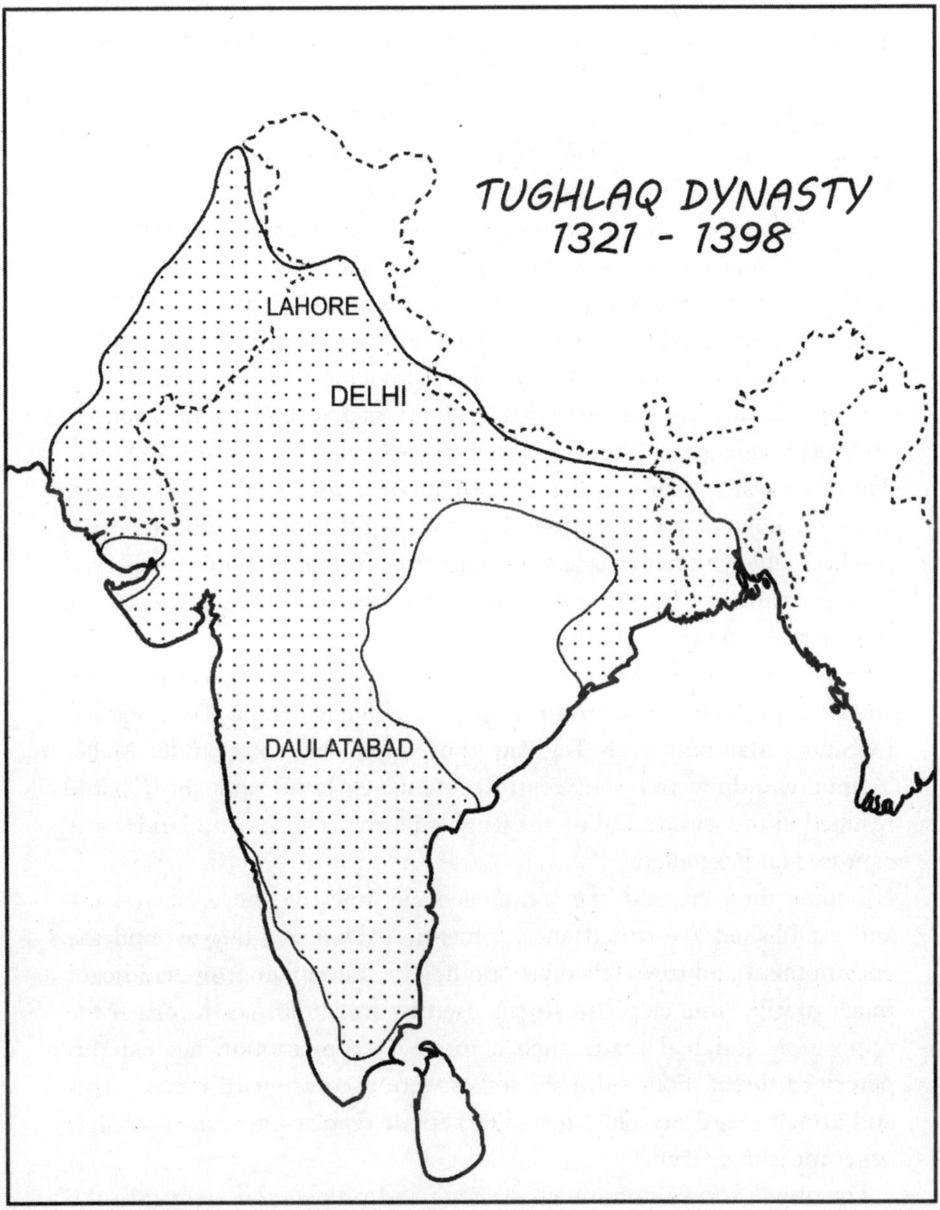
TUGHLAQ DYNASTY
1321 - 1398
LAHORE
DELHI
DAULATABAD

missiles, rocks, and javelins from the fort but ultimately had to surrender. The usual massacre was ordered and thousands of Hindus killed. Similar massacres were conducted at Sirsa and other places.

A weak kingdom is unable to organise a strong defence against an invading force. The Tughlaqs of this era ruled a weak central kingdom with little control on the frontiers of India. Taimur and his grandson were offered piecemeal resistance by frontier tribes, Khokhars, Rajputs and other small kingdoms and faced no formidable foe in their march to India. By the time they reached a position where they had to attack the seat of the empire, Delhi, they had had sufficient experience of fighting Indian armies and were also more or less intact in their strength.

After conducting further raids and massacres, his whole army of 100,000 finally assembled at Kaithal to focus on the capture of Delhi. The stage was set for another important battle for Delhi. This invading army made its way to Delhi via Panipat. In December 1398, the army reached Jahan Numa palace. Crossing river Yamuna, Taimur captured Loni Fort after a typically stiff fight but fruitless resistance put up by the Rajput rulers there.

On 12 December 1398, he came out to inspect the defences of Delhi and unexpectedly ran into an armed contingent of the Tughlaqs led by Sultan Mahmud Shah Tughlaq himself and his commander Mallu. Taimur withdrew but sent reinforcements. A bitter and short battle resulted in the withdrawal of the Tughlaq army, whose commander was captured and executed.

Taimur then crossed the Yamuna again towards the eastern bank and established a fortified encampment. A ditch was dug around the encampment and trees felled around it. The Taimurian army had heard much of the large elephant forces used by Indian armies to crush the opposition and had made such a move as a precaution against this perceived threat. Four pronged spikes were used as guard mechanisms and armed guard detachments were kept at regular intervals as well as other measures taken.

The above shows how much strategy and preparation went into the work of invaders who were destined to be successful conquerors. They were determined to succeed. Since the focus of their activity was always military in nature, their capabilities were well developed to analyse the kind of opposition they would face in India and think of ways to overcome it. They invaded with large, well prepared forces. Smaller opposition met on the way was crushed with resolution and massacres conducted ruthlessly to instil fear in the heart of larger defensive formations waiting further ahead. However, no matter what, these invaders did not rest on their reputation and were not to be found wanting in their preparation for the ultimate decisive battle. The defensive measures adopted by Taimur, a much feared conqueror, show how well thought out his plans were, how well prepared he had come but was still ready to take all precautions, never underestimating the enemy.

On the day of the battle, the Taimurian army formation was in three parts—centre and two wings. The advance guard was under Prince Rustam and the centre under Taimur himself. The Tughlaq army also came well prepared. It advanced with a great beating of drums and seemed to have come determined to fight. In the right wing was Muinuddin and in the left Taghi Khan. There was a rear guard. Sultan Mahmud Shah was in the centre along with his Wazir Mallu Iqbal. To oppose the Taimurian army of 70,000, the Tughlaqs had assembled a force of 10,000 cavalry, 40,000 infantry and a large number of war elephants. The elephants were protected by iron plates with poisoned blades to harm the enemy. In addition there were fire and rocket throwers, equipping the army with firearms to attack Taimur's army. Therefore the forces were more or less evenly matched.

The army of Taimur consisted of a centre, left and right wings, an advance guard, a reserve and a rear guard. Taimur before the day of battle had collected his commanders and briefed them extensively on his battle preparations and how the battle itself was to be conducted.

The battle took place on 17 December 1398. The battle began with the Taimur advance guard launching a surprise attack on the rear of the Tughlaq advance guard. The Tughlaq advance guard lost the fight and had to retreat. In the meantime, the Taimurian right wing attacked the Tughlaq left wing. A shower of arrows was combined with a mass attack of heavily armoured cavalry. The Tughlaq left wing was destroyed. Also the Taimurian left wing attacked the Tughlaq right wing with the usual initial shower of arrows to render the elephant force useless. Again a charge followed, routing the Tughlaq right wing and chasing it to the gates of Delhi.

However the Tughlaq centre under Mallu gave a good account of itself and continued to hold its own against the Taimurian army. However, Taimur's strategy of enveloping and defeating the Tughlaq army from the wings was succeeding. Taimur also continued to attack enemy elephants with arrows, rendering them amuck and then cutting them down with swords. The Tughlaq centre continued to fight hard but soon found themselves under increasing and unbearable pressure. The Tughlaq army fell back in disarray giving up the fight and the Tughlaqs lost the Battle of Delhi as well as the control of the imperial capital. The Sultan fled to Gujarat, and Mallu Iqbal, elsewhere.

Taimur marched in triumph into Delhi and ordered a general massacre of the populace. The massacre went on unhindered for days. A ruthless massacre of non-Muslim populations and immense looting happened for days. Delhi had not seen a sack and massacre like this before. A weak king with a weak kingdom had failed to defend its people as well as the integrity of the land. The result was there for all to see.

Meerut and Panipat were captured with similar results, as was Hardwar. The same fate awaited Hindu Kingdoms of Kangra and Jammu with massacres and forced conversions. The massacre of non-Muslim populations, loot and rape were the norm. Once the back of the main army was broken, the whole country and its populace were defenceless against a rapacious conqueror. This was perhaps the most frightening, rapacious and massacre-driven invasion of India. The Shivalik hills were invested. Jammu was attacked, conquered, and its Hindu king converted.

In many ways it happened because the Tughlaq dynasty had outlived its days of strength and power and was led by a weak ruler, no match for Taimur in the art of war. It had insufficient resources and plans or the power to intercept such a large and powerful force coming towards India. There were no strong garrisons and commanders to slow down or repulse the incoming force. The final battle was fought at the doorstep of Delhi, they say somewhere near the site of present day Safdarjung airport. It should have been fought further up northwest and even if lost could have resulted in a retreat to a more defensible position. Once lost, there was no way Delhi could have been further defended and saved. This was a far cry from the forward defensive strategy adopted successfully by Allaudin Khilji against the similarly rapacious Mongol invaders. Luckily Taimur had only come to invade, massacre, destroy loot, and not to stay. He went away, leaving a ghost town called Delhi.

Chapter VII

Babur's Battles: Panipat and Khanua

It is said that India's fate was decided on very critical occasions by the battlefields of Panipat, where three decisive battles were fought. One established the Mughal Empire, another restored it and the third pushed back the dreams of the Marathas to control Delhi by over a decade.

The Tughlaq Sultanate was decimated in the Battle of Delhi by Taimur Lang. Mahmud Shah Tughlaq's defeat meant the onset of a new dynasty called the Sayyids. It lasted 37 years and was at best tenuously clinging on to the throne at Delhi. The next truly big dynasty was the Lodhi dynasty whose name is borne to this day by the famous Lodhi Garden, Lodhi Estate, Lodhi Road and until sometime back by the Lodhi Hotel. Little would this dynasty have realised that its name would stretch far into the future as landmarks in a large modern Indian state.

Bahlol Lodhi was the founder of this dynasty and lies buried near Chiragh Delhi today. His successor was Sikander Lodhi, the founder of Agra in AD 1504. Next in line came Ibrahim Lodhi, the last of the Muslim Sultans before the advent of the Mughals, as historians view the Islamic Sultanates. The era of the Great Mughal Empire started after Sultan Ibrahim Lodhi and the platform for that was the First Battle of Panipat.

What encouraged Babar to attack India was his desire to establish a personal empire for himself as well as the weakness he perceived in the Afghan Sultanate run by Ibrahim Lodhi. Ibrahim Lodhi inherited the Sultanate of Hindustan from his illustrious father Sikander Lodhi. However, this Sultan's rule started with a fault line. He was forced to divide and give away a part of his empire to his brother Jalal Khan who became a parallel ruler at Jaunpur. Having done so, Ibrahim realised this cardinal error and refuted this treaty which had been painstakingly constructed by intervening Afghan nobles. Jalal Khan, understandably, opposed this development and what followed was a battle between brothers with nobles taking sides. Jalal Khan was defeated, took initial refuge at Gwalior and thence proceeded to Gonda where the ruling Raja obligingly captured him and delivered him to Ibrahim Lodhi. Ibrahim, of course, wasted no time in dispatching him to death by getting him poisoned.

One military achievement of Ibrahim Lodhi was his defeat of the Tomara kingdom of Gwalior, something his father could not achieve. Lodhi's army, led by Azam Humayun Sarwani, defeated Vikramjit Singh, the ruler of Gwalior. But the military achievements that Ibrahim Lodhi could claim were cancelled out by the sheer ineptitude he exhibited in his dealings with the Afghan nobility.

The Afghans were not a people who accepted overlordship easily. It had to be earned. Sikander Lodhi earned it. Ibrahim Lodhi inherited it under the assumption that he deserved it. However, he mishandled the Afghan nobility. He infuriated a certain section of Afghan nobility by repudiating the treaty he had reached with his brother, Jalal Khan. Then he started showing signs of casting suspicion on senior and respected Afghan nobles. He imprisoned Miyan Bhua, a *vazir* who had served the Lodhi Sultans diligently for close to thirty years, merely on account of his old age. He then made the error of appointing Miyan Bhua's son as *vazir*. He imprisoned a noble, Azam Humayun Sarwani, on the suspicion that he had helped Jalal Khan escape from Gwalior and also imprisoned his son, Fateh Khan. In addition, he imprisoned and did to death the rest of his own brothers. These actions led to an open military revolt by the Afghan nobility.

Islam Khan, the second son of Azam Humayun, revolted. The area around Kanauj passed into the hands of the rebels who defeated a couple of armies sent against them by Sultan Ibrahim. Not to be deterred and being a brave warrior, Sultan Ibrahim himself took the field against the rebels. It was a particularly bloody battle where Afghans had to take sides. Relatives fought relatives and the flower of Afghan soldiery perished in the battle. Ibrahim Lodhi won the battle but by now Afghan nobility had lost faith in him and were afraid of his vindictive conduct.

Ibrahim Lodhi on his part continued to plague the Afghan nobles, getting big nobles like Azam Humayun Sarwani, Miyan Bhua and Husain Khan Farmuli either murdered or imprisoned to death. Bahadur Khan, a prominent governor of Bihar, declared himself independent as Sultan Mohammed and collected a fearsome army. He defeated armies sent against him by Ibrahim Lodhi. The eastern part of the Afghan empire and therefore its economic and military resources were lost to Ibrahim Lodhi.

Ibrahim Lodhi appealed to Daulat Khan Lodhi, Governor of Punjab, for help. Daulat Khan Lodhi sent his son to assess the intentions of Ibrahim Lodhi and his assessment was negative. Daulat Khan Lodhi therefore refused to help Ibrahim. Alam Khan, uncle of Ibrahim, based in Gujarat, was also ill disposed towards Ibrahim Lodhi. The Afghan nobles, Daulat Khan and Alam Khan, therefore united in the cause to overthrow Ibrahim Lodhi.

However, they made a fundamental error. They invited Babar, the ruler of Afghanistan, to attack Delhi and defeat Ibrahim Lodhi. The basis for this, apart from their hatred for Ibrahim, was the fond belief that Babar was a seeker of fortune and not an empire builder. He would defeat Ibrahim, take his share of loot and turn back, leaving Delhi for Afghan nobles other than Ibrahim. Thus, the Punjab part of the Lodhi Empire was also lost to Ibrahim Lodhi. It was therefore a considerably weakened Lodhi Sultanate driven apart by internecine quarrels that lay in wait for a formidable adversary called Babar. It was weakened by internal dissensions and a Sultan who had an impolitic approach to issues.

At the same time, another formidable power was rising to the southwest of the Delhi Sultanate. These were the Rajputs who had once ruled the heartland of North India, lost it to the invading Muslim armies and had retreated to the hills and deserts of Rajasthan, split into multiple kingdoms like Mewar and Marwar but not given up on their martial spirit and abilities. They had continued to fight armies sent by the Delhi Islamic Sultanates, sometimes defeating them, sometimes losing their forts, but always managing to recover them. At last, under a series of capable rulers like Rao Hammir, Rana Kumbha and others, the kingdom of Mewar grew the strongest and under the formidable Rana Sangha managed to acquire a quasi-leadership role in a Rajput confederacy.

Not only did Mewar grow strong enough to resist invasions from the Delhi Sultanate but it also adopted an aggressive and proactive stance towards the neighbouring kingdoms. Its immediate and hostile neighbours were Gujarat to its south and Malwa to its southeast. It had various battles with both these Sultanates, defeating Mahmud Khilji

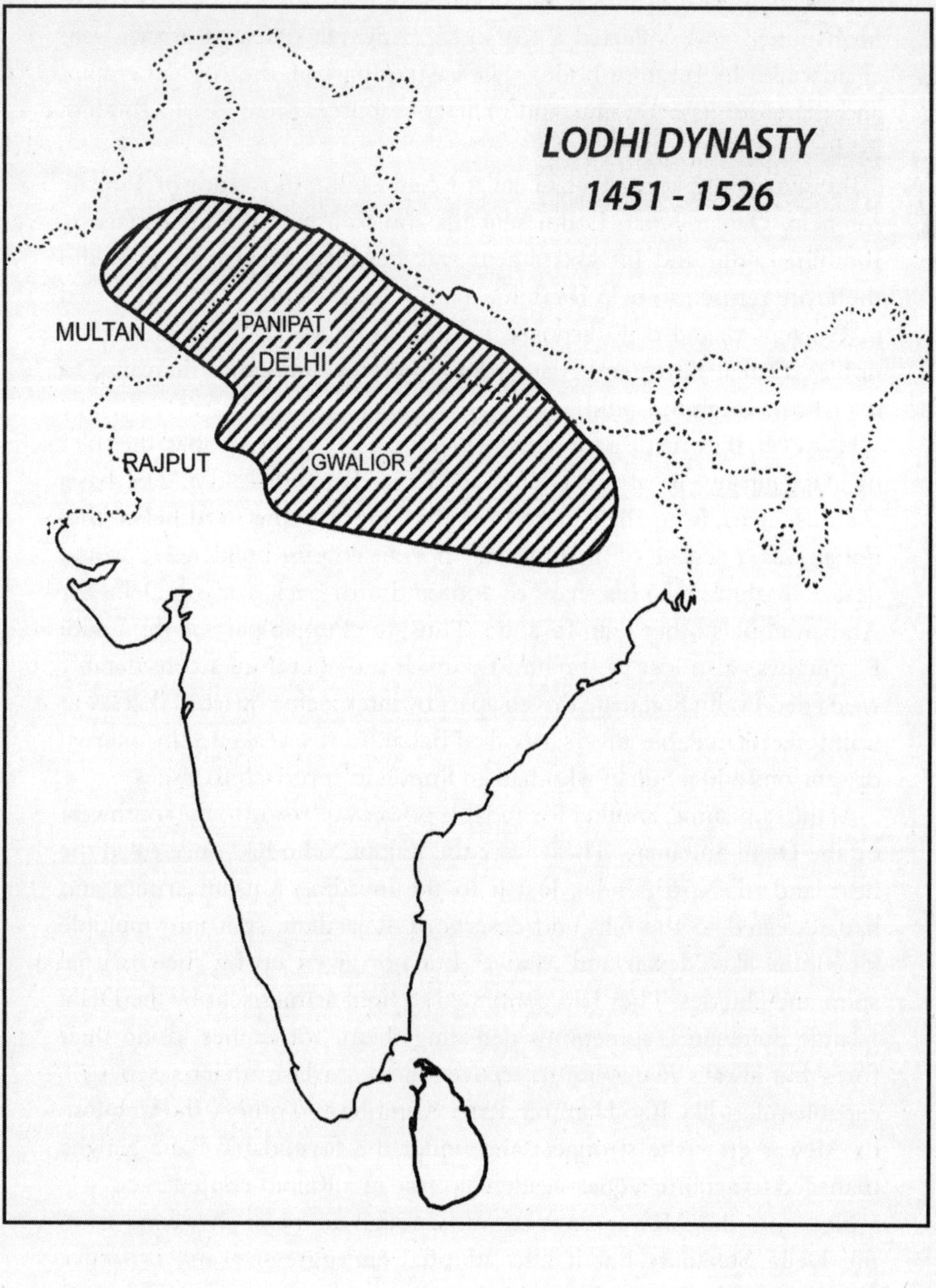
LODHI DYNASTY
1451 - 1526
MULTAN
PANIPAT
DELHI
RAJPUT
GWALIOR

The Dargah of Hazrat Nizamuddin Auliya - present day.
(Photograph copyright © Rajeev Katyal, 2016)

Qila Rai Pithora, the erstwhile fort of Prithviraj Chauhan.
(Photograph copyright © Rajeev Katyal, 2016)

The historic Qutub Minar.

(Photograph copyright © Rajeev Katyal, 2016)

Babar after attending a reception in his honour at Samarkand, leaving for Bustan Serai.

National Museum - New Delhi Collection (Acc no: 50.336/44)

Ramparts of Purana Qila, the old fort of Delhi built by Humayun and Sher Shah Suri.

Humayun's tomb.
(Photograph copyright © Rajeev Katyal, 2016)

Graves at Humayun's tomb—a Mughal necropolis.
(Photograph copyright © Rajeev Katyal, 2016)

Emperor Jahangir testing the strength of penance of Gosain Nirmulji and Bhagvanji.
National Museum - New Delhi Collection (Acc no: 47.110/359)

Grave of Allaudin Khilji.

(Photograph copyright © Rajeev Katyal, 2016)

Alai Minar: The construction of this tower was started by Sultan Allauddin Khilji, to rival the Qutub Minar.

(Photograph copyright © Rajeev Katyal, 2016)

Grave of Sultan Shamsuddin Iltutmish.

Ramparts of Tughlaqabad—cursed fort of Sultan Ghiyasuddin Tughlaq
(Photograph copyright © Rajeev Katyal, 2016)

Ramparts of Firozshah Kotla, fort of Firozshah Tughlaq.
(Photograph copyright © Rajeev Katyal, 2016)

Tomb at Lodhi Garden.
(Photograph copyright © Rajeev Katyal, 2016)

Inner courtyard of Firozshah Kotla.
(Photograph copyright © Rajeev Katyal, 2016)

Emperor Shahjahan at the marriage of his eldest son, Dara Shikoh.
National Museum - New Delhi Collection (Acc no: 58.58.38)

Dara Shikoh viewing acrobats.
National Museum - New Delhi Collection (Acc no: 52.32)

Shah Shuja, the third son of Emperor Shahjahan.
National Museum - New Delhi Collection (Acc no: 48.5/13)

Dara Shikoh with a Sufi fakir.

National Museum - New Delhi Collection (Acc no: 50/14/11)

Timur with his nobles.
National Museum - New Delhi Collection (Acc no: 47.131)

Ruins of Siri Fort, city of Allaudin Khilji.

of Malwa and Sultan Muzaffar of Gujarat or forcing stalemates and agreements weighted in favour of Mewar.

Rana Sangha was different from other Rajput rulers. He had the capability of building a military force that could wage war on multiple fronts. He could lead a normally fractious Rajput polity united in battle against adversaries. He had ambitions to bring Hindustan under the control of a Rajput rule and of creating a Rajput kingdom to replace a Muslim Sultanate. He, in fact, was moving forward in that direction. He started to move aggressively towards Delhi and started grabbing territory of the Lodhi Sultanate. Ibrahim Lodhi reacted with counter aggression and the armies of Mewar and Delhi clashed. The Rajput chief proved more than a match for the Lodhi army, defeating it on multiple occasions, notable being the battles of Dholpur and Khatauli because of which the Rajputs captured territory as far as Bayana.

Lodhi was now beset with a breakaway East, a rebellious and treacherous Punjab, a breakaway Gujarat, a hungry Rajput adversary and an ambitious Badshah of Kabul, Mohammed Zahiruddin Babar. This was hardly an enviable position and Ibrahim seemed to be heading towards inevitable doom. Moreover, all these adversaries seemed to be joining hands against him. Daulat Khan invited Babar to invade and defeat Lodhi Sultan. Rana Sangha did not seem averse to the idea as long as Babar came, conquered and withdrew. Ibrahim Lodhi obviously did not want Babar anywhere near the scene. The stage was set for another battle to decide the fate of Delhi. And what a fateful battle it was!

Babar was born in AD 1483. His father was Omar Sheikh Mirza. He inherited the kingdom of Farghana at Samarkand but lost it to his Uzbeg adversaries. Driven to defeat in Central Asia, Babar got an opportunity to interfere in the fractious politics of Afghanistan. He captured Kabul in AD 1504, then Ghazni and Kandahar, and by AD 1507 became the Badshah of Afghanistan. Inspired by tales of Taimur, his ancestor, he also aspired for an empire and thought of invading and conquering India.

Babar faced an India which was without a strong central controlling authority. It was divided into several powerful kingdoms engaged in mutual warfare. Ibrahim Lodhi was fighting internal dissensions from Punjab and the East. Rana Sangha was fighting Gujarat, Malwa and Delhi. Gujarat was fighting Malwa. The South was ensconced in a world of its own behind the Vindhyas with the Vijayanagar kingdom fighting with the Sultanates of Bijapur, Golconda, Ahmednagar, Bidar and

Berar, who in turn were fighting among themselves. A divided India was again waiting to be conquered. The inevitability of its defeat was hardly surprising.

Babar's first few incursions into India were exploratory, getting deeper each time but testing the waters. He never made for the heartland of India initially. In the second invasion he reached Peshawar but turned back. He invaded Punjab in his third incursion and is said to have reached as far as Sialkot. The fourth time saw him reaching Lahore. He was getting closer to Delhi each time. The fifth time was in AD 1525. Babar was now ready to fight the battle for Delhi. He was going for the crown of Sultan-e-Hind.

Babar strengthened his forces of Afghanistan with fresh and hardy recruits from Central Asia, always a ripe recruiting ground for battle -hardened warriors. Sending an initial foraging party under Jahangir Quli Khan, Babar followed with the main body. His advance was swift and determined. He passed through Peshawar, Sialkot, Lahore, Ropar and reached Ambala, capturing territory and recruiting fresh volunteers on the way. His force and strength were increasing continuously.

Babar was now reaching the gates of Delhi and Ibrahim Lodhi could no longer ignore him. The Delhi Sultan was never one to shirk from battle. This had been evident from his earlier track record. He dispatched advance parties to deal with the Mughals but unfortunately these met with reverses. Hamid Khan of the Lodhi Sultanate was defeated by the advance right wing of the Mughal Army led by Humayun, who was barely into his adulthood. Daud Khan, leading another Afghan detachment, was similarly defeated. Nothing remained between the invading army of Babar and the Delhi Sultan. Ibrahim Lodhi too advanced to give battle. The two armies camped near each other at what was fated to be the decisive field of Panipat, perhaps the most legendary battlefield in India other than Kurukshetra, not too far from it. The fate of the crown of Delhi was to be settled in close proximity to where it had been about 4500 years before.

The method employed by each side for preparing for the battle could not have been more starkly different. To Ibrahim Lodhi, this was just one more enemy of the Delhi Sultanate to be fought and defeated. His army relied on numbers, massed cavalry and elephants, a surging horde of striking proportions. Babar was much more diligent, had done quite a bit of homework and had very clear and well thought out plans.

Babar realised the destructive impact the ferocious and battle-hungry Afghans could have with their massed cavalry charges on his army. He was also immensely apprehensive of the impact of the couple of thousand elephants that the Lodhi army had. His entire plan was therefore focused on three things—a defensive layout that blunted the speed of charge of opposition and its mass attack; the use of artillery and matchlocks that could fire and halt the charging enemy at a distance making hand to hand confrontation difficult for the enemy; and thirdly, the use of flying columns from the flanks and wings that would encircle and destroy the enemy from the sides while fire was poured into them from the front.

Babar claimed that his army was 12000 and that of Lodhi 100,000. It seems to have been an attempt to understate his own strength and overstate the enemy's so as to show a greater disparity and claim greater credit. Babar seems to have referred to his cavalry strength and did not include the gunners, matchlock men and other soldiers he gathered on the way from Kabul. Historians estimate his strength in the vicinity of 25,000 and this seems to be a generally accepted figure. Lodhi's army is stated to have been at 100,000 along with 2000 war elephants. This seems to be an overstatement. The Lodhi Sultanate, on account of internal revolts in Bengal, Gujarat and Punjab as well as in other parts, was emaciated. There seems to have been a regular army of around 50,000 cavalry, between 1000 to 2000 elephants and hastily gathered peasant-based infantry with swords and other assorted weapons. The strength could not have been more than 70,000 with a large part of questionable quality.

The armies moved towards each other and were camped in the vicinity of Panipat for a week from 12 to 19 April 1526. Babar prepared extremely well for this battle. He had already realised that the strength of the Delhi army lay in its speed and the mass of charge led by elephants and cavalry of ferocious Afghan soldiers. He devised techniques to fend off this charge and blunt its ferocity and effectiveness. He settled his army in such a way that his right flank was protected by the town of Panipat and left flank by ditches in the dry bed of the Yamuna. The Afghan army therefore had its chances of turning and routing the flanks of the Mughal army considerably reduced. In fact, abatis of fallen trees with branches projected outwards were further placed in the dried bed of the Yamuna, giving even greater protection and blunting an impetuous enemy charge.

FIRST BATTLE OF PANIPAT

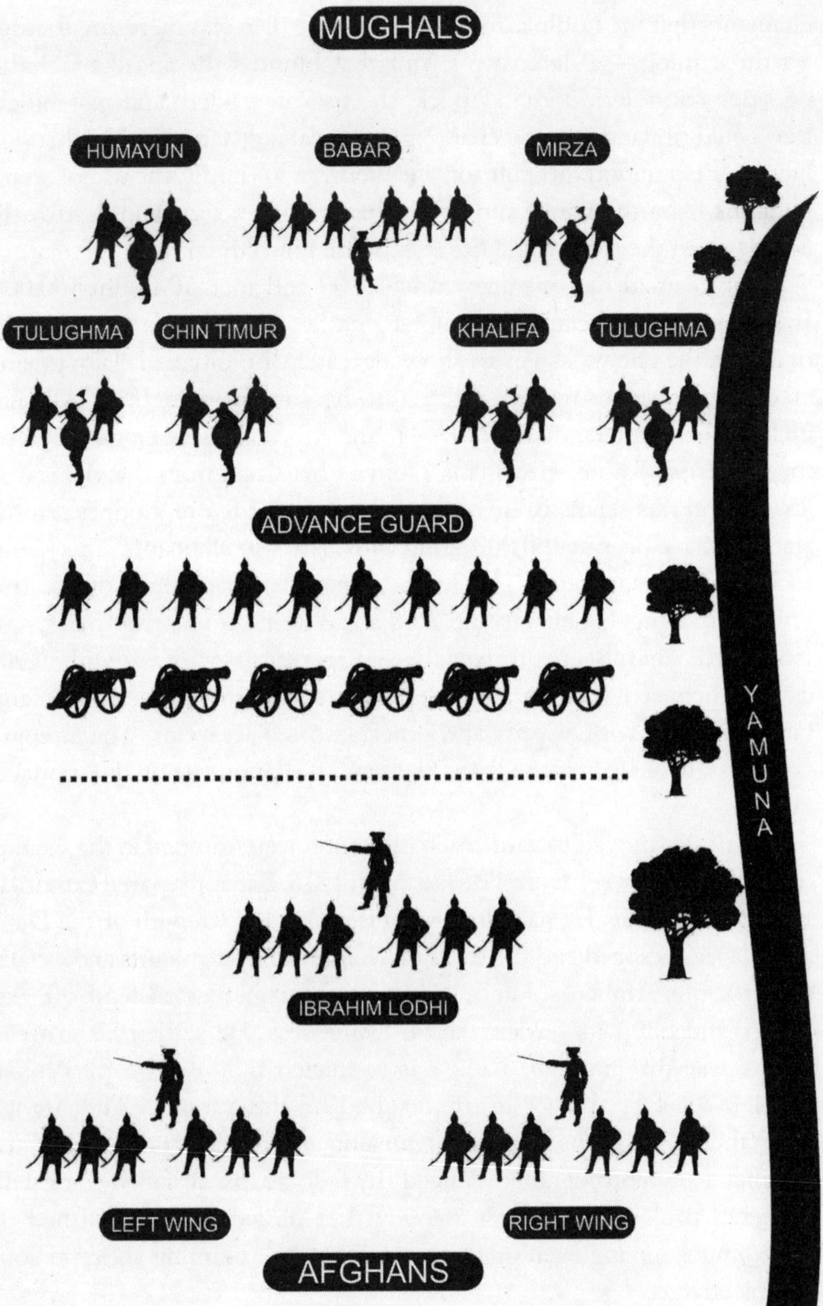

Babar devised a Rumi method, used by Ottoman Turks, where 700 gun carriages called *Araba*s were placed across the front of the Mughal army tied together by ox hide. In between groups of tied carts were placed tripod barriers of strong wood. It was behind these breastworks that Babar placed his most formidable weapons—his cannons, swivel guns and matchlock men. Placed behind breastworks, these men were protected from enemy cavalry and elephant charges but were free to pour withering fire into a massed, advancing enemy. Babar, as one can see, had done excellent homework to protect both his front and flanks from the main strength of the enemy, which was a massed, speedy charge which is akin to a modern army tank and armoured carrier attack. Preparations for a battle could seldom have been better.

However, Babar's preparations were not wholly defensive. Between wider gaps in the carriages, there was space for 150 cavalry at a time to launch attacks and counter charges. Moreover, the way Babar deployed his army gave him an ability to create smaller parts which could be used in a flexible mode depending on where the requirement arose. His army formation behind these defensive formations was composed of different parts.

Babar placed himself in the centre, commanding the ghol. There was a further sub division of the centre with the right centre under Chin Timur and left centre under Mir Khalifa. The *Baranghar*, right wing, was under his son Humayun assisted by Khwaja Khan. The left wing, *Jaranghar*, was under the combined command of Mohammed Sultan Mirza and Mehdi Khwaja. There was the *Harawal*, an advance guard under Khusrau Kokaltash and a reserve to the advance *Iltimish* under Abdul Aziz. In addition there were the far flanks with mounted horse archers on the left and right to encircle the enemy and execute the *Talughma.*

The advancing Afghans were in a simple formation with a centre, left and right, and Sultan Ibrahim Lodhi was himself in the centre. Before the battle he is said to have distributed gifts and wealth lavishly among his nobles.

The First Battle of Panipat, a battle for the control of Delhi, was fought on 21 April 1526. The Afghans covered four miles in three hours and went straight into attack. The Afghan left wing attacked the Mughal right wing hoping to break it and roll up Babar's army from the right. Babar sent in reinforcements which were helped by the protection afforded to his right by the town of Panipat. The Afghans came up in speed but were stopped in their tracks by the Mughal gun carriage defence system that did not allow them to go through. The Afghan cavalry, upon confronting this defensive barrier slowed and stopped and the Afghan cavalry coming from behind, not realising this, barged into its own by now stationary advance cavalry thus creating confusion and turmoil in Afghan ranks. Babar's cannons, swivel guns and matchlocks poured fire from a distance into this confused mass of Afghan army and wreaked havoc. The elephants panicked due to the fire, light and noise of the Mughal artillery and trampled the Afghan soldiery instead of the Mughals. Babar's cavalry sallied forth through gaps in the breastworks to engage and rout the Afghans.

In the meantime, Babar ordered the execution of the *Talughma* from his right flank on to the Afghans. These mounted archers encircled the Afghan left at great speed and poured arrows at great frequency and quantity into the Afghan mass. The same *Talughma* was executed from the Mughal left wing and the Afghan army got completely encircled. The Mughal artillery and matchlock men continued to pour destructive fire into the Afghan army and their left and right wings and centre pressed forward to engage the Afghan cavalry. This was where the contest was fierce even as Afghans could engage in some hand to hand combat at a lesser disadvantage. Babar had to skillfully time and deploy his flexible right and left components at this stage so as to blunt the fierce attempts by the Afghans to recover lost ground.

However, the battle was clearly turning in the favour of Mughals who encircled and attacked the Afghans from both flanks, poured artillery and matchlock fire from the front and sallied forth from protected breastworks to engage the enemy in hand to hand combat. The Afghan army suffered tremendous losses and started getting massacred. Ibrahim Lodhi got to know of the desperate state of affairs by mid-day. He may have been a general inferior to Babar but a coward he was not. Advised to withdraw, he steadfastly refused and led a counter charge of 5000 soldiers to try and redeem the situation. This was far too little and too late and more like the attempt by Napoleon to use the Imperial Guard as a last ditch resort at the Battle of Waterloo. The Afghan army was routed and Ibrahim Lodhi had to sacrifice his life at the battlefield of Panipat. About 30,000 to 40,000 Afghans are said to have died. Humayun moved forward to capture Agra and Babar captured Delhi. The battle for Delhi had been won by the Mughals.

Clearly it was a lesson to be learnt that no kingdom or state can be defended forever through a mindset that is lost in complacency, does not analyse the moves the enemy is making, relies on methods the invader is prepared for and is more prepared to be surprised than create a surprise on its own. It is a lesson not worth forgetting as it happened recently as late as 1999 in Kargil.

An invader with lesser resources but having only one purpose—to concentrate these resources for war—can easily fancy its charges against a richer, bigger but ill-prepared and complacent state. The use of artillery and matchlocks for the first time in North India was, of course, the decisive factor but so were the battle tactics. It was a lesson future Indian armies would not learn either—in the Third Battle of Panipat, the Mughals against Nadir Shah and traditional Indian armies against the British. Of course, being avidly intent on getting surprised, as happened in 1962 and in Kargil in 1999, is a typically maddening Indian characteristic. The fact that internally there are dissensions and revolts is a constant factor always advantageous to the enemies of India.

Babar's job was still not done. He had come to India as an invader but not to loot. He had come to conquer and rule. India was the destination where Babar was intending to establish his final kingdom, the empire he was keen to set up. Therefore, all those Afghan nobles who had fondly hoped for a noble conqueror to come, deliver them from the tyrannical Ibrahim Lodhi and obligingly go back, were in for a shock. As were later all those foolish kings and princes in India who revealed such touching faith in the British against their own countrymen. Witness the support given by the Marathas to the British in the war against Tipu Sultan, only for the British juggernaut to come back and overwhelm the Maratha Confederacy later.

Khanua

Rana Sangram Singh, who desired to re-establish a Rajput kingdom in Delhi, had also hoped Babar would go back. Realising it was not to be, he decided to contend with the Mughal invader on the battlefield. He moved forward to fight Babar and gathered a tremendous host of cavalry, Rajput chieftains and 500 elephants for the upcoming battle. Moreover, seeking to settle scores with Babar, Afghan nobles like Mahmud Lodhi, younger brother of Ibrahim Lodhi, Hussain Khan Mewati and others too came with substantial contingents to join Rana Sangha and try and expel Babar. Rana Sangha had between 80,000 to 100,000 cavalry and 500 war elephants at his command.

The first connect between the Rajputs and Mughals happened at Khanua where an advance party of Mughals under Abdul Aziz fought a Rajput cavalry contingent. Much to their consternation, the Mughals were worsted in the engagement, many of them were captured and the rest took to their heels. Another contingent of the Mughals was similarly defeated. Tales of Rajput chivalry and their prowess in battle began to take a firm grip in the minds of the Mughal army. Unlike the previous campaign where advance parties of Lodhi Sultanate had been defeated by Mughals in Punjab, this time the Mughals had been at the receiving end. The Mughals were also feeling the heat of the plains of India and begged Babar for a retreat to the cooler climate of Afghanistan. Mughal morale dipped and an astrologer in Kabul predicted the defeat of Babar.

Babar realised that he had both an internal and an external enemy to contend with. The external enemy was Rana Sangha who, with his Rajput host, presented a far more formidable military challenge than the Ibrahim Lodhi-led Afghan army. Moreover, Rana Sangha had initial victories to boast of against the Mughals. The internal enemy was the fear of defeat that seemed to grip the Mughal army vice-like. Babar showed his true leadership abilities. He made a rousing speech to his army pledging either victory or martyrdom. He famously renounced wine and broke the jars and goblets in front of his army. He swore on the Koran with them to fight to death. This dramatic gesture is said to have revived the sagging morale of his army and they took to preparing for the battle in earnest.

Babar expected a battle more or less on the same lines as Panipat in terms of enemy strategy. Therefore, not surprisingly, his preparations were also similar. This time, instead of 700, he had 1000 carts tied together by ox hide. There were tripods between carts with sandbags hanging behind which stood the matchlock men ready to discharge their furious firepower. The swivel guns and cannons were placed in protected positions to discharge fire into a charging enemy. Babar was in the centre with 10,000 chosen cavalry. The right wing was under Humayun with 500 cavalry, the left wing was with Mehdi Khwaja with 3000 horses. Flanking parties with 1000 mounted archers were in position on both flanks to deliver the *Talughma* and encircle the enemy host.

The battle was preceded by intense negotiations for a month to determine if war could be avoided and boundaries determined beyond which each side could claim sovereignty. These negotiations broke down and both sides moved forward to give battle on 17 March 1527.

The Rajputs as usual had not bothered to understand enemy tactics. They seemed neither to have given thought to nor discussed the new introduction to India of cannons, *zarzban* and matchlocks. It was not thought important to understand how a furious frontal assault by Afghans, similar to what Rajputs planned, was broken up by the murderous fire of these weapons which did not give an opponent the facility of close combat. There was an unshakeable faith in the Rajput bravery, skill and ferocity to overcome such seemingly miniscule and unimportant challenges. This was despite the presence of Afghan contingents in the Rajput army who could have rendered advice on this. This was in direct contrast to how well Babar thought through enemy tactics and prepared for them in spite of inferior numbers.

The Rajputs went straight in and attacked the right wing of Babar. Babar sent in reinforcements and simultaneously opened fire from his cannons, *zarzban*s and matchlocks. Also a new large cannon designed by Ali Quli threw a large hot stone on the Rajputs which tore into a surprised enemy wreaking havoc. The surprise attack and the effect of firearms dented the Rajput charge. The Rajputs attacked with their usual bravery in waves. However, the guns and matchlocks wreaked terrible destruction. The Rajputs also came upon determined resistance from the Mughal right wing and could neither penetrate it nor break it. The Rajput centre also surged forward in a similarly hopeless cause. The new technology of battle caused massive destruction in Rajput ranks as the guns and matchlocks would not allow the Rajputs to come at close quarter and denied them the advantage they would have got in hand to hand combat with the Mughals.

Rana Sangha then shifted his emphasis to the left and charged Babar's left wing. The results and the fate of this part of the battle were the same as before. The Mughal cannonade and musketry tore holes in the Rajput host and the Rajput strength, hitherto committed to the right, centre and left, began to deplete. The Mughals now launched the *Talughma* from both flanks that tried to encircle the Rajputs and discharge murderous arrows into their host. The Rajputs, undaunted by this new development, turned around and faced this new challenge and continued to fight.

Rana Sangha, himself engaged in the battle, had by now suffered multiple wounds. The legendary warrior who is said to have had 80 wounds on his body and had lost an arm and a leg, collapsed from loss of blood and was carried away from the battlefield by his chiefs. So as not to cause dismay in the Rajput army, a look-alike Jhala chieftain was mounted on an elephant to sustain Rajput ranks. The Rajputs made a last final death or victory charge on all fronts. Babar realised the time had come to press forward for victory.

He led his 10,000 cavalry central reserve in a final charge. Simultaneously, his cannons, *zarzban*s and matchlock men moved forward pouring forth a withering fire. The Mughal flanks too closed in. The Rajputs fought back with typical valour but it was a lost cause. They were slaughtered, and retreated. Surprisingly, a part of the retreat was orderly and Rana Sangha and a remaining part of the Rajput army successfully reached the safety of Mewat hills. Babar celebrated his victory by building a pyramid of enemy skulls. Rana Sangha vowed that this was a temporary setback and that he would come back to fight and regain his kingdom. However, tragically, he died shortly afterwards, either due to wounds or due to poisoning, killing all hopes of a Rajput revival.

Delhi had a new Sultan, a Badshah, who had earned the right to the throne by fighting two bloody but successful battles for Delhi. More importantly, it was another very important inflexion point in the history of India. A new invader had come, not to loot but to stay and build an empire. An empire that was to become the richest in the world, an envy of the other nations of the globe, the Grand Mughal empire, one which would give stability to India for at least a couple of centuries.

Yet again a foreign invader had triumphed. And in spite of having richer resources between the Lodhis and Rajputs, the Indians had lost.

The victories achieved by Taimur Lang against the defending Tughlaq dynasty and by Babar against the Indian kingdoms are prime examples of how a weakened nation can neither defend its territorial integrity nor prevent an invader from coming in, taking over total control and doing what he wishes to do.

In Ghiyasuddin Tughlaq, Mohammed bin Tughlaq and Firozshah Tughlaq, Hindustan had strong monarchs who not only defended the frontiers well but pushed the empire to an all-India status in terms of territorial reach. In the process, strong armies roamed the hinterlands of India as well as the frontiers. The Tughlaq rule also had a dark side when it came to atrocities against Hindus and other religions.

However, as happens to every imperial dynasty, infighting broke out amongst the Tughlaqs. The successors of Firozshah were unworthy, and sons and grandsons of the deceased Sultan fought among themselves for the crown, often setting up rival claims for the throne. Normally in such situations, one of the princes emerges as the strongest, makes better alliances, gathers and handles military resources better. Slowly he overcomes the others and then emerges as the next Sultan and strengthens the empire. In this case it was not to be.

This infighting gave a chance to nobles and other forces to get involved and in this struggle the palace guards are said to have played a big role. After considerable fighting, Nasiruddin Mahmud Shah came to power. However, in the process, the empire, which had already begun crumbling during Firoz Shah's time, disintegrated completely. Most provinces broke away leaving only a shell.

Taimur seized this opportunity. He would not have been able to do so against Ghiyasuddin Tughlaq but Mahmud Shah and his rump of an empire was easy meat. Taimur moved in through the northwest, crossing all important rivers and did something special. He arrived at the outskirts of Delhi to fight the battle for Delhi in Delhi itself. Only one battle had to be won and the imperial capital was his.

It was not that the Tughlaqs were badly endowed in military resources. They came out with a large army, determined to fight, had armoured elephants and fire weapons with specially trained soldiers. They gave a bitter fight. In fact, the centre fought well but the wings gave way and the Tughlaq army met with defeat. A bloodthirsty conqueror entered Delhi, specially singled out the non-Islamic population and indulged in wholesale massacre.

Unworthy successors and infighting caused the death of a dynasty.

Similar was the case with the Lodhi dynasty where powerful Bahlol Lodhi and Sikander Lodhi were replaced by a weaker Ibrahim Lodhi who could not keep a turbulent flock called the Afghans together. Bengal and Gujarat were lost and a rival claimant in Daulat Khan Lodhi came on the scene. This also coincided with the restoration of Rajput grandeur, military prowess and ambition through the personage of Rana Sangha who missed out being the emperor of India by a whisker.

This is a typical case where not only has the central kingdom weakened but there is power vacuum and there are rival contenders, all equally strong who can win the central throne. There were rival Afghan factions, Rajputs and a Mughal invader. In this case, the rival Afghans could have united and presented a solid front but it was not to be. Common cause between the Rajputs and Afghans was out of question. So the invader had to pick on his opponents one by one. If the invader is resourceful and a great military leader, then fortune tends to swing his way. Especially if he is armed with military resources and technology that is new to India and has a shock capability.

Babar brought in cannons and match locks, which Indian armies had never faced before. The Afghans and Rajputs were good at the use of elephants and mass cavalry charges. However, when these heavy charges had no chance of coming anywhere near the enemy owing to being kept away by artillery and guns, the Indian war tactics proved useless.

The same happened with the British who picked first Bengal, then Awadh, then Mysore, then Scindia, then Holkar and then finally the Sikhs, one by one. The British obviously had better trained, disciplined and drilled armies and were led by capable generals. But they had been defeated before by Indian armies and could have been defeated again.

The need for unity in facing invading forces, the need to understand, analyse and counter their tactics, calls for unceasing devotion to building national unity and defence. India has witnessed this scenario time and again and needs to avoid a future repeat.

CHAPTER VIII

Hemchandra Vikramaditya and Panipat

DELHI IN THE MID-SIXTEENTH CENTURY CHANGED HANDS between the Mughals and Afghans in turns. It first came under Humayun who inherited it from Babar. Humayun, an otherwise good general and soldier, had at times a tendency towards indolence, neglecting what in modern management parlance may be called the urgent and important. Unfortunately, he had to confront a military genius in the form of Sher Shah Suri, an Afghan commander.

A first soldier king of his age, and in terms of military and administrative accomplishments second only to Akbar, Sher Shah defeated Humayun repeatedly and forced him in abject state out of India. Sher Shah won the battles for Delhi against Humayun. Capturing Delhi and ruling from what is now called Purana Qila, Sher Shah had a short but scintillating career. He transformed India's transport system by rebuilding the Grand Trunk and other important routes. He revitalised the revenue collection system. He also created a stronger postal system and ruled the North, East and Central India's major territories, thus creating an Afghan empire. Unfortunately for the Afghans, this amazing genius died early in a siege of Kalinjar and gave way to Islam Shah. Thus ended the career of an emperor whose rule could well have been talked of in the same breath as that of Akbar for its military and administrative achievements.

Sher Shah Suri was succeeded by his son Jalal Khan who took on the title of Islam Shah. Islam Shah did not prove to be an unworthy successor. He conquered territories further east and also brought about a more unified state. He successfully thwarted a weak and ineffectual attempt by Humayun to regain Delhi.

His successor and son Firoz Shah was a minor and was soon killed and dispossessed by his uncle Mubarriz Khan. Mubarriz assumed the titled of Mohammed Adil Shah. This, unfortunately for the Afghans, led to a free for all and the Afghan empire split into four parts. One part obviously went to Adil Shah beyond Agra to Bihar. Ibrahim Shah captured Delhi and Agra. Another captured Punjab, the gateway to the Heartland of Hind, and declared himself Sikander Shah Sur. There was an independent state declared by another contender in Bengal called Mohammed Shah. It was a time ripe for Mughals waiting impatiently in the wings. A lesson in how petty sub-nationalistic politics and stupid individual aspirations counteracting central unity result in the downfall of not only the central empire but also of these sub-nationalists who fondly imagine the time has come to build their own independent states.

An internecine struggle developed among the Afghans for control of the Indian empire. This was not to escape being noticed by Humayun who was keen to recapture the lost empire of the Mughals in Hindustan.

At this point, in came a person called Hemu. Hemu is a character least written about and analysed by Indian historians. But Hemu clearly is one of the most fascinating characters to emerge out of Indian history. This was a time when the contenders for the throne of Hindustan were Islamic rulers—Mughals waiting impatiently in Kabul and the Sur contenders vying among themselves, oblivious of the impending danger from the Mughals. The only Hindu empire of any consequence, in fact of great consequence, was the Vijayanagar empire in the South but with hardly any aspirations towards the North. At this time, for a Hindu entity to emerge and became an emperor of Hindustan, in the process leading an Afghan army in battle, would have been considered a foolish thought. But this was precisely what Hemu achieved. It was a truly meteoric rise followed by an equally tragic and unfortunate fall.

Hem Chandra was born in a Hindu family in a village near Rewari in southern Alwar. Hemu was not only educated in Sanskrit, Hindi, Persian, Arabic and Arithmetic but possessed an outstanding physique thanks to a self-imposed exercising and wrestling regimen.

Hemu started his career as a supplier of store items to the army of Sher Shah Suri including supplying saltpetre. Sher Shah's death resulted in the ascension of his capable son Islam Khan to the throne of Delhi. Islam Khan, in fact, proved more than a match for the Mughals, thwarting an attempt by Humayun to invade India.

Hemu rose to prominence under Islam Shah. Islam Shah gave recognition to Hemu's talent and initially appointed him as *Shahang-i-Bazar* (Market Superintendent). This gave Hemu control over

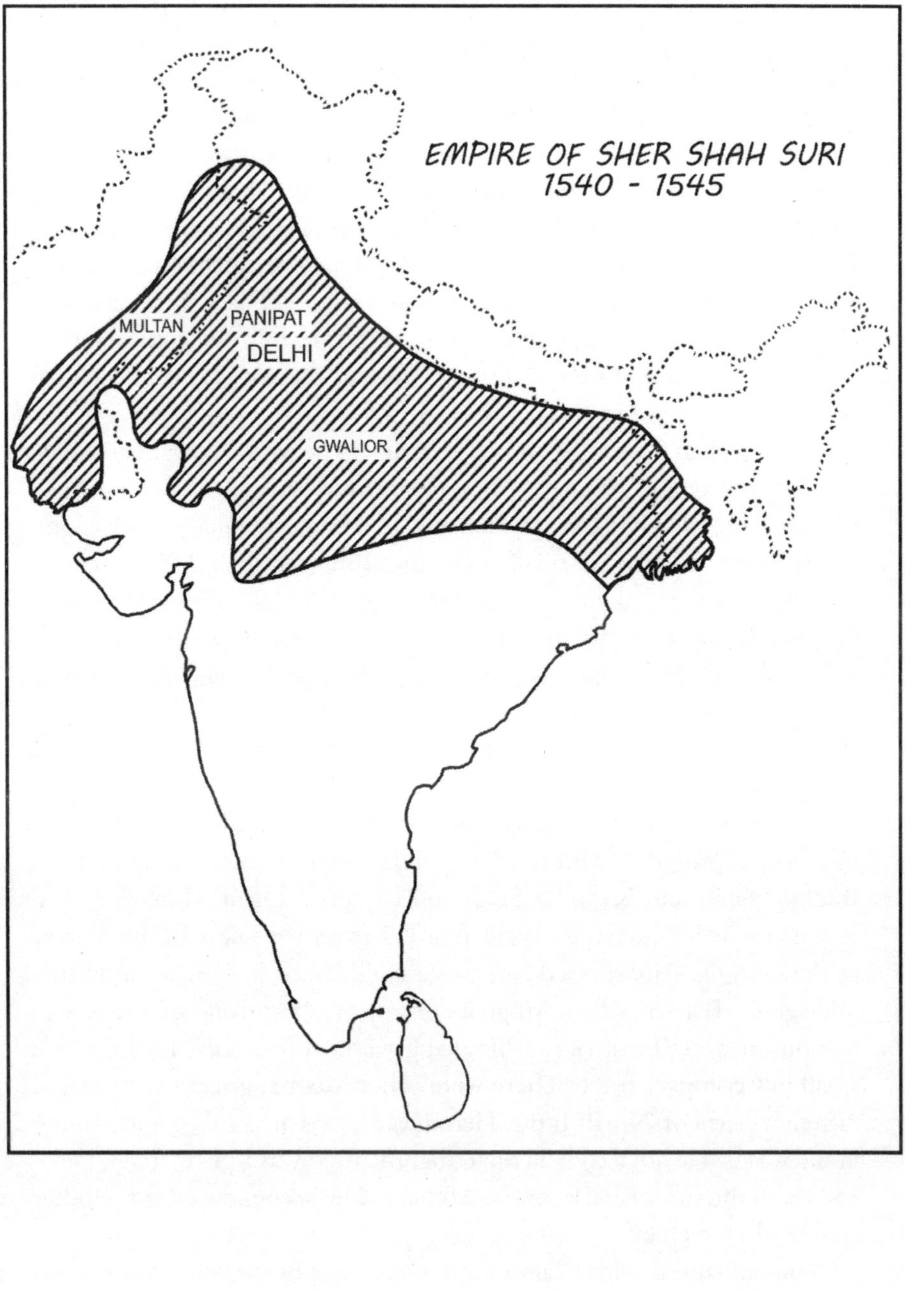
EMPIRE OF SHER SHAH SURI
1540 - 1545
MULTAN
PANIPAT
DELHI
GWALIOR

commercial interests and also earned him the ear of the emperor. Hemu advised Islam Shah on a variety of matters. He used to supply him with secret information and therefore became an intelligence gatherer for the Sultan. Then Hemu rose to become Chief of Intelligence or *Daroga-i-Chowki* (Superintendent of Post). Islam Shah died early.

Islam Shah was succeeded by his twelve-year-old son, Firoz Khan, who was killed within three days by Adil Shah Suri. The new king, Adil Shah, was an indolent pleasure-seeker and a drunkard who faced revolts all around. Adil Shah took Hemu as his chief advisor and entrusted all his work to him, appointing him the prime minister and chief of his army. After some time, Adil Shah became almost insane and Hemu became the *de facto* king.

Many Afghan governors rebelled against the weak king, Adil Shah, and refused to pay the taxes, but Hemu quelled them. Ibrahim Shah rose against Adil Shah but was defeated by Hemu on multiple occasions. While in the process of finally defeating Ibrahim Shah, Hemu got the news that Muhammad Shah was attacking Adil Shah who was in great danger. Hemu broke off the engagement with Ibrahim Shah and rushed to the aid of Adil Shah. The battle occurred at Chhapparghatta near Kalpi. Muhammad Shah was on way to victory against a helpless Adil Shah when Hemu arrived and attacked his army in the rear putting it to rout. Muhammad Shah is said to have been killed in the battle.

Sikander Shah Suri meanwhile had managed to get the better of Ibrahim Shah and captured the throne of Delhi. Humayun's forces defeated both Ibrahim Shah and Sikander Shah and captured Delhi. Humayun died in January 1556 due to an accidental fall from the stairs of his library at Purana Qila. His son, Akbar, was a child based in Punjab under the tutelage of Bairam Khan. Mughal control on the throne of Delhi was tenuous at best. Tardi Beg, a Mughal governor, protected Delhi with a small but compact force. There were other Mughal governors based in different parts of North India. Hemu was based at Gwalior and waiting in the wings. He advised Adil Shah that the time was ripe to attack Delhi and claim the throne back for the Afghans. The scene was set for another epic battle for Delhi.

Hemu advanced with a large force consisting of 50,000 cavalry, 1000 elephants, 50 cannons and 500 falconets towards Delhi. He had a mighty reputation of having won 22 battles for Adil Shah. He had a large force moving inexorably towards Delhi. The Mughals citadels standing in the way fell like nine pins as terrified Mughal commanders abandoned their posts in sheer fright at this formidable host coming at them led by an audacious commander. Etawah, Bayana and Sambhal all fell to Hemu. Finally the run halted at Delhi where the Mughals decided to give battle.

This battle for Delhi was on a smaller scale but significant as it gave Hemu control of Delhi and established him, although very briefly, as an emperor. Tardi Beg had a force of 3000 heavy cavalry with which he came out to give battle against the much larger force of Hemu. Tardi Beg himself commanded the centre. Iskander Beg commanded the left wing and Haider Mohammed the right wing. Abdullah Uzbeg commanded the advance guard. The heavy Turkish cavalry launched the initial assault on the right wing of Hemu and was very successful. 3000 Afghans were killed.

However, the Mughals mistook this charge for victory and started looting the enemy camp. Hemu regrouped and asked his left wing under Allahdad to attack the Mughal right wing. This had limited success. Hemu seeing his right wing destroyed and left wing under a stalemate, launched a furious assault at the Mughal centre with 300 elephants and his chosen troops. The Mughals could not withstand this heavy frontal attack and broke and fled. Hemu had captured Delhi, albeit temporarily, from the Mughals. This was a direct battle fought for Delhi in Delhi itself near Tughlaqabad and resulted in the fall of Delhi to Hemu.

Hemu anointed himself as Raja Hemchandra Vikramaditya. Very interestingly, at a time when Muslim powers were vying for the control of Hindustan, it was a highly talented Hindu King who captured power with a mixed army of Afghans and Rajputs. How this strange circumstance happened and how quickly Hemu consolidated and started applying his administrative and military skill is another subject.

The Mughals were in complete disarray. Their force was too small to handle Hemu's much larger army. Tardi Beg fled to join Akbar and Bairam Khan. He had gone back to his doom. Bairam Khan, more to settle earlier personal scores, had Tardi Beg executed for his failure to retain Delhi, although Tardi Beg could have done little about it. There was a general advice for Akbar to retreat to Kabul, consolidate and come back to handle a formidable adversary. Bairam Khan stoutly opposed this and propounded his own reasons to move forward and give battle for Delhi. His advice prevailed and the armies of the Mughals and Hemu moved forward to a highly awaited clash for a battle for Delhi at Panipat.

SECOND BATTLE OF PANIPAT
AKBAR'S ARMY
SIKANDER UZBEG
ALI QULI
ABDULLAH UZBEG
ADVANCE GUARD
RAMAYYA
HEMU
SHADI KHAN KAKAR
AFGHANS

A 20,000-strong Mughal army advanced for this fateful encounter and was bolstered on the way in Punjab by additional Mughal contingents of forces who had been earlier defeated by Hemu. The force swelled to 25,000. Hemu advanced with a 50,000 strong army of cavalry, 500 elephants and 50 cannons. A huge mistake was made by Hemu who sent his artillery under the guard of Mubarak Khan in advance. This important arm should have been under heavy protection for ultimate use. Hemu may have fallen prey to overconfidence. This entire pack of artillery fell into an advance Mughal party and their usage got transferred from Hemu to the Mughals, an event of immense importance to the outcome of the battle.

The Mughal army was under the overall command of Ali Quli Khan. Akbar was young, and safely ensconced 30 kms. away behind the battle scene, something to take note of. Not once during this time of great uncertainty and turbulence did the Mughal notions waiver as to who was to be preserved as their emperor in the event of victory. It was perhaps this unity in adversity, this focus of winning back an empire under the successor of Babar and Humayun that was to play an important part in the ultimate outcome.

The Mughal left wing was under Abdullah Uzbeg, the right under Sikander Uzbeg. Ali Quli himself commanded the centre and there was an advance guard under Hussein Quli and Shah Quli. There was a reserve of 6,000 horses under Shah Badagh and Abdul Mali. The overall commander of the Mughal Army in the Second Battle of Panipat was Ali Quli Khan.

Hemu had a simpler centre, left and right combination. The left wing was under his own relation Ramayya and the right wing was under Shadi Khan Kakkar. Hemu himself was poised in the centre with 30,000 horses and 500 elephants to deliver the usual decisive blow.

The battle took place in winter on 5 November 1556. This was a very important battle because it was a single battle here that decided the fate of the Mughal empire for years to come. The importance of this battle was that it helped fill a big power vacuum in Delhi. The situation was not like the First Battle of Panipat that required even tougher follow up battles for Babar or the Third Battle that ended in creating a vacuum and resultant confusion for the throne of Hindustan.

Hemu took the offensive as was his wont. His left and right wings pressed the Mughal right and left wings, which gave way steadily under the pressure but did not disintegrate. The Mughals responded by launching the *Talughma*s which wheeled around Hemu's army and enveloped from both flanks, ultimately attacking also in the rear, showering arrows and rapidly attacking with their mounted horses. Hemu's army began to suffer from the mounted archers and the fire of Mughal artillery. His commanders were killed. Ali Quli seized the chance and sent his cavalry to attack Hemu in the flanks thus further putting him under pressure. The Mughals were using the same tactics that had won them battles earlier in India, rapid flank attacks, mounted archers and frontal artillery fire. And these tactics seemed to be working.

However, the quality of the opponent they were up against was different, a much more fierce, mobile and resourceful commander. Hemu counter-attacked and turned back the Mughal offensive. His countercharge blunted the Mughal flanking tactics and neither their *Talughma* nor their flanking cavalry charges had the usual effect. Hemu had neutralised the tried and tested Mughal battle tactics and his main force was still intact. He now collected it together to deliver the typical central blow that usually won him the 22 battles he had fought so far.

Hemu advanced forward with his 500 war elephants and central cavalry, his elite force, to destroy the Mughal army. He had blunted their advantage and now was poised to deliver the final blow. His furious charge unnerved the Mughals as his elephants and cavalry wreaked havoc within the Mughal ranks. The Mughals were on the back foot and Hemu was ready to claim another famous victory. The Mughals fought back with their cavalry and arrows and the battle became fierce. But the tide was turning in favour of Hemu and so was the battle for Delhi. Hemu was inexorably moving forward for the kill and the Mughals, having already lost to him on numerous occasions earlier, were anticipating the worst. At this stage occurred a freak event that was to prove decisive.

The man the Mughals proposed as their emperor was safely 30 kilometers away from the battlefield; he could live to fight another day even if his army lost. The man the opposing army proposed as their emperor was himself in the thick of battle because that is how he had fought and won so far. If he was lost, so was the cause opposed to the Mughals. And that is precisely what happened.

An arrow came from somewhere and hit Hemu in his eye, piercing deep. The circumstance was helped by the fact that Hemu was perched on his unusually tall, favourite elephant, Hawai, and thus was a more plausible target. Hemu, made of stern stuff, refused to give in. He pulled out the arrow, tied a scarf to stem the flow of blood and carried on bravely. But the die was cast. The bleeding continued and a badly wounded Hemu fainted. Hemu collapsed. His army lost sight of the commander and fled in confusion. The Mughals captured Hemu who had collapsed and took him to Akbar. The Mughals had won the day and the crown of Delhi was theirs. Hemu was produced before Akbar and Bairam Khan advised Akbar to execute Hemu. Akbar refused to kill an adversary who was half dead. Bairam Khan himself took off Hemu's head. The battle for Delhi had gone in favour of the Mughals.

This battle brought to the fore a man recognised as one of India's greatest ever emperors. It also finished off an individual who was perhaps no less talented and capable. The defeat and execution of Hemu led to the extinction of an individual highly qualified to lead India. Another case of what if? It also brought to power a person also highly qualified to lead the country—Mughal-e-Azam Jalaluddin Mohammed Akbar.

Chapter IX

Samugarh

The reign of Akbar brought growth and stability to the Mughal empire. He grew to become one of the greatest monarchs of Indian history. The succession of his son Salim, better known as Jahangir, was smooth. Jahangir gave a long and stable reign to India although the succession battle to him was bloody as his successor, Khurram, later to be called Shah Jahan, won a bloody battle with his brothers and had Shahryar and other prisoners executed. Shah Jahan again had a long and stable reign.

However, it was when the reign of Shah Jahan reached its end that things became really unstable. After that, almost every succession to the Mughal throne was decided after a horrendous internecine struggle that resulted in deaths of many royal princes who were claimants to the throne, the only survivor being the one who succeeded to the throne.

The contest for succession to the Mughal throne had indeed become messy and bloody. It then became a norm for the throne of the Mughal empire to be decided by a bloody contest with the cry—*"ya takht ya tabut"* (either throne or tomb)—being repeatedly used to describe the struggles for the throne. Only one of the successor sons of the Mughal emperor would survive in the ensuing bloody conflict to sit on the throne at the end of such contests. The rest would lose their lives in bitterly, though bravely, contested battles. The tragedy was that each of these battles left India weaker as each battle weakened the strong central Mughal empire.

So when Shah Jahan was nearing the end of his reign, a contest seemed imminent. He had four sons who were Dara, Shuja, Aurangzeb and Murad. Each of them had aspirations for the throne. Each of them felt he was the one most capable of taking over.

Dara Shikoh was the favourite of Emperor Shah Jahan. He had always been kept near to himself by the emperor. He had received excessive love and affection from Shah Jahan and he had reciprocated in full. He had been kept by the side of the emperor through thick and thin and was called Shahzada Buland Iqbal. He was extremely educated, knew multiple languages and was secular, which is what Mughal emperors, Akbar onwards, had become. He had not only studied and written books on Islam but had also studied Christian, Jewish and Hindu religious scriptures. In fact, he was specially inclined towards Hinduism although it was not to change his own faith. He was so learned and involved that he had made a deep study of the Vedas and had led the translation of Upanishads from Sanskrit to Persian. He wrote a work on how Hinduism and Islam were two paths to the same objective and he called the book *Majma ul Bahrain*—Mingling of Two Oceans. He spent a lot of time in the company of Hindu holy men as well as that of Sufis, his association with the eccentric Sufi, Sarmad, was well-known.

Dara, in fact, was famous for saying that Paradise is where no mullah resides. He was articulate, civil, pleasant and courteous. He was liked by all and was very popular with the people. Shah Jahan had made it very clear that Dara was the man he had chosen as his heir. Dara was, in fact, entitled to sit on a throne in the Mughal Darbar though he never did so in the presence of Shah Jahan. He was given a lot of powers in handling the affairs of the realm which he did with due deference to Emperor Shah Jahan.

On the face of it, all seemed to be going in Dara's favour. He controlled the Mughal wealth and affairs at the Central Court. He was polished and good at handling administrative affairs. He had the emperor's clear favour. He had military resources at his disposal. He was liberal and liked by the population. He was secular and likely to hold a complex country like India together, weaving together the magic thread of Hindu-Muslim unity. He was open to new ideas and could well have led a more modern version of the Mughal empire. Most importantly, he had an excellent successor in his elder son, Suleiman Shikoh, who shared his father's qualities, had Shah Jahan's trust and moreover unlike his father was militarily capable.

However, it was not all hunky dory for him. Dara was also a proud person whose intellectual prowess made him haughty. So he could also be rude and contemptuous towards the Mughal Omrah. He enjoyed their respect but to what extent he enjoyed their empathy is a question mark. Also, because he had been kept by his side by Shah Jahan, Dara had very limited direct military experience of battles. He had military resources but not the battle-hardened experience to handle them. In a contest for the Mughal throne most likely to be decided by battles, Dara would not be able to give the same kind of leadership which his brothers could. In fact, it was this aspect that disturbed Shah Jahan most.

Shuja was the second eldest and had been mostly confined to the rich but distant provinces of Bengal, Bihar and Orissa. He had done a competent job and moreover commanded military and financial resources thanks to his governorship of the Eastern Provinces. One factor in his favour was that he was in military terms a daring and experienced commander. This was likely to stand him in good stead in the ensuing contest. His weak point was that he was pleasure-loving and therefore less inclined to show promptitude in action when faced with the choice of pleasure versus urgency. Nevertheless, Shuja was considered a serious contender for the throne.

The youngest was Murad. He was the governor of Gujarat and was a ferocious warrior, known for his personal bravery and strength. Among all the brothers he was the most capable of leading personally in battle based on his military skills and bravery. However, he was also the least capable of handling political intrigues, being a bit out of depth in such dealings. Murad, therefore, was the least likely to succeed Shah Jahan, as a succession battle involved political manipulation as much as military capability.

We now come to the most interesting character, Aurangzeb. Aurangzeb represents an inflection point in Indian history. He was the last of the Grand Mughals. As a contender for the throne, everyone including Shah Jahan acknowledged him as the one most likely to succeed in the ensuing battle for succession to the Mughal throne, purely because of his personal military capabilities and experience.

Aurangzeb was, from the beginning, hostile to Dara and the relationship between the two blood brothers was more like the one between the Kauravas and Pandavas, one of intense mutual dislike, mistrust and hatred. Aurangzeb even accused Dara of trying to get him killed in the earlier years of his life through manipulating an elephant fight. Aurangzeb also nursed a dislike for his father and never got along with him. In fact, the dislike was heartily reciprocated by his father.

Consequently, Aurangzeb was always kept away from the court as well as fatherly affections, with accusations being exchanged. Shah Jahan would accost Aurangzeb with dereliction of duty, disobeying commands, never transmitting to Mughal court the full treasure captured in wars and even stealing the best mangoes meant for Shah Jahan. Aurangzeb would accuse Shah Jahan of partiality towards Dara and of not placing an iota of either trust or affection on his third son. This created two mutually recriminatory parties—Shah Jahan and Dara on one side and Aurangzeb on the other. Aurangzeb also felt that Dara poisoned Shah Jahan's mind towards him and indulged in machinations against him.

The result of this was a tableau for the future where Dara would be backed by the resources of the Mughal court and Shah Jahan when he would make his bid for power and Aurangzeb would have to rely on his own resources wherever he was and these were likely to be considerable, in order to pit himself against Dara.

In the process occurred another development which would decisively direct the course of Indian history. Aurangzeb identified himself with anything that stood against what Dara stood for. Dara was secular. Dara spent time with Hindu fakirs and studied Hindu holy texts, translating them. Aurangzeb, although he would have been inclined from the very beginning towards Islam, transferred his hatred of his brother in terms of accusing Dara of reducing the impact of Islam on India. He accused Dara of undermining Mughal authority, which he felt represented the rule of Islam. Therefore he started accusing Dara of being anti-Islam, who if he came to power, would transfer the allegiance of the empire from Islamic rule to a multi-religious regime. Aurangzeb postured himself as the champion of Islam and let out that he greatly feared that the advent of Dara on the throne would mean the ruin of the Islamic character of the Mughal empire. This was apart from his accusations that Shah Jahan and Dara were mismanaging the government anyway. This accusation of Aurangzeb against Dara of being anti-Islam had the secret empathy of the Mughal nobility, most of which was Muslim.

Another very critical aspect was the military aspect. Dara had spent all his life in the Mughal court and apart from a not too successful stint at Kandahar against the Persians, had rarely distinguished himself in the battlefield. Aurangzeb was the direct opposite. Because he had been kept away from the Mughal court, he had taken the hardship postings—Kandahar, Deccan, Samarqand and numerous other battle fronts. He was a battle-hardened general who had led his soldiers coolly and calmly in battle facing personal danger. In the worst of situations, he could

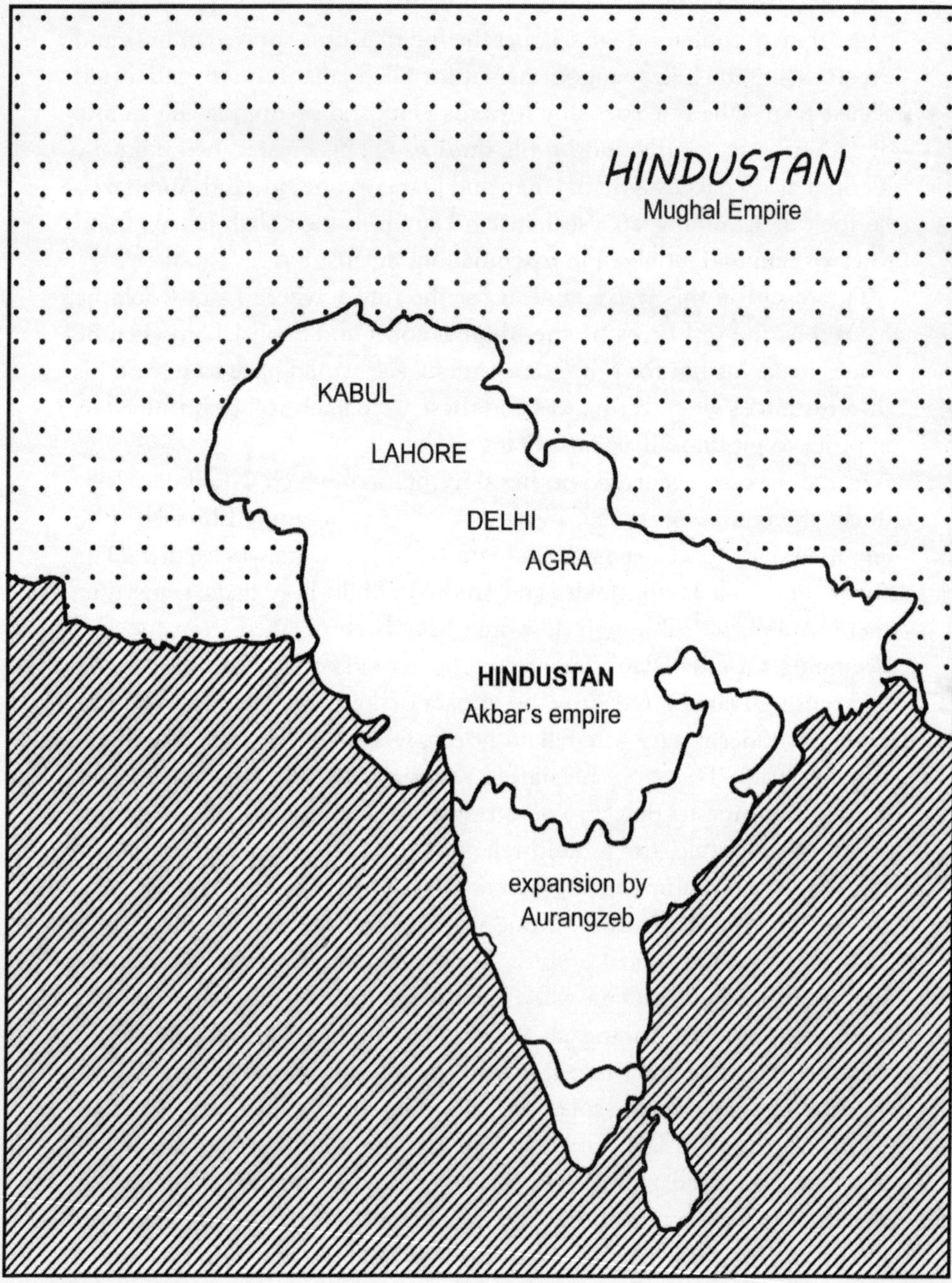
HINDUSTAN
Mughal Empire
KABUL
LAHORE
DELHI
AGRA
HINDUSTAN
Akbar's empire
expansion by
Aurangzeb

be relied upon to calmly rally his troops and lead them to victory. His courage in the face of showers of enemy arrows from the Uzbegs in Samarqand while he conducted his prayers on the battlefield was the stuff of legends. If it ever came to a direct battle pitting Dara as a general against Aurangzeb as a general, the odds would be in favour of Aurangzeb.

The nobles of the Mughal court, opportunistic as ever, had to contend with Dara and show respect to him, his intellect and administrative capacities. But they kept in touch with Aurangzeb, knowing the issue ultimately could be decided in his favour and they may have to deal with him as the emperor.

This was how it was in 1657 when Shah Jahan fell seriously ill in September and people feared for his life. Dara and Aurangzeb were the chief contenders and Shuja and Murad followed in that order. The final contest would be between Dara and Aurangzeb. A battle for the throne of Delhi was imminent with the issue undecided.

Dara had on his side the support of Shah Jahan, the resources of the Mughal court, its key military generals, the army and his own intellect and abilities. His weakness was primarily a lack of military acumen and experience. Aurangzeb did not have the fatherly support and affection, and no central resources. But he had financial resources gathered during his campaigns in the Deccan, a battle hardened army and experienced commanders. However, he also had his own military skills, ability to win battles as a general and most importantly a cool and calculating mind well orchestrated to win a battle for Delhi.

Shuja had resources of Bengal, Bihar and Orissa, experience as a military commander and administrative ability. But compared to Dara and Aurangzeb, his resources and abilities were more limited and he would need a great deal of luck and daring to win. Murad, inspite of his indomitable bravery would fight with more brawn than brains and was not likely to succeed to the throne of Delhi.

Shah Jahan fell ill and rumours abounded about his demise. Dara took complete control of the Mughal court and nursed Shah Jahan to wellness. Rumours spread and disturbances broke out. Shah Jahan even got up to show himself in the balcony to people but there were suspicions that it was a look-alike and this appearance did not calm the matters or make the rumours die.

Shah Jahan gradually recovered his health and took a royal flotilla down the Yamuna. However the die was cast. The three princes, Shuja, Aurangzeb and Murad had decided that whether Shah Jahan was dead or alive mattered little. The control of the Mughal empire was in Dara's hands and unless they moved fast, Dara would be the next emperor. Machinations and preparations began in earnest in the drive towards Delhi.

Dara's focus was to consolidate his hold. He realised that there were three other contenders for the throne who would leave no stone unturned to realise their dreams. He also wanted to prevent any possibility of them getting together and combining against him as that would pit three forces against his one. And he was not wrong.

Aurangzeb was the shrewdest and held his cards initially close to his chest. He was the person considered most likely to succeed but he played things as if he did not want the throne. His stance was that the empire would be in great danger if Dara, the lover of infidels, was to come to power. The forces of Islam, which according to Aurangzeb were the foundation of the Mughal empire, would weaken and so would the empire. Aurangzeb was therefore in correspondence with both Murad and Shuja. He gave out that he was least interested in being the emperor and that was something that could go to the others or be divided as per mutual agreement. But according to Aurangzeb, the priority for him, Shuja and Murad combined was to rid the empire of the evil presence of Dara and save Islamic glory.

Aurangzeb therefore hung around in the Deccan getting his resources ready but inciting both Murad and Shuja to unite against Dara. Shuja and Murad were impatient and they declared themselves emperors, Murad in Gujarat and Shuja in Bengal. So very interestingly, there were three people who called themselves emperors in India—Shah Jahan, the actual emperor, and Murad and Shuja who had declared themselves emperors while their father was still alive ruling India. At the same time, the two most favoured contestants to the throne were Dara and Aurangzeb, neither of whom called himself emperor yet.

Dara was not sitting ideal. Although he lacked direct battle experience, he was not to be found wanting in stratagem. He decided to prevent his three brothers from uniting and also becoming more powerful. So he had orders sent to Deccan to the commanders of the army of Aurangzeb that they were to return to Delhi. By this he hoped to weaken Aurangzeb's army. And that is what started happening much to Aurangzeb's alarm.

No matter how hard he tried, his commanders started to obey the royal command from Agra and started returning. The last straw on the camel's back was the recall order to Mir Jumla, a highly experienced noble on whom Aurangzeb counted much. Aurangzeb tried hard to prevent Mir Jumla who evidently insisted on returning. Aurangzeb had no choice but to put Mir Jumla under detention, though he did the same most respectfully. Murad in the meantime, given his wont, became impatient for action and a contest. He kept telling Aurangzeb to move forward and finally Aurangzeb decided to cross the frontier that was considered important to cross for any army from Deccan intending serious business in the North—the Narmada River.

Dara was watching this movement carefully and he had tried to weaken both Aurangzeb and Murad by a clever stratagem. He asked Murad to vacate Gujarat which was a source of money and power to him. He asked him instead to take over Berar that was under the control of Aurangzeb. He had hoped to set off one brother against the other. It failed as by now Aurangzeb and Murad had bonded tightly and Dara's machinations proved fruitless.

Already an order had been issued to commanders in Aurangzeb's Deccan army to return north. Many commanders complied and when Mir Jumla also wanted to comply, it forced Aurangzeb's hand. He could not afford to lose any more commanders and especially one as capable and wise as Mir Jumla. His army was being forced to disintegrate. He forcefully captured Mir Jumla, thus preventing his northward flight and moved forward.

In the meantime, the danger from the East manifested itself more directly and earlier. Shuja decided to seize the first mover advantage. He advanced on the imperial capital to defeat the imperial forces and seize the capital. In fact, it is said that it was he who first gave the famous war cry for the imperial throne—*Ya takht ya tabut*—either throne or tomb. Dara decided to eliminate the less difficult threat from Shuja first and then marshal his entire resources to concentrate on the more formidable threat from the South emanating in the form of the Aurangzeb and Murad combine.

Dara sent an army of 20,000 under his highly talented son Suleiman Shikoh assisted by two of the Mughal army's ablest commanders, Mirza Raja Jai Singh and Diler Khan to confront Shuja. Shuja was by now, in January 1658, closing in on the imperial capital. He was attacked in a very prompt manner by Suleiman Shikoh and put to flight. He should have been decimated on the spot at Varanasi but escaped due to instructions from Shah Jahan. While the old emperor wanted Dara to win the throne, out of fatherly love, he did not wish to see the destruction of his sons. So his instructions were for no physical harm to come to Shuja. Shuja escaped and was chased all the way to Mungher in Bihar. This drew away from Dara highly critical resources at a very important juncture. If the imperial forces had had orders to decimate Shuja, the result of the contest with him would have been decided nearer to Agra, making it easy for the Mughal forces sent to tackle him to return and join Dara in his forthcoming epic battle with Aurangzeb. As fate and Shah Jahan's instructions decreed, it was not to be.

The army he had sent to defeat Shuja was the flower of the Mughal royal army. Along with it he had sent his son Suleiman who had much more military talent than his father as well as two very capable generals in Mirza Raja Jai Singh and Diler Khan. This army went too far east to chase Shuja and was not going to be around by the time Dara came face to face with Aurangzeb. This meant that Dara went to fight Aurangzeb weaker than what he should have been. Suleiman was still in Mungher in May when Dara had Aurangzeb breathing down his neck and in no way could have returned in time to help his father.

In the meantime, it was not as if Dara had stood idly by and done nothing to prevent Aurangzeb. He sent forward an army under two very capable generals to confront Aurangzeb. These were Raja Jaswant Singh of Jodhpur and Qasim Khan. The idea was to take care of Shuja, delay Aurangzeb by confronting him with Jaswant and Qasim, then get back the army led by Suleiman Shikoh, Mirza Raja Jai Singh and Diler Khan, combine forces and defeat Aurangzeb. He could have moved forward with Jaswant Singh's army and tackled Aurangzeb with a larger combined force of both his and Jaswant Singh's army. However, the strategy was to delay Aurangzeb and then meet him along with Suleiman Shikoh, Mirza Raja Jaisingh and Diler Khan. This caused Dara to meet Aurangzeb eventually with a force less strong than was desirable.

Aurangzeb crossed the Narmada on 13 April. He was joined by Murad in the last week of April at Dipalpur. They moved forward towards Ujjain. Herein arose another contradiction which showed the indecisiveness of both Shah Jahan and Dara to deal with the rebel princes. Had they been decisive, the only sensible course would have been to eliminate them.

But just like the instructions of Shah Jahan were to turn Shuja back and not decimate him, similar ambiguous instructions were issued to Jaswant Singh, thereby confusing him totally. Jaswant therefore could not take any offensive posture save one of deterrence. Against a commander of Aurangzeb's calibre, it was to prove suicidal.

Jaswant could not move forward and prevent the confluence of Aurangzeb and Murad. If he had done so, Aurangzeb would have been deprived of an ally whose performance in the final battle proved crucial to its success. He had to wait and then as per Shah Jahan's instructions plead with Aurangzeb to go back. Aurangzeb was much smarter and told off Jaswant Singh, in the process making it very clear that as a commander in the Mughal army, he had no business confronting a royal prince. Taken aback, Jaswant told Aurangzeb to retreat or face a battle. However, Jaswant Singh's mindset still remained one of deterrence and not of attack.

Jaswant took a defensive position at Dharmat, 22 miles from Ujjain. He seemed to have chosen a position where he put a drain behind his army, thus restricting his movement and also selected a broken ground for the deployment of his army, restricting the mobility of the famed Rajput cavalry. He had also in the process, ceded level ground to his rival Aurangzeb, affording him greater mobility for his forces. The other disadvantage which Jaswant Singh inflicted on himself was to place less reliance on artillery which Aurangzeb made better use of during the ensuing Battle of Dharmat. An inbuilt disadvantage was that the other commander called Qasim Khan sent along with him seemed to have played a dubious role in the battle, openly helping the cause of Aurangzeb.

Again the intention of the imperial army seemed deterrence or delay, not elimination of the enemy. Aurangzeb and Jaswant had a furious battle lasting eight hours. Jaswant Singh deployed an advance guard of 6,000 Rajput cavalry, split into six units of 1,000 each under a commander. On his left was Qasim Khan with 4,000 cavalry which deserted Jaswant Singh and took no part in the battle. The centre of Jaswant Singh's army was 7,000 Rajputs and 10,000 Muslim soldiers. The right wing was commanded by 10,000 cavalry under Rai Sisodia. A reserve of 5,000 Rajput cavalry was placed behind. Little emphasis was placed on use of artillery. So Shah Jahan and Dara had largely relied upon a force of Rajputs to confront Aurangzeb at the first tier of defence.

Aurangzeb had an advance guard of 8,000 heavy cavalry to match the Rajput advance guard. It was led by his son Mohammed Sultan. Murad formed the right wing. There was a left wing and the centre was personally commanded by Aurangzeb. He had placed cover on his right and left flanks. His personal bodyguard was deployed as a reserve. Aurangzeb decided to make extensive use of artillery unlike Jaswant Singh.

The artillery employed by Aurangzeb commenced the battle by opening fire on the Rajput advance guard. The Rajputs were jam-packed while moving forward and started suffering heavy casualties. They realised that if they remained static, they would be exposed more and more to this withering fire and be decimated. Therefore, taking their lives into their hands, he launched a frontal suicidal attack on the Mughal artillery and advance guard. They tore through in typically reckless Rajput style, taking their lives in their hands. They threw themselves into the cannon mouths and cut down Aurangzeb's gunners. They put the Aurangzeb advance guard to flight and reached the centre of his army, cutting down opponents. They almost won the day as there was disorder and flight in Aurangzeb's army. However, either Jaswant Singh was not aware of their success or he showed poor generalship as he failed to move his centre and reserves forward to support the successful charge of his advance guard and enabled Aurangzeb to recover the situation. A push forward by Jaswant Singh of his main army to supplement the success of his advance guard could have put the Aurangzeb army to flight and decided the day in the favour of imperial forces.

Aurangzeb, like a seasoned general, threw forward his centre and reserve to stem the onslaught of the Rajput advance guard that had lost a lot of numbers and soon the tide swung against Jaswant Singh. The right and left flanks of Aurangzeb surrounded the Rajput army and began enveloping them in side thrusts. At the same time, Qasim Khan showed treachery and moved away from battle exposing the left flank of Jaswant Singh and sharply reducing his numbers. Murad, on Aurangzeb's right wing, took advantage and attacked Jaswant Singh on his left. Aurangzeb's artillery came in to attack and damaged Jaswant Singh's centre.

Jaswant Singh realised he had lost his advance guard, his left wing had deserted him and he had further been attacked and destroyed on his exposed left by Murad. His army was surrounded by Aurangzeb's enveloping flanks and his centre was being torn apart by the enemy artillery. The day was lost and he decided to give up the Battle of Dharmat as a defeat and retreated gathering his remaining forces.

Given that the latter battle with Dara lasted less number of hours, Jaswant fought obstinately. The battle took place on 25 April 1658. However, it is said that Qasim Khan refused to help him in battle and Jaswant lost 6,000 Rajputs that day along with the battle and had to retreat. The way to Agra was clear for Aurangzeb and only Dara stood who could try and stop him. Suleiman Shikoh and Mirza Raja Jai Singh were very far way. The road was set for what was literally a battle royal.

A word on Aurangzeb. Although everyone recognised him as one of the two chief contenders to the throne, he himself gave out that he was least interested. His line with his two brothers, which at least Murad on the face of it seemed to have swallowed hook, line and sinker, was that Aurangzeb's only desire was to rid the empire of the evil influence of Dara. After that, he wanted to retire to pursue holy contemplation and either Murad or Shuja could take over the throne. He continued to address Murad as Padishahji and the foolish Murad gloated over his imagined emperorship, calling Aurangzeb in return Hazratji. Little did he realise that he was playing into the hands of a consummate schemer.

Aurangzeb, having safely taken care of Jaswant Singh, now moved forward to Agra. Dara at once wanted to go and give battle. But Shah Jahan seemed ambivalent. His chief problem was his love and apprehension for Dara. He clearly thought that Dara would make an emperor superior to Aurangzeb. But in his hearts of hearts he also knew, having been an ace general himself, that on the battlefield Aurangzeb was a superior general to Dara. He knew that Dara stood little chance of beating Aurangzeb in direct battle unless he was supported by generals who could help him match Aurangzeb on the field of battle.

He therefore pleaded with Dara to wait for Suleiman Shikoh, Mirza Raja Jaisingh and Diler Khan to join him. He also advised Dara to wait it out inside the Agra fort until Suleiman reached him from the East. However, Dara realised that waiting would subject him to a siege by Aurangzeb and trap him. He also realised that to be seen as an emperor, he would have to earn it by bettering Aurangzeb in battle. So he pleaded with Shah Jahan to be allowed to go and join battle with Aurangzeb without further waste of time.

Dara had lost very good resources in the army that went east to combat Shuja under Suleiman. He had lost an able leader in Jaswant Singh and his formidable Rajput army. If he had had these resources, it would have been easier to tackle Aurangzeb. However, he still set out with an army of 50,000 blessed with good artillery, matchlock men, brave generals and warriors. He left the fort on 28 May 1658 at an hour declared auspicious. He rode some way on a chariot before getting onto an elephant. The whole army moved forward after a very emotional farewell from Shah Jahan to Dara. Shah Jahan clasped Dara to his bosom and then raised his hands upwards in prayer to the almighty.

Dara rode forward and reached the Chambal to a place called Dipalpur. His attempt was to stall Aurangzeb from crossing the Chambal until Suleiman came to his aid. He guarded all the fords and forced Aurangzeb to think. So far Dara's strategies had been correct. He had tried to weaken Aurangzeb but succeeded only partially as the astute rival had managed to keep the bulk of his forces intact. He had tried to create a rift between Aurangzeb and Murad but could not succeed as the two brothers were too bitterly opposed to him and Aurangzeb had convinced the gullible Murad that he wanted Murad to be the emperor. Dara's strategies were being effectively countered by Aurangzeb. Dara had to simultaneously take care of a menacing Shuja approaching from the east while containing Aurangzeb advancing towards the north. He had succeeded with Shuja but Aurangzeb was a different kettle of fish. Ambivalent instructions from Shah Jahan thwarted a determined Jaswant from proactively stopping Aurangzeb and Aurangzeb smashed through his defences. With Suleiman Shikoh too far away with some of Dara's best soldiers and generals and a powerful force of Jaswant Singh routed, Dara's strength was considerably reduced when he went to battle against the foremost general of the age in Hindustan.

So time and again, Dara had his best laid plans thwarted by an audacious, astute and ruthless competitor like Aurangzeb. Time had now come for a face to face contest of military skills. And here Dara's inexperience of fighting and leading actual battles was to prove a major handicap. No matter how well equipped his army was and no matter how well he planned the entire strategy to win the empire, he was clearly outclassed by a seasoned rival who was used to leading armies against enemies in Samarqand, Kandahar, Deccan and Central India. The outcome of the forthcoming events was to be decided by who would manage the battle tactics and situation better and here Aurangzeb was rather well placed.

Faced with a blockage across Chambal, Aurangzeb swung east 60 odd kilometers and crossed Chambal with the help of a local leader. He was now in a position to reach Agra directly. Dara's position at Dipalpur across the Chambal was now untenable. Aurangzeb could bypass him to Agra and had outsmarted Dara again. Dara hurriedly pulled back his defences and retreated towards Agra. He chose the plain of Samugarh about 15 kilometers from Agra and reached an entrenched position awaiting Aurangzeb. Aurangzeb reached Samugarh with an exhausted army on 7 June 1658. Dara's army was fresh. A more experienced commander would have taken advantage of the tired state of Aurangzeb's army and attacked straightaway. He infact moved forward but stopped inexplicably. He missed a clear opportunity and would pay for it dearly. Dara would live to rue this ghastly mistake of not launching an immediate attack on an exhausted enemy host.

The armies confronted each other again the next day on 8 June. This time both armies had rested. The armies advanced towards each other and an artillery duel commenced. Then Dara's left wing under a legendary warrior Rustam Khan Dakhani and Dara's youngest son, Sipihr Shikoh with 10,000 men attacked Aurangzeb's army. They tried to fall on the opposing army but were met with determined artillery and musket fire. They swung left and attacked Aurangzeb's right, inflicting great damage. At the same time, Dara's right under Chhatrasal Hada with Rajputs attacked Aurangzeb's left, commanded by Murad. A bitter battle ensued and Aurangzeb's left, just like his right, seemed in danger of disintegrating. Murad was specially targeted and received many arrow wounds and his howdah was pierced by arrows. Aurangzeb had to rush special reinforcements towards Murad; such was the extremity of danger.

The situation became especially desperate for Aurangzeb when the courageous Rajputs tore through his personal bodyguard. Rup Singh Rathore cut his way through to Aurangzeb's elephant and tried to cut the ropes that tied his howdah to the elephant to bring Aurangzeb down to the ground and eliminate him. However, Aurangzeb's personal bodyguard restored the situation and killed Rup Singh Rathore, in spite of Aurangzeb protesting to spare the gallant Rajput.

At this stage, the aggressive impact of Dara's left and right wings had done considerable damage to Aurangzeb's army and the stage seemed set for delivering the coup de grace. Dara had seen the opportunity and he decided to move forward to deliver the killing blow and rout the army of Aurangzeb from the field.

Battle of Samugarh

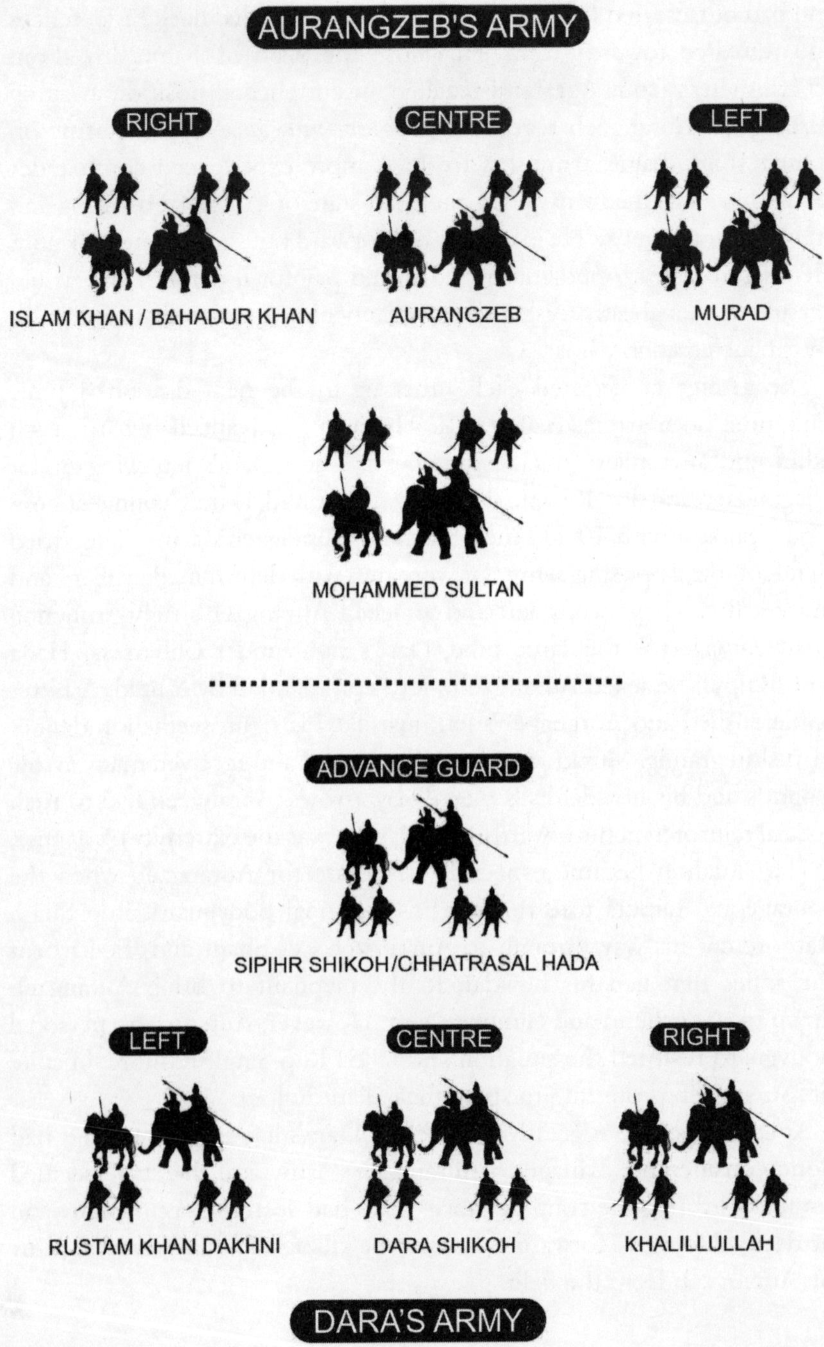

Dara advanced forward with his 20,000 strong centre and reserve. However, this is where he made a crucial mistake. He put himself between his artillery and Aurangzeb's army thereby rendering artillery support from his own army ineffective. By this time, Dara's own army had met with serious reverses. The charge of his left wing had been successfully contained by Aurangzeb's army and Rustam Khan Dakhani killed. The charge of Dara' right had also been neutralised with Murad personally killing Chhatrasal Hada with an arrow. Aurangzeb was now ready for a counter-attack.

Dara realised that the coup de grace faced the possibility of failure. He swung to the left to hit Aurangzeb's right but was met by determined fire. He tried to counter it with his own artillery but that could not fire through his own troops. He swung to the right and went for the jugular by trying to take on Aurangzeb's centre directly.

It was at this time that he made the biggest judgement of error. A man called Khalilullah advised him to get off his elephant and lead the final charge on Aurangzeb on a horse. Khalilullah reasoned that Dara made an easy target on the elephant. Dara's inexperience cost him the battle. Once off the elephant, he was not visible to his army. Aurangzeb and Murad were still seated on their elephants and were visible to their army. Dara's army mistook his non-visibility as his demise and a rumour started that he was either dead or had fallen wounded. Consternation spread throughout Dara's army and they felt all was lost. They also saw Dara's retreating elephant further confirming the rumour. All was then flight for Dara's army. A helpless Dara saw his army melt away and the battle was lost for him. Aurangzeb advanced and Dara ran for his life.

He reached Agra but would not go in front of his father owing to the shame of his defeat. In vain Shah Jahan entreated him to come in, gather his defences for another battle and wait for Suleiman Shikoh to come to his aid. But Dara was not made of stern military stuff and could not take a defeat in his stride and gather his wits for another battle. He turned to Delhi and then fled to Punjab.

Aurangzeb in the meantime cut off the water supply of the Agra fort forcing a defiant Shah Jahan to surrender. Shah Jahan was made captive. Aurangzeb and Murad chased Dara. On the way, the future "Padishah" Murad was forced into a drunken revelry by Aurangzeb, captured and made a prisoner. He was later interned in Gwalior fort and forced to drink *pousta*. He tried in vain to escape but was put to death.

While Aurangzeb was busy chasing an escaping Dara in Punjab, a new danger arose in the east. Shuja had still not been finished off. He decided to take advantage of Aurangzeb's departure to the West and moved towards Agra. Opposing him was a weaker force led by Aurangzeb's son Mohammed Sultan. However Shuja moved slower than required and gave enough time for Aurangzeb to move back and join his son Mohammed Sultan in taking on Shuja. The army that Aurangzeb led was three times the army brought in by Shuja. Aurangzeb had 65,000 men as against 22,000 brought in by Shuja who lost an opportunity of handling Aurangzeb's forces in two installments, first Mohammed Sultan and then Aurangzeb himself.

On the morning of battle, Raja Jaswant Singh, who had fought Aurangzeb at Dharmat, but now joined his standard, deserted Aurangzeb with his 15,000 men, plundering the Mughal camp on the way. Aurangzeb was taken completely by surprise but remained unfazed. He was a cool and composed commander who realised that he still enjoyed more than 2:1 superiority against his rival.

Sayyid Khan, who commanded the right wing of Shuja, advanced forward and attacked Aurangzeb's left wing. He unleashed an impetuous and successful charge and drove back Aurangzeb's left and converged onto his centre where Aurangzeb himself was. The charge was led by three infuriated elephants that carried heavy iron chains in their trunk which were swung menacingly, compelling Aurangzeb's armies to draw back. Aurangzeb's army was in flight when he ordered his reserves to counter-attack Sayyid Khan on his sides thus reducing his momentum. However, the elephants kept charging forward, creating havoc. They even reached Aurangzeb's personal position and one elephant moved forward to attack his elephant, thus exposing Aurangzeb to mortal danger. Luckily, Aurangzeb's bodyguards were able to control the infuriated beast and averted the danger to Aurangzeb.

Aurangzeb then turned his attention to his own right wing that was under attack from the left wing of Shuja commanded by Prince Buland Akhtar. Aurangzeb reorganised his forces and repelled the left wing of Shuja. Shuja's right and left wing collapsed, his centre was jolted by Aurangzeb's advance guard and Shuja realised the day was lost. He retreated for dear life. Aurangzeb had him followed inexorably like he did with Dara and finally forced him to retreat to Arakan where Shuja lost his life at the hands of local kings.

Suleiman was deserted by the opportunistic Mirza Raja Jai Singh and Diler Khan, took refuge in Garhwal, was captured by Aurangzeb and made to die a slow death through drinking *pousta*.

Murad had been executed. Suleiman done to death and Shah Jahan captured. Dara was left and he fought a series of retreating battles with Aurangzeb, before deciding to escape to Persia via Baluchistan. He was betrayed by Malik Jiwan, a man whose life he had saved once. He was brought to Delhi with his son Sipihr Shikoh, his wife Nadira Begum having already expired. He was incarcerated and finally killed, his head sent to Shah Jahan as the latter sat down for dinner and the unfortunate prince had his body hung from the Khooni Darwaza.

Aurangzeb had already assumed emperorship in July 1658 in a simple ceremony in Shalimar Bagh at Delhi. He made a grand enthronement ceremony in May 1659 at Delhi. Aurangzeb won, Dara lost. It was *Dara ki shikast, Aurangzeb ki fateh*. In the process, while the Mughal empire had a strong emperor for 38 years, it also had an emperor who divided India, setting off the majority Hindu population against what they perceived as injustice. He left behind an impoverished treasury. Aurangzeb won and maybe India lost. The Mughal emperor may have lasted longer with an inclusive Dara and a capable Suleiman to follow him. What if Dara had won the battle for Delhi at Samugarh and crowned himself in the Red Fort? That is a big what if of Indian history. But for now, it was *takht* for Aurangzeb and *tabut* for Dara.

Chapter X

Jajau

They say all good things come to an end. And the death of Aurangzeb sounded the death knell of the Grand Mughal Empire. An empire that had taken close to 30 years from 1526 to 1556 to lay a firm foundation and which flourished for 151 years under powerful monarchs like Akbar, Jahangir, Shah Jahan and Aurangzeb, was about to start coming apart. An empire that protected India against foreign invasions of the Persians, Afghans, and Uzbegs, and made powerful European nations like Britain, France and Portugal gape in awe at the grandeur of the Mughal court, begging for trading rights within the dominions of the Great Mughal as it was called, was now going to start declining. Shah Jahan had decisively defeated a European power like the Portuguese when it dared to take on a military power that boasted of 900,000 soldiers at its command. Aurangzeb's general, Shaista Khan, and other commanders had taught the British a lesson in the war called the Child's War when they had dared to take on the mighty Mughals only to ask for pardon later. The Mughal empire at its zenith, under a strong central rule, was what made India unconquerable in that time and age.

This powerful edifice, which gave security and integrity to a large part of the land mass of the Indian sub-continent, was now ready to crumble. And what brought about this unfortunate happening were a number of factors. One prominent factor was the narrow-minded and needlessly expansionist policies followed by Aurangzeb that bled the empire's treasuries dry through incessant warfare to expand the empire's territories, especially in the Deccan. Deccan was, in fact, a big obsession for Aurangzeb. Another was his none too friendly policy towards Hindus that brought up internal rebellions from the Rajputs, Marathas, Sikhs and Jats. The earlier Mughals had managed to keep a lid on these tendencies through judicious and secular policies. Thirdly, the fate of the next Mughal emperor was now entirely decided by the sword in which the most powerful triumphed and the others were vanquished. This created a series of internecine struggles in quick succession that resulted in the obliteration of the best of Mughal generals. If these generals had survived, they would have made the Mughal empire handle internal insurrections as well as external aggressions and helped maintain its integrity. When push came to shove, there just weren't enough Mughal generals militarily capable of either handling the Marathas, Persians, Afghans or the British. Fourthly, as the empire flourished, the Mughal princes who came later, were fonder of wine and women than the battlefield. Therefore the next generations of Mughal emperors, unlike the earlier ones who were outstanding generals, were military nincompoops. The power went to the *vazir* and nobles and the emperor became a puppet. The empire was decimated as it became incapable of handling either external invaders or internal rebellions.

The first nail in the coffin of the empire was the Battle of Jajau. Aurangzeb expired in March 1707. Three of his sons survived the nonagenarian monarch. The first was Mohammed Muazzam. His mother was Nawab Bai. The next in line was Mohammed Azam, born to Dilras Bano. He was also called Azam Shah or Azam Tara. The third and youngest was Kam Baksh, son of Udaipuri Bai.

Mohammed Muazzam had seen military service in Deccan campaigns and Konkan. He was militarily capable but owing to the suspicious nature of Aurangzeb, had to suffer incarceration based on suspected disloyalty, quite a habit with Aurangzeb. Muazzam had two sons—Mohammed Muizuddin and Mohammed Azim. He had gained experience in the rough terrains of the Northwest in Afghanistan and Punjab. He was posted as governor of Kabul, a hardship frontier posting for the Mughals, engaged as they were in intermittent conflict with the Persian empire on that front. He was near Peshawar when he heard the news of his father's death. His two younger sons, Rafi-ul-Qadr and Khujista Akhtar were with him. His son, Muizuddin, was at Multan and the other, Azimushshan, was in Bihar. If one were to look at geographical proximity, then Muazzam was in the Northwest and ready to make a move for either Agra or Delhi. His sons were on the western and eastern flanks at Multan and Bihar, ready to join him in a pincer movement towards the Mughal capital. In terms of proximity to the twin seats of the Mughal empire, Delhi and Agra, Muazzam was better placed.

Muhammad Azam was the more aggressive and daring son. He had amassed a lot of wealth during his governorship at Ahmedabad. Suspicious of this, Aurangzeb had instead posted Azam's son, Bidar Bakht, to Ahmedabad and recalled Azam nearer to him. So in terms of imperial proximity, Azam was better poised to declare and take control of the imperial army. Plus, he had the flower of the Mughal army and commanders with him.

Kam Baksh, the youngest son, had a running feud with Azam Shah and also happened to be Aurangzeb's favourite. Fearing for his safety after his death, Aurangzeb sent him as *subedar* to Bijapur, separating him from the dangerous and aggressive Azam.

It is rumoured that Aurangzeb may have left a will declaring the division of the empire among his three sons. However, the great empire was not ready for such a peaceful division. It was destined to have a single emperor for some more time, the fate to be decided on the battlefields of India. The battle for Delhi was not to be decided by a will but by the sword.

Azam Shah had been commanded by Aurangzeb to go to Agra from Aurangabad near where Aurangzeb expired later. Azam Shah deliberately moved very slowly, and was not too far when he got the news of his father's death and hurried back. Aurangzeb's body was taken to Daulatabad and buried in a simple ceremony in a tomb in Khuldabad, much in keeping with the lifestyle of one of the most powerful kings on this earth at that time. Azam Shah, who had been welcomed by most of the nobles of Aurangzeb's entourage, was now commonly assumed by all in the huge Mughal encampment to be the next emperor. In a typical simple Mughal ceremony, the *khutba* was read in his name and he was declared emperor. Most Mughal nobles supported him but some stayed away, not sure of the future turn of events.

Azam Shah was guilty of having a haughty character. He disdained some sane advice offered to him like pressing for the loyalty of a powerful noble, Ghaziuddin Firuz Jang, and also moving ahead fast for capturing the imperial capital. Ghaziuddin Firuz Jang, a veteran and highly revered Mughal commander refused to accompany him and the same was done by his son, Chin Qilich Khan. Chin Qilich Khan's brother, Mohammed Amin Khan, also made only a show of supporting Azam Shah by participating half-heartedly in the march forward and subsequently deserting midway.

However, Mohammed Azam Shah had the support of the *vazir*, Asad Khan, and his competent son, Zulfiqar Khan. Zulfiqar Khan was a much-decorated general and was destined to play a historic role in the forthcoming struggles for the throne of the Mughals at Delhi.

However, Mohammed Kam Baksh, the youngest, was not to be left behind and promptly declared independent sovereignty at Bijapur.

Azam Shah then proceeded from Aurangabad to Burhanpur. His march commenced on 17 March 1707, barely two weeks after the death of his father, Aurangzeb. Asad Khan and Zulfiqar Khan are said to have become reluctant participants and Chin Qilich Khan, son of Ghaziuddin Firuz Jang, left for the South. Therefore, the support of key Mughal nobles was much reduced and Azam Shah was deprived of important resources as he moved forward to capture Agra and Delhi.

Azam Shah intended making straight for Agra where all the Mughal treasures were kept and where the *subedar*, Mukhtar Khan, was his son Bidar Bakht's father in-law with more loyal officers present to support him. He reached Aurangabad on 2 April 1707 and Burhanpur on 24 April.

Azam Shah's son was at that time in charge of Ahmedabad. Bidar Bakht, being at Ahmedabad, proposed to Azam Shah that he be allowed to go straight to Agra and capture the city, its fort and resources for Azam Shah, thus giving him the undoubted edge in the forthcoming struggle for the throne. Agra was the place where the treasure built by generations of Mughal emperors was kept and whoever got hold of that treasure had the largest resources of the empire at his disposal. Then it would be easier for that contestant to buy loyalties and raise resources for the conflict for the throne.

However, Azam Shah also suspected that once having captured Agra and its treasures and having his father-in-law, Mukhtar, as *subedar-e-Agra* for support, Bidar might wrest the crown for himself. Bidar was therefore ordered to join his father instead at Gwalior. Bidar raved bitterly at the decision but hastened to do his father's bidding, being joined there by Raja Jai Singh of Amber. The reason for this was that Azam Shah had long suspected the loyalties of his son, having once intercepted a message between Bidar Bakht and Aurangzeb, purportedly aimed against Azam Shah.

This decision of not allowing Bidar to capture Agra could be said to be the single most important factor that decided the fate of the ensuing battle. There was a typical risk versus return inflection point and the risk of Bidar assuming power himself dictated that Bidar should not proceed to Agra even though he had reached Gwalior. One and a half months passed in the process and in the meantime Muazzam had moved to Lahore. This delay would prove to be crucial in deciding the fortunes of the impending struggle.

Bidar Bakht had reached Shahjahanpur in Malwa on 5 April and could have reached and captured Agra from there. However, bound by his father's orders, he had to cool his heels and his father reached him somewhere in the middle of May. Only then was he allowed to move forward.

This unfortunate decision was supplemented by disastrous news that Mohamed Azim, the second son of Muazzam, had managed to capture Agra, its resources and its considerable treasures, in fact the cream of the wealth of the Mughals. With this, the pendulum swung in the favour of Muazzam. Muazzam placed more trust in his son and reaped the benefits. The point of contest now became the Chambal River. Bidar Bakht wanted to cross this river, much like Aurangzeb had to fifty years earlier, to make a thrust on the twin seats of Mughal power—Delhi and Agra. Mohammed Azim sent forward a strong force to prevent the crossing. The stage was set for another battle for Delhi.

Azam Shah had reached Sironj and from there sent a force under Zulfiqar Khan and other chiefs to reinforce Bidar Bakht and to advance on Gwalior. Azam had reached the vicinity of Gwalior when he got the news that Mohammed Muazzam and his son Mohammed Azim had taken firm control of Agra, it treasures and its resources.

Mohammed Azim meantime had moved his forces forward to prevent an advance of Azam Shah's forces across the river. Bidar Bakht was keen to cross the river but Zulfiqar Khan had advised against it. There was a fierce clash of opinions, in the end the prince prevailing and managing to cross Chambal at unguarded fords and putting the opposing camp to flight.

Muazzam had come to know only on 22 March of his father's death as he was placed far from where the death occurred in the Deccan. He intended making his way to the Mughal capital and had already alerted Munim Khan, *subedar* of Lahore for his aid. Mohammed Muazzam had obtained tremendous cooperation from this Munim Khan, *diwan* of Kabul, who helped him with men, resources and the means to cross the river Indus. Muazzam crossed both Indus and Ravi and arrived at Lahore. He left Lahore on 5 May 1707 and made his way to Delhi. He captured Delhi on 1 June 1707 and thus won another round of the battle. He got hold of the treasure at Delhi. He had by then assumed a rival imperial authority and titled himself "Bahadur Shah", having captured Delhi and its treasure. However, the road to the throne of Delhi lay via Agra and Muazzam proceeded in that direction. His three sons—Muizuddin, Khujista Akhtar and Rafi ul Qadr—were with him.

Muazzam reached Agra on 12 June 1707. The commandants at Agra, Mukhtar Khan and Baqi Khan presented themselves, the fort and its treasures to him. The entire fortune at Agra, hoarded over centuries of Mughal rule, estimated to be between 13 and 24 crores, fell in a single swoop to Bahadur Shah and virtually decided who would sit on the throne. Add to this the reputed treasure from Bengal of about 10 crores brought by Mohammed Azim and we have an idea how well stocked Muazzam was in terms of money. This treasure was taken out in part and distributed liberally among chiefs and soldiers to enhance the loyalty and commitment before the forthcoming contest.

Bahadur Shah, alias Muazzam, now advanced to give battle to his brother Azam Shah or Azam Tara as he was called. The forces on both sides were considerable. Just the advance guard sent to prevent crossing of Chambal under Mohammed Azim's command had 80,000 men. Azam Shah also advanced forward. Both sides advanced towards Dholpur, south of Agra. Azam Shah's vanguard was commanded by the unfortunate Bidar Bakht, who had been prevented by his mistrusting father from capturing Agra. Bidar was supported by Zulfiqar Khan, Rao Dalpat Bundela and Ram Singh Hada. His brother, Wala Jah, followed with 25,000 men and other chiefs.

Azam Shah moved forward to join Bidar Bakht and when the two met the total force came to 110,000 men. A pay hike was given to soldiers and a further hike was promised upon capturing Agra.

Both the would-be emperors marched towards each other with massive forces. Each was accompanied by their full retinue of sons. It was the searing hot month of June 1707, not easy for soldiery moving in heavy armour. A huge battle for Delhi was on the cards. Bidar Bakht moved forward in the vanguard with Zulfiqar Khan, Amanullah Khan, Rao Dalpat Bundela and Ram Singh Hada reinforcing him. On his right was Prince Wala Jah. Azam Shah was at the centre but three miles behind, again a crucial mistake. Bidar Bakht's army suffered from thirst and water and took a course intending to find water. In the process the forces got a bit scattered and lost touch with each other. Not the ideal situation to force a battle.

The battle for the throne of Delhi however began accidentally. It happened neither at the historic field of Samugarh, nor at Dholpur but at a place called Jajau. This battle in history is called the Battle of Jajau.

Bidar Bakht, from the very beginning eager to take the initiative and ever eager for battle, marched forward on his elephant with arrows and quiver. He commanded the advance guard. On the left was Zulfiqar Khan along with Ram Singh Hada and Rao Dalpat Bundela with Amanullah Khan in tow. Alongwith the advance guard marched Aziz Khan Afghan with Khan Alam Dakhini and Munavvar Khan. On the right wing was Prince Wala Jah. In the centre was Azam Shah himself, three miles behind. This force was moving towards Jajau hoping to encounter Muazzam's forces in the vicinity. Not only was the army well provisioned but also had capable leaders.

With the troops in desperate need for water, Bidar's men reached a village where there was a stream of water and step wells. Bidar proposed to camp here for water, replenish his forces and then move forward into an area where there was lack of water. He told a noble, Iradat Khan, to go back and inform Azam Shah of the news.

Iradat Khan came back after informing Azam Shah only to find Bidar nowhere in sight. Bidar had in fact came to know that the advance guard of Muazzam was camped nearby and in sight. The rival's advance tents were being pitched under the supervision of Prince Azimushshan and Rustam Dil Khan. Khan Alam Dakhini and Munavvar Khan advanced quickly on the advance guard of Muazzam and though they had one-tenth the strength of the enemy, succeeded in dispersing it through their quickness. Rustam Dil Khan surrendered and presented himself to Azam Shah. Azimushshan however decided to prolong the contest and sent word to his father to send for reinforcements. Bidar Bakht misunderstood the partial enemy retreat as a final victory and started beating the victory drums. Iradat Khan warned him to be careful as the battle seemed to have just begun. Bidar Bakht angrily told him off. In the meantime, Bahadur Shah got word of the enemy attack and without wasting time, redirected his forces forward to battle. Azam Shah's generals advised him to wait a day for battle but the haughty Prince replied in the negative and he too pressed forward. The problem for Azam Shah was that Bahadur Shah's forces reached to aid his son Azimushshan much faster than Azam Shah's forces reached Bidar Bakht to support him.

Azam Shah, on receiving news that the main battle had begun, dramatically flailed his arms, flashed a crooked staff and angrily gave orders to move forward to battle. In the meantime, Prince Azimushshan and Munim Khan came forward with their artillery and army. They engaged with Bidar Bakht's advance guard, which was somewhat disorganised and engaged in plunder. They let loose their cannonade and their artillery began to exact heavy casualties from Bidar's men. Bidar Bahkt's men were not organised to handle it. He started experiencing a heavy loss of men. Seeing this, Khan Alam Dakhini and 500 men on Bidar Bakht's side got ready to engage the enemy.

Thus we see that the Battle of Jajau was not a battle where the two gigantic armies reached a stated place, arrayed themselves for battle and began to fight in a formal manner. The two armies were advancing towards each other with the camps of each army split in parts and intending to gather at Dholpur. It was the advance guard of each side, on Muazzam's side led by his son Azimushshan and on Azam Shah's side led by his son Bidar Bakht, that came into accidental contact with each other and the battle therefore began accidentally. Bidar Bakht having got the better of initial exchanges moved forward imprudently. Bahadur Shah and Azam Shah both moved forward to aid their sons and Bahadur Shah was the first to reach, thus giving his side the larger and more formidable force immediately engaged in battle.

The forces now closed for hand to hand combat. Khan Alam Dakhini took his elephant forward to attack Prince Azimushshan and thrice tried to pierce him with his spear, failing in his attempts. The prince counter-attacked with his bow and arrow and killed Khan Alam Dakhini. Such was the bravery and contempt for life the Mughal princes and generals showed in the battles for the throne. Dakhini's brother was wounded by an attendant of Azimushshan called Jalal Khan. Amanullah Khan from Azam Shah's side hastened to the rescue but his elephant seat was set on fire by a rocket. Thus, the advance guard of Azam Shah's force started losing its key commanders. The right wing of Azam Shah, led by his son Wala Jah, got exposed badly. Prince Wala Jah, now feeling unprotected, went back under the cover of Bidar Bakht. Baz Khan Afghan attacked Zulfiqar Khan from Azimushshan's side. Zulfiqar Khan successfully repulsed his attack with heavy losses but in the process lost his trusted commanders, Rao Dalpat Bundela and Ram Singh Hada. Seeing the loss of their leaders the Rajputs fled and Zulfiqar Khan was forced to retreat under the protection of Azam Shah. From there he left the battlefield completely and left to join his father, Asad Khan, in the Deccan. Raja Jai Singh also saw his forces suffering and left Azam Shah's side, presenting himself to Bahadur Shah. The losing of key commanders in the advance guard, the loss of key Rajput generals like Rao Dalpat and Ram Singh Hada, the surrender of Raja Jai Sngh and the flight of Zulfiqar Khan from the field of battle, left Azam Shah's army with lesser forces and without able generals, leaving him to fight the battle alone.

It seems that Bahadur Shah had made for a far better campaign. Not only had he captured the treasures at Delhi and Agra, he had brought a far more cohesive force to battle. His generals stuck with him and his force moved forward to give battle, the moment it was joined, in a far more cohesive manner.

Azam Shah, too, seemed to have brought forward an equally formidable force. But he lacked the money to buy loyalty and his generals deserted him at crucial intervals right from the start of the march to the very day of the battle. Also, the speed with which he brought his entire force to battle on the fateful day was inferior to that of Bahadur Shah.

Azam Shah's forces were now under severe attack and clearly Muazzam was beginning to dominate the proceedings. Zulfiqar Khan's retreat swung the battle towards Muazzam. Raja Jaisingh Kachhwaha also made his way over to Prince Muhammad Azim and Bahadur Shah. In fact many commanders either started crossing over to Muazzam's side or retreating, exposing Azam Shah's position badly.

The battle now became very fierce and soldiers from both sides joined in mutual combat led by their commanders. This internecine battle, one of the many to be fought by Mughals for the contest of the throne of Delhi, was to cost them dearly. Experienced commanders, instead of leading forces against the enemies of the Mughals like the Afghans, Marathas and Persians, fought against and annihilated each other. So did the princes who were capable of leading Mughal armies in battle. What was left as the Mughal empire proceeded along in the eighteenth century were emperors, princes and nobles more at home in court craft and not in battle craft. No wonder the eighteenth century is a story of the decline of Mughal military might and India's descent into chaos.

Nuruddin Ali Khan, Mirza Namdar, Sayyid Hussain Khan and Inayat Khan died on Muazzam's side. On Azam Shah's side, Amanullah Khan, Tarbiyat Khan, Matalab Khan and Khudabanda Khan were killed. A major disaster struck the Azam Shah side when a musket ball came and killed his daring son, Bidar Bakht, dealing a body blow to his advance guard. Many more commanders continued to perish and Prince Wala Jah, who had taken refuge under Bidar Bakht, also fainted from loss of blood, after fighting relentlessly. He was then moved to be under his father's protection so that the losing contest could be revived.

Azam Shah now moved forward with his main body for battle. His son Prince Ali Tabar was struck on the arm but Azam Shah pressed on despite such reverses. His commanders continued to get slain but Azam Shah was now in the thick of battle. Arrows struck him but he pressed on, leading his elephant personally until he was struck in the forehead by a musket ball and perished. His army now fled in the general direction of Gwalior and got badly plundered and ransacked on the way. News reached Muazzam that his rival, Azam Shah, and Bidar Bakht were dead. Their army was in retreat and rout. He had won the battle for Delhi and could now safely call himself Bahadur Shah.

Bahadur Shah was presented the head of his brother, Azam Shah, which had been cut off by Rustam Dil Khan, who had until then been in the captivity of Azam Shah but in an opportunistic manner, switched sides again. The body of Bidar Bakht was also found. Bahadur Shah showed great character and issued orders for the safety of Azam Shah's harem, his ailing sons and his grandsons. The next Mughal emperor after Aurangzeb was now ready to take over as the Grand Mughal.

However, the contest had been costly. Not only had the defeated Mughal prince been slain but so too had been his sons. So too had powerful and fearless nobles. After Samugarh came Jajau and then many more. The cost the Mughal empire had to pay for deciding who would be the emperor was going to prove very harmful for the continuation of the empire.

CHAPTER XI

Lahore

BAHADUR SHAH DIED ON 27 FEBRUARY 1712 AFTER A REIGN OF FIVE years, weighed down by his struggles and age. His health had started deteriorating in January 1712 on reaching Lahore. He suffered from hallucinations and ordered mass killing of dogs, who literally swam across the Ravi to save themselves, knowing their lives were in mortal danger. He last gave an audience on 26 February.

It is a sad commentary on the affairs and stability of India that in spite of being ruled by a powerful empire, the strains of impending instability were already beginning to be felt. The succession of Jahangir to Akbar's throne, though not without some intrigue, was smooth. The decline started on Jahangir's death when Shah Jahan or Khurram had to literally fight his way to the throne. It aggravated further when the bloodiest of battles was fought between the sons of Shah Jahan, possibly the bloodiest conflict, when Shuja, Murad and Dara lost their lives and Aurangzeb emerged the victor. Same was the case when Aurangzeb died and it literally came to a *takht* versus *tabut* battle in which Azam Shah and Kam Baksh lost their lives and Muazzam emerged victorious to be crowned as Bahadur Shah.

Therefore, much to the detriment of India, the succession came to be decided by bloody battles. Perhaps it was inevitable as each prince and son of the dying emperor felt that he was best suited to the throne. He also secretly knew that once any other brother succeeded to the throne, the new emperor would ensure his other brothers were obliterated to prevent future threats to his rule. Therefore a contest was inevitable and each prince had his soldiers, treasure and camp followers with a core of loyal adherents, prepared to hitch their fortunes to his and to work for ensuring his success.

The problem was not the finances and weaponry lost in the ensuing battles because in a country like India that was rich in resources, these could be replenished during the subsequent years of rule through taxes on agriculture and trade. The problem was that in the process, generals and nobles, capable of leading men in battle, fought on either side. The conflict was bloody and fearsome. No quarter was either given or taken. The result was that in all such conflicts, the flower of Mughal military leadership perished one by one. Great nobles perished such as Suleiman Khan, Rao Dalpat, Zulfiqar Khan and Rustam Dil Khan, to name only a handful out of the large number that were killed.

The Mughal military leadership thus became devoid of talent. Later Mughal emperors had been brought up in the cozy comfort of the royal court at Delhi and became incapable of providing military leadership by themselves unlike Aurangzeb, Akbar, Shah Jahan, Babar and Humayun. A militarily hapless emperor became a pawn in the hands of the grand nobles. Gone were the days when heir aspirants like Khurram, Salim, Aurangzeb and Dara inspired fear and respect. Now it was the turn of the princes to become supplicants to nobles like Zulfiqar Khan. The decline of the Mughal empire had begun.

Immediately, various rumours regarding Bahadur Shah's death or severe illness started circulating. Commotion arose within the camp of the emperor as well as those of the princes and nobles. Each prince and grand persona, fearing for his own safety either repaired to the city of Lahore or set up a pitched encampment surrounded by faithful nobles and soldiery, either already existing or specially hired given the circumstances. Spies ran around trying to get information for their masters, adding to the commotion already created.

The emperor's health deteriorated. But so great was the fear and suspicion that none of the sons dared to be near the imperial camp, preferring to be in the safety of the pitched encampment that they had created, so that when the hour of reckoning arose, none of them should be found wanting in their preparedness to fight. Azimushshan, the most powerful among them, was the only one who bothered to be anywhere near his father. He too went away as the end came near, hastening to where his encampment was, telling his faithful to keep reporting until the end had come. The love for their father, if there was any, was overcome by personal ambition and fear for their own safety. So the Grand Mughal, Bahadur Shah I, died in the company of nobles like Zulfiqar Khan, Hamiduddin Khan and Mahfuz Khan, with none of his sons present.

He had four sons who would become contestants for the throne of Delhi after his death. Jahandar Shah, the eldest and the governor of Multan but not considered the strongest contender with hardly any financial and military resources. The second was Azimushshan, the governor of Bihar and Bengal, the man with the strongest resources at his disposal and the person considered most likely to be the next successor. In fact, he was the one who had played the most significant role in the elevation of his father Muazzam to the Mughal throne as Bahadur Shah. Not only had he ensured Agra and its treasures were captured first by the Muazzam faction but also been the advance guard that bore the brunt of the battle at the field of Jajau, resulting in the death of Azam Shah and his sons. The third was Rafiushshan, and the fourth, Jahan Shah. The latter two were apparently minor contestants.

It seemed very clear to everyone as Bahadur Shah's end approached that Azimushshan would take over as the next emperor of India. Azimushshan gave orders that drums be beaten announcing his elevation to the throne of Hindustan even as the emperor lay dying.

The emperor died on 27 February 1712 at the age of seventy. However, the dead body of this emperor of Hindustan suffered great ignominy. It lay unburied for almost 45 days until the battle of succession was decided, only being sent to Delhi on 11 April 1712 for burial near the Qutub Minar.

Nobles sent their wishes and among them was Zulfiqar Khan, a man of great military and political capability. However, on receiving a discourteous and discouraging reply, he made up his mind to work against Azimushshan and approached the other three princes. He reminded them that the resources and forces at the disposal of Azimushshan were more than those of the other three brothers combined and the three must unite if they were to escape an inevitable annihilation. The deal made was for Jahandar to become emperor of Hind. Rafiushshan was to take over Kashmir and the West including Multan and Kabul, and Jahan Shah was to be the king of the South beyond the Narmada all the way to the southern coast. Zulfiqar Khan was to be Grand Vazir. If Azimushshan were to be defeated, it was an arrangement that could hardly have lasted. In fact, it was as tenuous and weak as were the promises made to the princes, Murad and Shuja, by Aurangzeb before the Battle of Samugarh. Nevertheless, united in their fear of Azimushshan and intent on believing the unbelievable, the princes agreed to work together.

This circumstance constitutes a turning point in the history of the Mughals and also a beginning of the decline of imperial authority. For the first time, an entity other than one belonging to the imperial house was calling the shots. An important noble, Zulfiqar Khan, was in control and deciding the fate of the empire. He was to play the most decisive role in the ensuing battle for Delhi. In fact, he was to become a king-maker, setting in motion a trend that was to prevail in all subsequent battles for the throne at Delhi. The princes, potential heir-aspirants to the throne, would henceforth be made or unmade by such king-makers like Zulfiqar Khan, Sayyid brothers, Safdarjung, Imad ul Baksh, Ghulam Qadir, Marathas and ultimately the British. This gradual but irrevocable erosion of central authority was to lead to the ultimate collapse of the Mughal empire, an empire that had kept a strong and cohesive India under a monarchical authority, and ultimately lead to the capitulation of Hindustan to the British.

Zulfiqar Khan now exerted himself in boosting the morale of Jahandar Shah, Jahan Shah and Rafiushshan. Their alliance was weak and could break any moment. He had the three largest guns in Lahore brought in by oxen and gave away one to each of the three princes. He made them encamp close to each other and each day made them advance a short distance towards Azimushshan's encampment.

Azimushshan was however the soul of complacency. By his demeanour it seemed the throne of Delhi had already been decided in his favour. He had been advised to get the dangerous Zulfiqar Khan arrested and executed but he declined to do so. He was advised by his commanders like Raja Daya Bahadur and Mirza Shah Nawaz Khan Safawi to take the field, attack and rout the enemy forces. Azimushshan seemed hell bent on taking it easy. He had a low opinion of his enemies. He felt Jahandar Shah had very low capabilities and resources. He knew Rafiushshan to be a man who spent half his time adorning himself with clothes and jewels. He also felt Jahan Shah was conceited. To every entreaty by his followers not to waste time and attack, his simple reply in Farsi was *Andak Bashid*—Let us wait. It was a reply that was designed to drive them to exasperation and despair and Azimushshan to his ruin.

This conduct of Azimushshan is quite inexplicable. For a person whose daring, speed and enterprise had virtually decided the battle of succession in his father's favour, it is very difficult to explain such inaction. When Aurangzeb died and so many factors were loaded in the favour of Azam Shah, his father's rival, Azimushshan had moved with lightning speed to Agra, captured the city and its treasures for his father, then moved forward to guard the fords of the Chambal river against the crossing of Azam Shah and his son, Bidar Bakht. Initially surprised, he had resolved to sell himself dear and had asked for reinforcements, continuing to give battle to the advancing forces of Bidar Bakht. Having stayed put, his father's arrival and resources succeeded in turning the tide of battle and led to the defeat and death of Azam Shah.

It is very surprising that this same prince, who showed such alacrity in his father's cause, declined to do the same when fighting for his own life and for the throne for himself. It is amazing and shows a decline in either spirit or character or plain overconfidence and lethargy.

Azimushshan had, in fact, taken possession of the emperor's camp. Drums were beaten in honour of his succession. Nobles reminded him that he was not without enemies, that the other three princes were prepared to contest and he should not ignore that. To which Azimushshan gave a disdainful reply. He was also informed that it was important to arrest and execute Zulfiqar Khan who was an extremely powerful noble and not well inclined towards Azimushshan. The latter ignored this advice, scornfully replying that one single Zulfiqar Khan could do nothing, a lesson he only learnt to his cost later. The nobles, ignoring their master's complacency, hastened on their own to arrest Zulfiqar Khan and execute him. Zulfiqar was no idiot, came to know of the danger to himself and vanished from the scene for his own safety, only to cause mayhem later.

Azimushshan did send his son and soldiers forward and the other three princes feared an attack. However, he had only done so to bring back certain nobles to his camp. Azimushshan's advisers earnestly advised him that the other princes were ill-prepared, even now not united, and could be defeated in an attack which needed to be launched immediately. Azimushshan seemed to be in a dazed stupor, highly complacent and waiting for god knows what. He declined to attack, repeatedly saying *Andak Bashid*—Let us wait. As the hours passed, the other princes became more united and militarily stronger while despair grew in the camp of Azimushshan at his perceived inaction. Nobles began to despair of his cause and cursed themselves for aligning with a highly inactive prince.

Several days passed with Azimushshan making barely a move. The other three princes, Muizuddin, Rafiushshan and Jahandar Shah pitched their camps closer to each other, brought in more artillery and men, and started advancing closer to Azimushshan's camp every day. The latter would occasionally let his troops sally out or engage in desultory artillery duel with no decisive action, much to the consternation and despair of his adherents.

The battle itself was an extended affair and not something that got over as a contest in a single day. In fact, the contest for the throne was conducted over a few days, the final denouement happening quite some days after the contest was joined.

The armies got closer to each other purely on account of exertions shown by Zulfiqar Khan and the three princes who came closer and closer to Azimushshan's camp, giving the appearance that the latter was besieged. Due to exertions shown by Zulfiqar Khan and the frantic activities of the three princes who were showing unusual cooperation, it seemed that the combined forces of these three princes were moving in for the kill and had gone on the offensive. The hunter was becoming the hunted.

Azimushshan had thrown an entrenchment around his camp and had gone into a stupor of complacency. He had a low opinion of his brothers and considered his succession a foregone conclusion. He therefore remained where he was and got gradually surrounded by the armies of the three princes. He was going into a defensive shell, much the way Sadashiv Rao Bhao did at the Third Battle of Panipat and Mohammed Shah at the Battle of Karnal. He became the besieged party and was now seen to be fighting for his survival.

The battle now began not as a major battle with the entire armies operating but like a series of chess moves with the three princes sending out detachments for battle and same happening from Azimushshan's side. Since the three princes were as yet tentative and Azimushshan was indecisive, the battle swung back and forth with neither side gaining the advantage. It was by Mughal standards a rather strange battle with no decisive contest but a sickening pendulum swinging back and forth.

Abdussamad Khan, from the side of three Princes, attempted a night attack on the camp of Azimushshan but was made to retreat by an alert defence commanded by Suleiman Khan Panni and Shah Nawaz Khan.

On the first day of any serious contest, 15 March 1712, Shah Nawaz Khan attacked Jahandar Shah's positions with 2,000 cavalry. Abdussamad

Khan opposed him. However, Shah Nawaz Khan pressed home the advantage. The beleaguered force of Abdussamad Khan was rescued by the arrival of Jahan Shah. Shah Nawaz Khan had to retreat to the camp of Azimushshan for his life. Jahan Shah pursued Shah Nawaz Khan to Azimushshan's camp but was beaten off by Suleiman Khan Panni. Mukhtar Khan from Azimushshan's camp counter-attacked Jahan Shah and beat him back. Thus the first day ended with advantage to neither side but a curiously inactive Azimushshan. A devil's wish of inactivity seemed to have overtaken him as the battle fruitlessly swung back and forth. A few pawns had been exchanged but neither side was the victor. Azimushshan continued to waste his superior resources.

The second day saw Rafiushshan take the offensive at the head of 5,000 cavalry. He attacked Azimushshan's entrenchment. His men carried the day and defenders retreated in confusion. Rafiushshan troops now tried to enter the entrenchments but Suleiman Khan counter-attacked. Rafiushshan men retreated and now it was the turn of Suleiman Khan to emerge and take on the role of the attacker. He speedily put Rafiushshan to rout. Rafiushshan was saved by the arrival of Zulfiqar Khan and his men. The battle became fierce but Suleiman Khan found himself hemmed in by enemy forces and retreated to his entrenchment. Again, a fruitless swing both ways with no result. Gul Khan, an important noble on Azimushshan's side, lost his life in the battle.

Somehow, while Azimushshan had more resources, he seemed to have gone into a mental and physical shell, turning his camp into an entrenchment and Jahandar Shah's forces seemed to be display more vigour, initiative and speed.

An attempt was made by Shah Nawaz Khan on the side of Azimushshan to hire Qalmaq salves and send them at night to assassinate Jahandar Shah or Muizuddin and at least end the life of one of the contestants to the throne. The slaves were discovered by an alert lady camp-follower, Raiman, and put to flight, thus saving the life of Muizuddin.

The third day saw more fighting with Zulfiqar Khan coordinating the attacks of the forces of the three princes on the entrenchment of Azimushshan whose forces did not give in but got hemmed inside the entrenchment and could not come out to either give battle or take on an offensive role.

The third day saw the three princes take the initiative further. Zulfiqar Khan coordinated the attack. The army of the three princes brought their cannons closer and started pounding the positions of Azimushshan. An attack was launched by Raja Pirthi Bundela on Azimushshan's encampment. Kesari Singh opposed him. Kesari was winning the day when Rafiushshan sent reinforcements to push back Kesari Singh. Daya Bahadur was rushed from Azimushshan's side to reinforce Pirthi Bundela and the day was saved. Suleiman Khan Panni came out from Azimushshan's side to attack but was deterred by the presence of Abdussamad Khan. Azimushshan became even more desperately besieged with the three princes closing in for the kill.

By the end of the third day, the fortunes seemed to be swinging in favour of the three princes. They had begun to encircle the camp of Azimushshan who had gone clearly on the defensive. The morale in his camp was low. Zulfiqar was displaying exemplary battlefield tactics. He realised that the morale was low in the camp of his opponents and many people were in discomfort and planned to escape. Since the camp was near the river Ravi, he realised that most of them would escape by that side. So he let out word that he would remove the encircling guard and those that wanted to escape from the side of Azimushshan could take advantage and escape. The moment a number of nobles became informed of this escape route, believing Azimushshan's cause to be desperate, they made good their escape. Therefore leaders and men from Azimushshan's side got further reduced and only a few nobles stood steadfastly on his side. However these were men of substance like Suleiman Khan Panni, Raja Daya Bahadur. Shah Nawaz Khan Safawi and Kesari Singh.

By the fourth day, paralysis had hit the mind of Azimushshan. He could no longer think of taking the offensive. Zulfiqar pressed forward for the final battle. He ordered the entire combined army of the three princes for the battle. The entire formation was organised to give a final shape to the events. Zulfiqar Khan had been in touch with the followers of Azimushshan who by now were giving up all hope. He sent word to them that he would not bar their escape from Azimushshan's camp either to their own territories or to his own camp. Azimushhan's numbers became thinner by the moment.

On the fourth day, the army of Zulfiqar Khan and the three princes moved forward in order of battle. Jahandar Shah and Zulfiqar Khan commanded the centre. Abdussamad Khan and Jahan Shah were in the vanguard. Kokaltash Khan and Jani Khan commanded the right and left wings. Rafiushshan commanded the rear. This army advanced on the entrenchment of Azimushshan and there was an artillery duel for six hours.

Kesari Singh from Azimushshan's side attacked but was beaten back by Abdussamad Khan. Kesari Singh was shot down from his horse and another commander was lost. Abdussamad Khan and Pirthi Chand entered the entrenchment together. They moved forward but were opposed by Shah Nawaz Khan and Sulaiman Khan Panni. Shah Nawaz Khan was severely wounded with seventeen arrows sticking into him. Suleiman Khan carried on the fight valiantly but was constantly losing men around him. At last he also retreated but again and again came out fighting valiantly to retrieve a lost cause.

Meanwhile, Daya Bahadur, who had repeatedly been urging Azimushshan to attack, decided to get into an offensive mode himself. He first attacked Jahan Shah's positions and then those of Jahandar Shah. He was repulsed and shot down. His men retreated but were cut down by Rafiushshan's men. In fact, at this stage, the forces of the three princes were all over the camp of Azimushshan. They had either entered or had taken possession of the walls. Jahandar Shah or Muizuddin, Zulfiqar Khan, Abdussamad Khan, Kokaltash Khan were all either inside the entrenchment or on the boundaries. Kokaltash Khan and Abdussamad Khan had taken a complete offensive and entered Azimushshan's entrenchments. Suleiman Khan Panni, however, kept resisting.

Azimushshan's numbers were dwindling rapidly owing both to desertions and to battlefield losses. He was losing commanders. Of his original strength of 70,000 men, only 12,000 had been left on the last day and this number soon came down to 2,000 and then to 22. A hitherto impregnable host had been driven to around a score of men and a desperate Azimushshan resolved to sell his life dearly in a contest he had lost due to a fatal proneness to inaction. He decided to move forward and only Aminullah Khan remained faithful to him until the end, refusing to desert him even when his own son had deserted him.

An elephant was brought in for Azimushshan to mount but the animal did not oblige and another had to be brought in for the prince. He was advised by his followers to either fall back on Bengal where he had the resources or go to Dakhin where Daud Khan Panni would assist him. Azimushshan refused and it seemed was ready to fight to the bitter end.

In the meantime, a fierce wind arose and there was a sandstorm. In the middle of this confusion, a heavy artillery shot hit the elephant on which Azimushshan was mounted and it fled in utter panic towards the river Ravi taking the hapless prince with it. In vain did his followers try to stop the elephant but the animal charged through. It went over a high bank and vanished into the mud and sand below, drowning both the prince and itself.

Azimushshan was dead and the forces of the three princes had triumphed. Zulfiqar Khan was now the complete king-maker. However, the contest had not yet ended. It was just like the situation where Dara's defeat at Samugarh was not the end of contest for the throne. Dara had still to be personally eliminated, Murad was still alive foolishly believing Aurangzeb destined him to be the emperor, and a resourceful Shuja still remained alive for the contest from Bengal.

In this case, the other two princes—Rafiushshan and Jahan Shah remained alive and were in the contest either for the throne or for the spoils of war. However, they were in a very dangerous position as Jahandar Shah and Zulfiqar Khan were engaged in machinations against them.

The two unfortunate princes, Rafiushshan and Jahan Shah, kept entreating Zulfiqar Khan to fulfil his earlier promises of the division of the empire and the spoils of war. Zulfiqar Khan had no intention of keeping his promises as he intended making Jahandar Shah the sole emperor and himself the *vazir*. He kept giving evasive replies and further befooled the princes by behaving very obsequiously in their presence.

At last the two princes prepared for battle. It was now Jahan Shah and Rafiushshan, either individually or together against Jahandar Shah. Men were enlisted on both sides.

Rustam Dil Khan went to Jahan Shah and informed him in no uncertain terms of the danger posed to him by Zulfiqar Khan and proposed that the latter be made a prisoner and beheaded. Jahan Shah, obviously under the same delusions as the earlier unfortunate Azimushshan, refused. Zulfiqar Khan came to know of the plot and escaped. This was the second time luck had favoured him and Jahan Shah lost an opportunity he was later to regret bitterly.

Rustam Dil Khan advanced against Jahandar Shah. He brought into play an effective artillery fire and killed many men on Jahandar Shah's side. He then charged forward vigourously putting the enemy camp to flight. His charge was so furious and effective that it broke through the enemy army and he reached the position of Jahandar Shah, intent either on capturing him or killing him. He broke through Jahandar Shah's bodyguard. In fact, he and his men reached Jahandar Shah's elephant. Jahandar Shah's concubine ran away in a *palki* to Lahore, fearing the worst. Jahandar lay low in his howdah and hid himself from the approaching enemy. His mahout rose to the occasion and earnestly pleaded with the approaching attackers saying Jahandar Shah had fled. The foolish attackers, instead of checking out on their own and finishing off the task and therefore the battle, rode away, assuming the end of Jahandar Shah, who was then able to make his way to safety.

Jahandar Shah had almost lost the day and his life but survived to tell the tale. In the meantime, events took a turn for the worse on Jahan Shah's side. The prince, intent on taking the advantage and being an intrepid warrior, rode forward with his men. He intended reinforcing the advantage gained by Rustam Dil Khan for him. In the ensuing dust of battle, the wings and centre of Jahan Shah got separated and Jahan Shah found himself with very few men. They approached a position where several matchlock men of Jahandar Shah had hidden themselves while being put to flight by Rustam Dil Khan. Seeing Jahan Shah approaching, they thought themselves to be in a desperate position and regrouped to defend themselves, firing back resolutely. Jahan Shah, who had very few men with him, found himself under withering fire and lost his son and several men.

Zulfiqar Khan came to know of the rather surprising and quick turn of events. He found out that Jahandar Shah was in severe danger and in a position to lose both his life and impending kingship. He hastened out to support him only to be told that Jahan Shah himself was in the thick of battle and rather disadvantageously placed, being at the end of withering fire from Jahandar Shah's matchlock men. Zulfiqar Khan now resolved to turn that position to his advantage. He hastened forward to attack Jahan Shah and reinforce the efforts of the matchlock men. Jahan Shah's men and his own band of men wilted and soon Jahan Shah was shot dead. Zulfiqar Khan captured his body, cut off his head and triumphantly presented it to Jahandar Shah declaring him the victor. Jahan Shah had lost and now Jahandar Shah, with the wily and powerful Zulfiqar Khan, was left with only the hapless and foolish Rafiushshan to contend with. This battle for Delhi was drawing to a close. This was on 27 March 1712, a month after Bahadur Shah's death.

Rafiushshan, the other remaining prince, should have joined the cause of Jahan Shah. Unlike in the previous battle between the three princes and Azimushshan where over four fateful days the position swung gradually in favour of the three princes and way from Azimushshan, the second battle between Jahandar Shah and Jahan Shah was over in less than two days and the most decisive moments of the battle were on the second day, that is 27 March. Rustam Dil Khan almost carried the day in favour of Jahan Shah and could have dispatched a Jahandar Shah cowering in the howdah of his elephant. In fact, after delivering such a devastating attack and putting to rout Jahandar Shah's forces, he had reached Jahandar Shah's elephant. If only he had advanced a few paces and bothered to peer into the howdah, he would have found a doubled up Jahandar Shah and put paid to his life. Instead he believed a mahout, and turned around looking for fresh soldiers to kill. At the same time, if Jahan Shah had not been separated from his men in the dust, he would have been able to handle the matchlock men confronting him. He instead got lost and separated from his men in the dust and paid for it with his life.

In a sudden swing of fortunes the person who was about to be beheaded became the beheader and Jahandar gained his life while Jahan lost his. It could so easily have been different. Something similar is seen in the *Mahabharata*, where Guru Dronacharya believed the words of Yudhishthira that his son Ashwathama was dead rather than checking physically himself. Belief in the sanctity of Yudhishthira's words let him lay down his arms and Dhrishtadyumna, who was waiting for just such an opportunity, claimed Dronacharya's life.

Now came the turn of Rafiushshan. He had made the strategic error of not joining Jahan Shah. His followers advised him to let one side destroy the other and then either make terms with the victor or take that weakened person on. His astrologers advised him to wait anyway as their charts told them he was destined to be the ultimate emperor. These foolish words and advice rather than sound military thinking decided his action and he waited not too far from the field of action for the outcome of battle.

He soon found that Jahandar Shah had emerged triumphant and Jahan Shah was dead, much like Azimushshan. His men told him that Jahandar Shah's forces were tired and he should attack immediately and finish off the enemy. Others told him that fighting at night was not advisable.

Inaction overtook him and he decided not to press ahead with the attack which could have helped him become the emperor of Hindustan. He foolishly sent word to Jahandar Shah, Zulfiqar Khan and Kolkatash Khan, reminding them of the earlier treaty, little realising that all such talk had been waste and none of them intended to honour their word.

On 28 March, the next day, Rafiushshan desperately moved forward to give battle to Jahandar Shah's army. His confidant, Fatehullah Khan, went over to the enemy. Shamsher Khan from Rafisuhshan's army went forward to fight but soon met his death. Jahandar Shah's forces moved forward to give battle and Rafiushshan's army, composed of inexperienced troops fled. Most of his commanders who did not desert him fought for his cause to their death. At last Rafiushshan realised all was over bar the shouting. He came down from his elephant and went forward on foot, fighting and keen to sell his life in the thick of battle. He was soon shot dead, knowing he would not become the emperor but little realising that one day both his sons would.

Thus ended another Battle of Delhi, barely five years after the first that had happened after Aurangzeb at Jajau. Now the bodies of Bahadur Shah and the three dead princes—Azimushshan, Rafiushshan and Jahan Shah were sent to Delhi for burial in April 2012. This battle brought down a seemingly incontestable winner in Azimushshan and propped up an imbecile called Jahandar Shah. It happens when king-makers call the shots. Worthless aspirants come to the throne as puppets. It can be said that the real decline of the Mughal empire started with Jahandar Shah, possibly the most worthless occupier of the throne of the Great Mughals.

Chapter XII

Farrukh Siyar

The decline of the Mughal empire could be said to have started under the reign of Aurangzeb Alamgir when he ensconced himself in the Deccan and wasted the Mughal empire's energy and resources in conquering the Deccan. In the process he conquered Bijapur and Golconda and imprisoned and killed the Maratha warrior, Sambhaji. But he could not ultimately control the irrepressible Marathas and in the coming times they became the most dangerous foes of the Mughal empire. Also, the Rajputs, Jats, and Sikhs rose in defiance, perturbed by the religious intolerance practised by Aurangzeb. The empire's financial resources got dissipated in the struggle and its unitary character began to crumble. From then onwards the Mughal empire would be weakened by internal dissensions from constituents within Hindustan. Centrality of control has to be tempered by the wisdom of tolerance and allowing expression of freedom to different constituents for the sake of growth and fair play. Aurangzeb was a failure in this regard.

Aurangzeb, a man of pious character and tremendous capacity for hard work, was also blessed with military genius. But in the end, he showed himself to be a man who did a lot of things right but not the right things. The decisions taken to overextend himself in the Deccan and waste resources on a long conflict rather than focus on central governance and administration weakened the empire. Religious intolerance took away the faithful allegiance of Indian warrior kingdoms which had hitherto flourished under the Mughal umbrella. A schism was created between them and the central authority that led to military weakening.

By the time Bahadur Shah came to the throne, considerable damage had been caused. But the situation was not irretrievable. Babar and Akbar had built the Mughal empire with much less. However, Bahadur Shah, by the time he came to rule, was over 60 years old, and too old to make a long term impact. Most of his five year reign was spent in subduing his remaining brothers along with rebellious kingdoms. He died exhausted from these struggles by the time he was in his late sixties.

Jahandar Shah, who came to succeed Bahadur Shah, can be said to be the man under whom the honour and authority of the Mughal emperor crumbled the fastest. He spent his entire reign as a drunkard and a wretched character. He was a plaything in the hands of Lal Kunwar, a courtesan, who had a vice-like group over the emperor. She exercised more control over him than even the *vazir*, Zulfiqar Khan.

Illuminations using oil and clarified butter became the order of the day leading to severe shortages of these commodities. Grain became scarce and expensive. Lal Kunwar's relations and friends got grandiose titles, *jagir*s and monies. Her brothers became all-powerful. Proud nobles of the empire were insulted on the streets of Delhi by them. Trees were cut down in huge quantities to please the emperor. Drunken revelries were carried out until late night in the palace with the emperor completely involved in them. There was no governance. The emperor went shopping and drinking in bullock carts with Lal Kunwar, and one night even went missing from the palace, only to be found in the morning after a frantic search was launched.

In this debauched state of affairs, arose a new claimant to the throne, Muhammad Farrukh Siyar, a son of Azimushshan. He was present in the East. He had hardly any resources or backers. All the people his father had done favours to did not back him. However, he was pressed on by his mother to contest the throne and seek help and resources for the same.

At the same time, there were the Barrah Sayyid brothers—Hassan or Abdullah Ali Khan and Hussein Ali Khan. They belonged to the clan of Sayyids known more for their valour than for their brains. Their family had distinguished themselves in the field of battle over the years, the latest being Jajau where they fought on the side of Bahadur Shah. They had been badly injured in the battle but a subsequent verbal engagement with Muizuddin, the son of Bahadur Shah, saw them go into disgrace and out of favour.

At that time, Azimushshan, the second son of Bahadur Shah, came to their rescue. He got the elder brother Hassan or Abdullah the governorship of Allahabad and the younger one Hussein, the governorship of Bihar. It was to these Sayyid brothers that Farrukh Siyar appealed for help.

Help they did, but the result was a further weakening of the authority of the emperor vis-à-vis the nobles who controlled the actual reins of power. After Bahadur Shah, it was the king-maker rather than the king or the Mughal emperor who would call the shots in the Mughal empire. It may not have been realised at that time but this would prove to be a body blow to the unifying central authority of the Mughal emperor and a development that hastened the decline and fall of the Mughal empire. It is a lesson that the ultimate authority in the government also has to be the strongest, and not dependent upon another authority for the power of his position if the central authority has to provide capable leadership to the nation.

Farrukh Siyar's cause was deemed to be hopeless as he had hardly any armed force or adherents. However, taking her life in her hands, his mother went to meet the mother of the younger Sayyid brother Hussein Ali Khan, beseeching her for help. She took Farrukh Siyar's daughter with her and they both wept and cried for help, citing the support Farrukh Siyar's father Azimushshan had given to the Sayyid brothers. Hussein Sayyid's mother gave in and called him in to the room to listen to the entreaties of Farrukh Siyar's mother. She also joined in the chorus and before long Hussein Sayyid found himself giving in and promising help to Farrukh Siyar to seize the throne of Delhi.

Hussein Sayyid then sent word to his elder brother Abdullah Khan, asking him to join the cause. As luck would have it, Abdullah Khan had assumed governorship of Allahabad and Jahandar Shah had sent a new governor with a force to dislodge him. That attempt failed and further aggravated the grievance Abdullah Khan had towards the emperor. Abdullah gladly joined in. The tide of fortune now began to swing in favour of Farrukh Siyar with more and more men joining him with money, arms and ammunition. Prominent among them were Sidhhisht Narayan, a powerful zamindar of Bhojpur, Khwaja Asim, Saif Shikan Khan, Zainuddin Khan and Mehta Chabeli Ram. Farrukh Siyar now started advancing towards Delhi, crossing rivers, collecting money by hook or by crook on the way to pay his soldiery, gathering new resources and adherents. What started as a questionable exercise had now become a strong momentum to seize the throne at Delhi. It was enough to alarm a newly-crowned emperor, no matter how deep he was immersed in debauchery.

Jahandar Shah ordered his son Azizuddin forward to stop the march of Farrukh Siyar. Azizuddin moved forward and finally entrenched himself at a place called Khwaja. He threw a ditch around his camp and put up cannons to repulse the enemy, counting on winning a defensive battle. Farrukh Siyar's army marched forward, reconnoitered the enemy position at will and then made their plan of attack. An initial engagement was fought with artillery and matchlock duels. Before the day of the final battle, the two nobles sent with Azizuddin, not particularly known for their fighting prowess, panicked and advised the prince to retreat to Delhi. Azizuddin, to his credit, refused. The nobles were now determined to retreat and prepared forged letters showing Azizuddin that Jahandar Shah had died. Azizuddin took the bait and decamped with his women folk and some part of treasure towards Agra. The next day his army woke up to find itself leaderless and broke up in panic. It was each man for himself and the imperial force crumbled. Farrukh Siyar's army marched forward in triumph. Untold loot was captured and a hitherto impoverished, malnourished army came upon money to feed and reward itself—an example of how lacklustre and spiritless the Mughal princes had become in the face of battle, if you compare them with Aurangzeb and Shah Jahan, who had displayed audacity.

There was nothing standing in the way of Farrukh Siyar in his march towards Jahandar Shah. The stage was now set for another Battle of Delhi.

Jahandar Shah had by now arisen, though not regretfully, out of his stupor and from the spell cast by his concubine Lal Kunwar. He realised that he faced a formidable and sizeable challenge from Farrukh Siyar and that he needed to act in person to quell that challenge. He therefore started making preparations for the inevitable battle for Delhi. However, having overspent from an already depleted treasury, he could find nothing. So whatever money could be gathered, borrowed or dug out through the sale of jewellery, utensils, precious items and clothing was gathered and used to pay for soldiery and provisions. A march was commenced towards confronting Farrukh Siyar in the vicinity of Agra. Soldiers were promised money that was supposed to be lying in the Mughal treasury at Agra where on reaching none could be found.

However, it was not a mean preparation that Jahandar Shah mounted. Asad Khan was handed over charge and safekeeping of the city of Delhi. Abdullah Khan was given charge of the fort and personal effects of the emperor. Zulfiqar Khan, Kokaltash Khan and Jani Khan were put in the vanguard with artillery and 40,000 cavalry. Raja Muhammad Khan had 100 cannon with him. Other commanders of calibre were put in charge of centre, right and left of the gathered host. Jahandar commenced his march to Agra, firstly to lay his hand on the treasure supposedly lying there and secondly to force issue at a place considered auspicious called Samugarh where Aurangzeb had defeated Dara Shikoh.

However, there was disunity in the ranks of this formidable host estimated at 100,000 infantry, 80,000 cavalry and over 100 artillery. Few people had any confidence in, and respect for, Jahandar Shah. They had merely gathered around the banner of the Mughal emperor, but secretly wished for his defeat. This was on account of the eleven months of misrule and his utter capitulation to the charms of Lal Kunwar, considered a bazaar woman by them. Mohammed Amin Khan and Chin Qilich Khan had hardly any enthusiasm for taking part in the battle under the banner of Jahandar Shah. Kokaltash Khan, Zulfiqar Khan and Jani Khan were at daggers drawn, each wishing to see failure descend on the other.

The action became centered around the river Yamuna. Each side was encamped opposite each other, with neither of them willing to cross. There was confusion and consternation on Jahandar Shah's side with some people advising crossing and an attack on the enemy while the other advised caution and letting the enemy cross over and letting it fight the battle with its back to the river. Eid festivities went on and passed by with neither side showing any inclination for action.

However, Abdullah Khan from Farrukh Siyar's side, as was his wont, lost patience and decided to force a crossing. He marched down the river and found a shallow ford where he saw villagers crossing on foot. He drove through and crossed over with his men. The next day, Farrukh Siyar followed on his elephant and then followed Hussein Ali Khan and Chabela Ram.

The stage was set for a battle royal. Both sides took their positions. Zulfiqar Khan seemed to be the commander on Jahandar Shah's side and he created a vanguard in two parts, one under Kokaltash Khan of 15,000 men and the other in equal measure under Jani Khan. About 10,000 men were kept in support with the artillery positioned in the centre. Kokaltash Khan had a formidable adversary in front of him in Abdullah Khan and Jani Khan opposed an equally formidable Hussein Ali Khan.

Abdullah Khan sent a force headed by Chabela Ram, Muhammad Khan and Khan Zaman to attack Jani Khan who was moving forward. Kokaltash Khan was commanded to attack the wing commanded by Hussein Khan but instead wheeled around to attack Farrukh Siyar's centre. Hussein Khan's army clashed with that of Kokaltash Khan and a desperate battle ensued with Kokaltash gaining the advantage. Abdullah Khan sent forth reinforcements to support Hussein Khan but these were severely damaged by the artillery from Jahandar Shah's forces commanded by Raza Quli Khan. Hussein Khan, finding himself in desperate straits, got down from his horse and along with his men commenced battle standing on the ground, sword in hand. Abdussamad Khan charged with his Turani mounted archers and attacked Hussein Khan, who being wounded severely, fainted and fell to the ground. This was a setback for Farrukh Siyar. Kokaltash Khan had fought bravely and swung the tide of battle in favour of Jahandar Shah. All the commanders who had helped Jahandar Shah in winning the Battle of Lahore were again helping him overcome Farrukh Siyar.

Chabela Ram, on the other hand, continued his struggle with Jani Khan, though not with much success. Jahandar Shah's booming artillery was beginning to have an impact and Farrukh Siyar's men seemed to lose heart and ground. Zulfiqar Khan directed artillery fire on the position of Abdullah Khan and although the senior Sayyid's position worsened, he held his ground. At the same time, Zulfiqar Khan sent Mukhtar Khan to help Jani Khan against Chabela Ram. However, Chabela Ram and Muhammad Khan fought desperately and succeeded in killing Jani Khan and driving back a severely wounded Mukhtar Khan. Farrukh Siyar's forces began to regain some lost ground.

At this stage, Jahandar Shah still had the upper hand. Farrukh Siyar was at the centre with very few men to guard him. Abdullah Khan had a few men with him. Chabela Ram had got the better of Jani Khan but had himself retreated to join Abdullah Khan. Zulfiqar Khan had the cards of battle in his hand. He commanded a strong artillery and a fresh force of 25,000 men. He was repeatedly asked by his commanders to give the orders to attack either Abdullah Khan or attack and capture Farrukh Siyar, which would have decided the fate of the battle. At this time, the experienced and battle-hardened commander either displayed a lack of alertness or fortitude or seemed unwilling to support Kokaltash Khan out of sheer jealousy. He hesitated to attack and merely asked Chin

Qilich Khan to join Kokaltash Khan and then attack Farrukh Siyar in the centre. Abdullah Khan had by then been rejoined by Hussein Khan's troops, Chabela Ram and his men, and Muhammad Khan with their forces. He now had a force with which to try and do something effective.

A few things happened that evened things out more for Farrukh Siyar. Chabela Ram met and killed Kokaltash Khan, thus removing from the scene a commander who had done the most on the day to swing things positively for Jahandar Shah. Mohammed Khan advanced upon Raza Quli Khan, commander of Jahandar Shah's light artillery, and killed him in hand to hand combat. This gave breathing space to Abdullah Khan to try and seize the initiative as Jahandar had lost key commanders.

Abdullah Khan, joined by Chabela Ram and Muhammad Khan, made his way to the rear of Jahandar Shah's camp and attacked his tents and elephants including the women in his party. Mohammad Amin Khan and Chin Qilich Khan showed treachery and stood aside, letting Abdullah Khan go ahead. Thus, we had the primary commander of Farrukh Siyar's forces trying to seize initiative from a desperate position and showing great courage by attacking the enemy's rear and the personal camp of Jahandar Shah. Zulfiqar Khan, against his own character, seemed to show great uncertainty and lack of initiative in his actions. He could at this juncture have easily attacked Farrukh Siyar and captured him as he outnumbered the enemy six to one and had artillery support. Thinking the enemy was anyway in disarray and had lost heart, he instead stopped his attack and sounded drums of victory much before victory had actually been achieved.

Abdullah Khan heard the drums of victory and was confused. However, displaying great valour and single-mindedness of purpose, he pressed forward and attacked Jahandar Shah, badly wounding his elephant which ran amuck, killing friend and foe alike. Jahandar Shah tried to have his elephant controlled but in vain. He wanted to reach Zulfiqar Khan but could not.

Jahandar Shah somehow managed to come down from his elephant and get onto a horse. Just then fate intervened and turned what could have been victory into a rout. Lal Kunwar appeared on the scene in great concern for her paramour-emperor and persuaded him to get onto her elephant, as according to her the day was already lost and flight was the only option. This was while the perplexed Zulfiqar Khan was wondering where the emperor was. Jahandar Shah decamped with his beloved Lal

Kunwar on her elephant and instantly all was flight in his camp.

Zulfiqar Khan sent men to search for either Jahandar Shah or his son Azizuddin, in the hope of making a final attack on Farrukh Siyar and winning the day, a thought that had come to him rather late. All of this was to no avail as neither the cowardly father nor his pusillanimous son could be found. On the other hand, Farrukh Siyar showed courage and desperation for victory, staying in the field although in great danger himself.

However, it was not that Farrukh Siyar had won the day completely. Zulfiqar Khan still remained in the field as an opponent with a formidable force of 25,000 men. In fact, he was a potentially victorious general in search of a king and looked forward to leading a counter-attack. Such was his strength that not even the intrepid and aggressive Abdullah Khan Sayyid dared venture against him. At last Farrukh Siyar sent him a message that there was little point in Zulfiqar Khan continuing the contest. Either Zulfiqar wanted the crown for himself or he should be prepared to serve whichever Mughal prince had the good fortune of sitting on the throne.

Zulfiqar Khan now realised that it was pointless to stay in the battlefield as his master was absent. So he resolved to withdraw. Zulfiqar was advised by his soldiery either to continue the battle and defeat and seize Farrukh Siyar or to withdraw to the Deccan and use the resources of his deputy, Daud Khan Panni, to create an independent or a semi- independent kingdom. He took the advice of Sabha Chand and decided to withdraw towards Delhi. His soldiery resented this deference of Zulfiqar towards the advice of a man of words rather than towards that of his soldiers and said openly that it was a wrong move.

In the meantime, Jahandar Shah had been reunited with his concubine Lal Kunwar and shaved off his moustache and beard, moving incognito in a bullock cart towards Delhi. They begged for bread on the way and finally reached Mathura. From there they made their way to Talpat and reached Delhi on 15 January 1713.

Zulfiqar Khan, in the meanwhile, made his way to Delhi to seek counsel with his father, Asad Khan, the *vazir*. He told Asad Khan that he would find Jahandar Shah, move to Multan with him or to the Deccan, and raise a new army and attempt to retake Delhi.

Asad Khan had a different opinion. The *vazir* greatly prided himself on his own wisdom, his way with words and his experience in governance.

Asad Khan argued that it would be far better for both father and son to make peace with the new emperor, Farrukh Siyar. He went on to say that Farrukh would value the experience Asad Khan could bring to governance and honour him with a big position, and a suitable position would be found for Zulfiqar Khan as well.

During this time the hapless Jahandar Shah arrived at Asad Khan's house hoping for refuge, succour and support. He was curtly asked to wait at the gate outside while father and son continued to argue inside. Zulfiqar was firmly opposed to any enterprise that included reconciliation and ingratiation with Farrukh Siyar. He knew that he had been the leading party to the combination of the three princes who had fought against Farrukh Siyar's father, Azimushshan, and done him to death. He feared for his life at the hands of Farrukh Siyar and was not keen to put himself in his hands.

However, gradually the will and persuasive logic of the older man prevailed and with great foreboding Zulfiqar agreed to go ahead with Asad Khan's plan. This plan was to imprison Jahandar Shah and hand him over to Farrukh Siyar. This, Asad hoped, would be enough for both father and son to earn the goodwill of the new emperor. Accordingly Jahandar was brought in and made a prisoner. A letter was sent to Farrukh Siyar informing of the same and of the loyalty of both father and son to the new emperor.

Farrukh Siyar was, however, fearful of Zulfiqar Khan and his resources, and the ability of the latter to find an alternative emperor and lead him to a contest against Farrukh. He dispatched Abdullah Khan to understand how things were at Delhi. From Abdullah he got the news that all was well, Jahandar Shah had been captured and both Asad Khan and Zulfiqar Khan professed allegiance to Farrukh Siyar.

A much-relieved Farrukh Siyar then advanced to Delhi to take over the reins of power. A letter was sent to Asad Khan and Zulfiqar Khan professing kindly dealing and friendship. Jahandar Shah was sent to prison in the Red Fort along with Lal Kunwar. An order for his execution was passed. An attempt was made to first strangulate Jahandar Shah to death and when that proved none too successful, he was kicked to death by the assassins. Lal Kunwar was sent to Suhagpura, a place where Mughal widows were kept.

In the meantime, Sabha Chand, an adviser of Zulfiqar Khan, was sent for and imprisoned. This aroused the greatest alarm in Zulfiqar Khan who anyway was never in wholehearted support of his father's plan. He now had the greatest foreboding but was calmed down by Asad Khan.

The two went to meet Farrukh Siyar. Asad Khan went in first and was greeted warmly by Farrukh Siyar who conferred on him robes of honour. Then Asad Khan beckoned in Zulfiqar Khan who came in with his hands tied on his own, professing guilt and surrender. He was received kindly by Farrukh Siyar and the hands were ordered to be untied. Both father and son were embraced by Farrukh Siyar.

Then Farrukh Siyar advised Asad Khan to return home and indicated that he wanted Zulfiqar to stay. Asad Khan left leaving behind a shaken and fretting Zulfiqar. Farrukh Siyar excused himself and left the room and food was ordered for Zulfiqar Khan. After some time, on the pretext of shifting rooms, Zulfiqar was taken out and immediately imprisoned by 200 soldiers. Zulfiqar knew his end was near and his worst fears had come true. How he wished he had not listened to his father.

Now Farrukh Siyar kept sending a series of questions to Zulfiqar Khan intending to nail him down to some crime punishable by death. An exasperated Zulfiqar Khan started shouting, asking for his death. He was strangled to death, stamped on until lifeless and a dagger plunged into him repeatedly. His body was tied by its feet and hung for public display.

Farrukh Siyar, the new emperor, entered Delhi on 12 February 1713 on an elephant. The head of Jahandar Shah was carried high stuck on a bamboo stick. Zulfiqar Khan's body was dragged by an elephant.

Thus ended the imperial reign of Jahandar Shah, the shortest until then in Mughal history. It was a reign full of ignominy for a monarch who slid into a life of debauchery and became the slave of a concubine. Strangely, for a man known for his military experience and prowess in his earlier years, he showed a strange ineptitude for battle and a desire to flee the battlefield under the benevolent protection of a concubine. What is significant is that he bled the treasury dry, scarcely bothered to govern and undid all the respect the Great Mughals had commanded. Imagine a Mughal emperor going missing and then found early morning drunk in a bullock cart. No wonder the Mughal emperors after Jahandar Shah lost all respect and became playthings in the hands of experienced nobles.

This lack of respect resulted in Jahandar Shah being the first Mughal emperor to be assassinated, or rather, executed in cold blood and beheaded. His body was thrown in dirt and then buried in Humayun's tomb. The assassination of Mughal emperors, their summary removal at the whims and fancies of powerful nobles, their blinding and imprisonment became the order of the day. No Mughal emperor who fearlessly commanded the respect of the nobles and rulers of distant provinces sat again on the Mughal throne.

Along with the decline in the power and prestige of the Mughal emperors, happened the decimation of Mughal royalty and generals capable of leading Mughal armies in battle. Bidar Bakht, Wala Jah, Azam Shah perished in the Battle of Jajau and Kam Baksh died later. Azimushshan, Jahan Shah and Rafiushshan perished in the Battle of Lahore. Some formidable military talents like Zulfiqar Khan, Rustam Dil Khan, Abdussamad Khan, Kokaltash Khan, Rao Dalpat, Kesari Singh, Rustam Khan Dakhini, Rao Dalpat, just to name a few, died in these military struggles. The Mughal empire could not find princes and generals to replace such talent. Over a period of time, the kings, princes and nobles who began to hold the reins of power had hardly seen battles. When the Marathas, Persians and Afghans attacked, and the provinces proclaimed independence and semi-independence, there was no military leadership to handle such problems.

And with the decline of the Mughal empire started the decline of central authority in India, its break up later into fissiparous provinces, internecine wars that led to interference of Europeans and the ultimate enslavement of all India including provincial governments and independent states who ultimately became slaves of the British. The so-called independence of these provinces was a temporary illusion as the foreign invaders had to fight them individually and not as a united and strong India and such independent principalities could be overcome more easily. Loss of the central authority of the Mughal emperors undid India.

Chapter XIII

Karnal

I often used to travel by train between Delhi and Chandigarh. While travelling on one such journey, I was struck by the names of the stations passing by. The Shatabdi between Delhi and Chandigarh does not stop at all of these but the names of the various stations stuck in my mind. One of them was Taraoni. It is the place where the forces of Rai Pithora and Mohammad Ghori waged two furious battles, the first one ending in the defeat of Ghori and the second one laying the foundations for Islamic rule in India, following the defeat of Prithviraj Chauhan.

Something clicked in my mind as I remembered the names of other stations on the train route—Kurukshetra, Panipat, Karnal—each one associated with one or more battles that decided the fate of India, particularly by deciding who would be seated on the throne of Delhi and would control the seat which faced both northwest and also faced the Gangetic Doab, affording a passage into the heart of Hind. Battles in any of these cities decided the fate of who would rule Hindustan. These were battles for Delhi, be it the Mahabharata War for Indraprastha; or the famous battles of Panipat or Taraoni. This can safely be called North India's battle axis.

This was the road down which the invading armies of immense strength attempted to force their ways via Punjab and conquer Delhi. If they succeeded, they would rule Hindustan—be it Turks, Afghans, Mughals or anyone else. The importance of defending this battle axis could not be overestimated as the power centre had shifted from Pataliputra and Kanauj to Delhi. If the invader was repulsed, as for example during the times of Allaudin Khilji, the existing ruler would continue. If the Indian rulers moved forward powerfully and proactively as Akbar did towards Kabul, the invaders would be further pushed back and the security and safety of the nation strengthened for a substantial period. If the invader defeated the Indian ruler as happened with Ibrahim Lodhi, a new dynasty like the Mughals took over.

Sometimes an invader was not interested in capturing Delhi and ruling Hindustan. His objective was to pillage, massacre and loot the legendary wealth of India. One such conqueror was Nadir Shah.

After the overthrow of Farrukh Siyar by the Sayyid brothers, two brothers were appointed in quick succession as emperors—Rafi ud Darjat and Rafi ud Daulah. However, both died quickly and Roshan Akhtar was placed on the throne of Delhi, to rule as Mohammed Shah in September 1719.

Nadir Shah was the king of Persia, an ancient land that had been on many turns of history a powerful and rich empire. The Persian empire had enjoyed great prosperity and stability under the Safavids. Their great ruler was Shah Abbas. The Persians had a love-hate relationship with the Mughals. The Persians had rendered great help under Shah Tamashp to the Mughal emperor, Humayun, in reclaiming his throne. Each empire recognised the power and influence of the other as a rich and powerful Islamic kingdom. However, there was a constant strife between the two for gaining Kabul and Kandahar, each side getting the better of the other on different occasions. However, it was known that there was never a power differential between the two strong enough for one side to overwhelm the other.

The Safavids became weaker after their last great ruler, Shah Abbas, died and a succession of weak rulers came after him. An internecine struggle followed during which parts of the Persian empire came under Afghan rule. Nadir Quli, a man of humble origins, grew into an enterprising local chieftain and defeated the Afghans. This came to the notice of the Shah of Persia who took him in his service. Nadir became a Persian hero, leading a national effort to rid the country of Afghan rule. When the weak Persian imperial line ran out of steam, Nadir Quli became Nadir Shah, the emperor of Persia, in 1736.

Nadir Shah then proceeded to consolidate the Persian empire and conquered Armenia and Georgia, wrested back lands inside and on the borders of Persia and then proceeded towards Afghanistan to retake Kandahar. It took him a year but he succeeded. Now he was on the border of the Mughal empire. The Persian and the Mughal empires were face to face with the Persian emperor on the borders of India with a huge, well-organised and experienced military force. So had it been during the times of Akbar, Jahangir, Shah Jahan and Aurangzeb. But there was a big difference this time. There was a huge power differential in terms of military capabilities between the Persian and Mughal empires with the advantage lying with the former. The stage was set for one side to dictate terms to, and defeat, the other. The Mughal empire in Delhi was in a clear state of decline and of military unpreparedness under an ineffectual, pleasure-loving and weak Mohammad Shah Rangila.

The Mughal empire at this stage may have been into a decline, but the situation was not irretrievable. It was not a situation where Babar entered as an uncertain conqueror having defeated Ibrahim Lodhi but facing redoubtable enemies in Rana Sangha and the remaining Afghans. It was not a situation like Humayun's where he had to run away, try initial unsuccessful steps back and finally reclaim it from a weak and split Afghan leadership. It was also not a situation as faced by Akbar where he got back Delhi and then had to fight and penetrate into the rest of India. Mohammad Shah Rangila had considerable wealth. He had large military forces. True, he had lost control of Malwa, and the Marathas controlled large parts of Deccan. But the Mughal empire stretched all the way to Bengal. It was deep into Deccan via the Nizam. It still controlled the Northwest all the way to Kabul and the Afghan frontier. A strong emperor, possessed of military determination and administrative skills, would have taken control, marshaled the considerable resources and recreated the Mughal grandeur and taken the empire back to its original strength, thereby recreating a strong India governed by a strong central rule.

Mohammad Shah Rangila was a weak, pleasure-loving and indolent ruler. His empire wrested on three pillars: Nizam ul Mulk was the *Wakil-in-Muttaliq*; Qamaruddin Khan was the *vazir* and Khan Dauran Samsamdaulah Khan was the head of the army. Nizam was the one capable military leader. Khan Dauran was considered a carpet knight with no particular capabilities and record on the field of battle. Qamaruddin was a court flatterer. Another notable noble was Saadat Khan, Nawab of Oudh, with considerable resources. However, the military strength the Mughals relied on most were the Rajputs who had been totally alienated by the religious bigotry of Aurangzeb. The Sikhs had taken to arms and the Jats were rebellious. Moreover, the Marathas, under the brilliant Baji Rao I, were not only dominant all the way to Malwa but had also made a famous predatory raid to Delhi in 1737. The Mughal rule of Aurangzeb had turned the Hindus against the Mughal empire which could not count for much support from the majority population.

Nadir Shah had decided to invade Afghanistan. He invaded Kandahar and drove away the Afghans. He sent a messenger to the Mughal court asking for cooperation in stopping the Afghans fleeing into India so that these could be caught in a nut cracker between the Persians and Mughals and be destroyed. The first envoy was Ali Mardan who was assured by the Mughal court that the Mughal forces would stop the Afghans and drive them back into the Persian army thus ensuring their destruction. A second envoy sent was called Mohammad Ali Khan seeking a similar assurance. Simultaneously the Persians renewed their assault and drove through the Afghans all the way. However, the Persian army stopped at the border of the Persian empire as they had no instructions to go forward. They found no Mughal forces positioned to stop the Afghans, as had been promised to the Persians. They complained to Nadir Shah who sent another envoy to the Mughal court, Mohammad Khan Turkoman, who asked for similar assurances. The envoy was asked to be in Delhi for forty days but had to wait for a year getting no concrete reply. The Mughal court was in a perennial state of indecision and gave evasive answers, hoping the Afghans would defeat and drive way the Persians, thus obviating the need for an answer. However, the Persians conquered Kandahar and Nadir Shah recalled his envoy to Delhi, thus setting the stage for another battle for Delhi.

The state of the Afghan frontier can best be described as one of utter neglect and lack of foresight from Delhi. Kabul was controlled by the Mughal empire. There were the restless Pathan tribes of the Northwest who had been kept under control by the strict military posture and presence first of Aurangzeb and then of his son Muazzam. These emperors patrolled the frontier with their troops keeping the tribes under leash and also by judicious use of money to the turbulent clans. Amir Khan was a noble praised by Aurangzeb for his effectiveness. He was succeeded as governor by Nasir Khan. But his son, also called Nasir Khan, was ineffective. He was either busy hunting or praying. Patrolling ceased. The soldiers' salaries fell into arrears. The rule of law ceased. The soldiers clamoured for money. The leading noble, Khan Dauran, was asked for money and reminded of the need to keep the northwest gateway to India under control, a plea that he derided and dismissed with contempt. Circumstances could not have been better for an invader to make ingress into India.

Zakariya Khan was the governor of Punjab and expected to be the second line of defence after the first line formed by the imperial army posted under the governor of Kabul. He was also in the Turani party and bitterly opposed by the influential Khan Dauran, leading the Hindustani party in Delhi. Khan Dauran neglected to strengthen the Punjab governorship thus also weakening the second line of defence. Thus conditions were created easing the path for Nadir Shah to gatecrash into Delhi.

Nadir Shah now decided to enter Mughal territory. It was crossing the Rubicon. He stormed Ghazni and attacked Kabul. The Mughal fortress commander, Sharza Khan, unexpectedly offered resistance and fought for seven days but then proved to be no match for such a large and well-equipped force and had to capitulate in June 1738. Nadir Shah then captured Jalalabad in September 1738 and sent a messenger to the Mughal court seeking an explanation for the lack of response. The messenger unfortunately got murdered.

Nadir Shah then moved forward. To his credit, the Mughal governor assembled a force of 20,000 and tried to stop the huge Persian army at the Khyber Pass. However, the result was a foregone conclusion. The irregular part of the Mughal force melted way but the regular part gave resistance for quite a while before it was defeated and its leaders captured. Gone was the forward defence policy of the Mughals whereby they always moved forward not only to deter the Persians from advancing on the Northwest Frontier but also pushed them back, capturing territory. Sometimes the emperor in person and mostly a notable prince of the Mughal court held the responsibility of defending the Northwest. The Mughal court was always seized of the importance of defending this frontier against the Persians and Afghans.

However, there was an indolent and careless Mughal emperor lost in his pleasures. He had given way to nobles who held that frontier to be of little strategic importance. The defence was left to ill-paid and ill-prepared troops under Mughal governors who did not excite the attention of the Mughal court. This had created a differential when the entire Persian host appeared on this frontier to invade India. The Mughals had no preparation to stop the Persian advance to the gates of Delhi.

Having wrested Kabul and other areas of Afghanistan from the

Mughals, the Persians had laid bare the Northwest Frontier. Now only the Punjab lay between the Persian host and the city of Delhi. The imbecile emperor, Mohammed Shah, had still little idea of the immense threat posed by the Persian army and was relying upon his weak governors to repulse the Persian army. Nadir Shah invaded Punjab and crossed its five rivers before attacking Lahore. Zakariya Khan, the governor of Punjab, set up an initial defence under Kalandar Khan that was overrun, and then faced Nadir Shah with his artillery at Lahore. There was fighting and an attempt to stop the Persians but after a few days, seeing no support from Delhi, Zakariya Khan offered submission. He was treated well by Nadir Shah but a fine was levied on Lahore. This was in January 1739.

The Mughal emperor should have moved forward and aligned his main forces with those of his governors thus stopping the Persian army in its tracks but instead he just sat back. The Mughal strength was getting decimated and the Persian onslaught was getting stronger. Nadir Shah again wrote to Mohammad Shah of his "friendly intentions" but complained of utter neglect by the Mughal court to his overtures.

Nadir Shah gave away Punjab to plunder and its well-known towns were reduced to penury, ashes and dust. Lahore, Jalandhar and Gujarat were some of the towns of Punjab laid waste. Law and order plummeted in Punjab and the whole state came to waste and ruin. This is how a badly defended nation starts losing control, firstly of its frontier provinces and then the centre to which the enemy starts eating its way.

Nadir Shah now marched forward towards Delhi and moved down the Indian battle axis from Sirhind to Ambala. Here he came to know that the Mughal emperor had finally been shaken out of his complacency and moved forward with a large army.

The Mughals had learned of the fall of Kabul in June 1738. It was in December that the Mughal Emperor ordered his three favourite courtiers—Nizam, Khan Dauran and Qamaruddin Khan—to move forward. They were given a crore of rupees and asked to move forward. They spent a month outside Delhi. They finally moved forward urging the emperor to join them, which he eventually did in January at Panipat. They finally decided to halt and fortify themselves at Karnal and wait there to give battle to the oncoming host of Nadir Shah. Saadat Khan, the governor of Oudh, was expected to come and reinforce the Mughal host with an army of 30,000. The Mughal emperor also wrote to the Rajputs and Marathas under Baji Rao to come to help but apart from mere empty words, no help was forthcoming. The Mughal position thus finally became an entrenched position at Karnal with a mud wall of many kilometers dug around for protection with soldiers and artillery posted along it to deter the enemy.

The Mughal army had placed itself in such a position that it had its front and right protected by a jungle and the Ali Mardan canal. It had Karnal town to its rear. To the east of the canal was the Yamuna River and between the canal and the river was flat plain suitable for cavalry manoeuvres. The Mughal army was not therefore lacking in water supply. However, by enclosing itself in an entrenched position, it had denied itself any mobility whatsoever, and willy-nilly got itself surrounded by a large Persian host with its supplies cut off. The Persians, with their highly mobile cavalry, surrounded the static Mughal army, developed a potential to cut it off from Delhi and also started capturing prisoners for information and the supplies of the Mughal army. The vast Mughal host with its fighting combatants and its large camp following became devoid of grain, that too in its own empire.

The Mughal army formed itself in a way that on the extreme right was Khan Dauran, Nizam was in the vanguard, the emperor in the centre and Vazir Qamaruddin Khan in the left. However, it lacked unity of command. It did not have one single commanding figure vis à vis the Persian army where Nadir Shah was fully in command.

No wonder the Mughal army developed a siege mentality and became paralysed with fear and lack of action, mortally afraid of Nadir Shah and his army. Therefore the arrival of Saadat Khan from Oudh with his fighting men became a highly desirable event and all waited for him to arrive. This the latter duly did with 30,000 fighting soldiers and a long camel train with baggage behind him on the night of 12 February 1739. Having come in a great hurry to the aid of his emperor, Saadat Khan left behind his cumbersome baggage train, which got duly captured by Nadir Shah and when Saadat Khan arrived, it was to his great consternation that he learnt of the baggage loss. A great urge to engage the enemy and recapture his baggage train seemed to overcome the noble from Oudh. He immediately resolved to go to battle much against the advice of Nizam who felt quite sensibly that neither was the Oudh contingent prepared for battle, nor were the imperial troops in a battle ready condition. Moreover, since only three hours were left for the end of day, there wasn't even enough time to fight a battle. He, the veteran of many a conflict, advised that the main battle be fought the next day, after the troops from Oudh had rested. It was the opinion of all that it was best his army rested, and the whole Mughal army got ready as a unit and then moved forward cohesively as a large host to defeat Nadir Shah.

A visibly excited Saadat Khan refused to budge and immediately issued forth to attack Nadir Shah with whatever he could muster, which amounted to not more than 2,000 combatants. Khan Dauran, who was to the right, was ordered to assist him. Khan Dauran's own troops were hardly ready and when the call came to move forward, not more than 5,000 could be found.

So here was this highly amusing spectacle of a huge Mughal army, marshalled for battle for a month, suddenly having a split in decision making with the most experienced general's advice being disdainfully disregarded, and only a small fraction of it issuing forth to battle against what was possibly Asia's finest army, while the main army stood silently in perplexity to the left of it, composed of the Mughal centre and left, not knowing what to do!

Saadat Khan had meanwhile hastened forward to engage the Persian army. Nadir Shah moved forward himself with 3,000 handpicked cavalry and sent a 100 soldiers ahead to lure the Mughals into battle. Nadir Shah's army came forward and there was an exchange of arrows and musketry. The Persians, who had formed an ambush, made a tactical withdrawal luring Saadat Khan further forward. The Oudh noble charged and then suddenly the Persian screen in front of him melted away and he found himself surrounded and subjected to incessant fire from the *jazail*s and *zambaruk*s of the Persians. Men around him died but he continued fighting, discharging arrows from the elephant he was on. A young Persian rode up to him, addressed him in familiar terms and pouncing on the back of his elephant, carried him off to captivity.

Khan Dauran in the meantime had hastened to the aid of Saadat Khan but could not connect up with him and had to fight a separate battle. Khan Dauran's soldiers fought on horse and on foot against the murderous fire from Persian *zambaruk*s and *jazail*s. Soldiers continued to fall on the Indian side and the bravest of Indian soldiers fought with their swords, to death. Khan Dauran was mortally hit on the face by a fireball and was with great difficulty brought back to the Mughal camp.

The most amazing aspect of this battle was that it was hardly a battle. The main Mughal army under the emperor and Nizam just stood to one side with the main army and the artillery clearly disinterested in the battle. It was either paralysed with fear, did not know what to do or was under instructions to wait and watch. The net effect was that by end of day, one big Mughal noble, Saadat Khan, was captured, Khan Dauran was mortally wounded, about 15,000 Mughal soldiers were killed and the Mughals suffered a severe setback on the battlefield although their main army was intact. The Persians lost close to 3,000 men.

It was, however, a Mughal defeat not so much in men and material as much as in spirit. The terrified army went into mourning and then on guard to ward off a Persian attack. The rather amusing fact was that Nadir Shah, who could claim a victory of sorts in the day, hardly had the nerve to attack this immense Mughal host. Mohammad Shah Rangila and Nizam, if they had so wished, could have still made a fight of it the next day and restored parity, if the Mughal army had been led by more daring and imaginative leadership. However, led by a cautious and scheming general and a hopelessly inept emperor, they retired into a siege mentality and decided to resort to negotiations to ward off Nadir Shah.

Nadir Shah asked the captured Saadat Khan for advice. The latter counselled him to talk to Nizam who was henceforth invited with promises on the Koran as to his safety. The latter arrived at the Persian camp, was received with respect and the negotiations commenced. The skillful Nizam prevailed upon Nadir Shah to receive 50 lacs as the tribute for withdrawal. The terms of deal were settled followed by a visit by Mohammad Shah to Nadir Shah's camp. Mohammad Shah returned much to the relief of his camp from the Persian camp.

Nadir Shah prepared to depart after receiving the money when a horrible blunder happened on the Mughal side. Khan Dauran died and the elated Nizam prevailed upon the imbecile emperor to declare Nizam's son, Firuz Jang, the *Bakshi* and then owing to some confusion, he himself became the *Mir Bakshi*. Saadat Khan heard of this and was enraged. This hatred and anger at being bypassed turned into treachery and he informed Nadir Shah how Nizam had made a fool of him in the negotiation. He further told Nadir Shah that untold wealth lay in Delhi and that he should demand 20 crores, not 50 lacs.

Nadir Shah again resorted to stratagem and recalled Nizam for further discussions. Nadir Shah demanded 20 crores from the Mughals and a flabbergasted Nizam, amazed at this turn of events, could only protest helplessly. The emperor was also called later and both were imprisoned. So were more and more Mughal nobles. The giant Mughal army was rendered completely leaderless and told to look after itself. This happened by 25 February when even the ladies of the Mughal empire were taken into custody. The soldiers had no choice but to flee and left in disarray, each man for himself. Thus a spectacle unfolded where a giant Mughal army came to fight a formidable Persian army, fought only with a fraction of strength at its disposal, got paralysed after an initial setback, got the emperor and its rest of leading nobles imprisoned, with the balance huge army forced to melt away.

What was left with was a complete disintegration of the imperial army and the road to Delhi completely open for the Persians to march in with a captive Mughal emperor. Nadir Shah's subsequent sack of Delhi, massacre of its citizens, loot of crores of treasure and the carrying off of the Kohinoor Diamond and Peacock Throne are well-known incidents. But the Battle of Karnal ended as a defeat for the mighty Mughal army and the sack of the imperial capital.

Nadir Shah entered Delhi on 9 March. The Mughal emperor, Mohammed Shah, became a mere waiting servant on him and Nadir Shah became the temporary ruler of Delhi. He was received royally. The Persians soldiers started camping around Delhi and doing the rounds of the city.

On the afternoon of 10 March, a rumour spread that Nadir Shah had been assassinated. This was coupled by altercations between the Persian soldiers and the armed citizens of Delhi who were militarily aggressive by nature. Armed clashes started and the Persians, unfamiliar with Delhi, got the worst of it with clashes continuing until 11 March. Close to 3,000 Persians got slain.

Nadir Shah got news of attacks on his soldiers but at first refused to believe them. When persistent news came in, he realised it was true. He decided to take swift action. In full armour he rode to the Roshanadaulah mosque, unsheathed his sword and ordered a general massacre and loot. It is a lesson for all those who believe in cozying up to invaders from inside India believing their interests are better served by aligning with foreign masters. Ultimately the entire country suffers.

The massacre continued almost the entire day. Men and children were butchered and women raped. Ultimately Mohammed Shah went with leading nobles and folded hands in supplication to request Nadir Shah to stop the massacre and finally the Persian king relented.

After that the Persian king took way wealth, estimated at close to 50 crores laden on thousands of horses, elephants and camels, to Persia including the famous Peacock Throne and Kohinoor Diamond apart from jewels, cash and other valuable items. Mughal vaults containing wealth of generations were opened and looted. The Mughal nobles had to pay up heavily. Rich and poor alike were assaulted and plundered and made to pay up. India paid a heavy price for the breakdown in the central imperial authority and capability.

The net result of the defeat was a complete depletion of the imperial treasury and a perceived weakening of the imperial authority and power. Bengal, Oudh and Punjab became semi-independent. Mohammad Shah became weaker. Nizam retired to the South to take care of his own problems. Afghanistan went into the hands of foreign powers and henceforth a foreign invader made Afghanistan the base for attacks on Punjab rather than having to conquer Kabul and its nearby territories. This is what led to the Abdali invasions and led to the complete disintegration of Mughal authority. It was to lead into a vacuum in central authority, a partial takeover by the Marathas under Scindia and then a complete take over by the British for 150 years.

Chapter XIV

Panipat: The Third Battle

It is considered to be one of the biggest and largest battles fought on this planet in the eighteenth century. Perhaps no other battle in Indian history has been written about or remembered so much possibly because it is fairly recent in Indian history which itself is several millennia old. The battle is also well-documented and Kashi Raj Pandit, a witness, has given a direct account of it. Another reason is also because it decisively changed the course of Indian history.

By the 1750s the Mughal empire only existed in name. The Mughal emperor, Alamgir II, was a mere puppet in the hands of a wily *vazir,* Imad ul Mulk, who himself was lacking in character, resources and armed strength. Around the Sultanate, many powerful potentates existed. There was Jat Raja Surajmal, south of Delhi, with his mud-packed strongholds and his Braj Bhoomi dominions. Then there was Najibullah, who controlled areas east of Delhi through his Rohilla Afghans, and there were other Rohilla Pathan chiefs as well. To the northwest were the surging Sikhs with Ala Singh as a major leader, not completely organised or a comprehensive military order yet, but full of energy, bravery and uncontrolled aggression. Further to the east was the super rich kingdom of Awadh, controlled by Shujauddaulah and possessing North India's largest army and unmatched wealth. There were Rajputs in Rajputana much weakened by repeated Maratha onslaughts and therefore glad to be left alone, no longer considered big power players in the politics of North India. Then there were the British who were virtually in control of Bengal, Bihar and parts of Orissa, carrying on an uneasy relationship with the Nawab of Bengal and about to start becoming serious players in India after the Battle of Plassey. However, until then, no one had assessed them as major players on the Indian power scenario.

The two major contenders were both considered by forces that were present in the North to be usurpers on the tableau of Northern India. These were the Marathas and the Afghans. The Marathas had become the most dominant military force in India, led by the Peshwas at Pune and having the Bhonsle, Scindia, Holkar and Gaekwad *subedar*s supplying considerable military muscle. The Bhonsles were confined more to Central and Eastern India but the Scindias and Holkars used Central India as the base to lead Maratha investiture of the North often going into Rajputana, Gangetic Doab, Punjab and of course in and around the Mughal capital of Delhi. They supplemented the huge forces the Peshwa periodically sent under his brother, Raghunath Rao, to subdue, ransack and extract money from the North Indian rulers. The Marathas, because of their aggressive military pushes and need for money, had a split image in the eyes of powers concentrated in and around Delhi—that of protectors and pillagers, at times welcome and at times hated.

The other major contenders were not even Indians. These were the Afghans whose aggressive nature had been given a military organisation by the pearl of pearls—Ahmad Shah Abdali, an erstwhile lieutenant of Nadir Shah. Abdali led many expeditions into India and save for the first invasion where the Mughals defeated him completely, had become unstoppable.

The Mughal empire thus suffered from multiple atrocities—infighting in Delhi, non-compliance from its feudatory chiefs in Suraj Mal, Najibullah and Shujauddaulah, invasions and depredations from Marathas and Afghans and a general loss of power, prestige and wealth. This empire alternately suffered from raids of Abdali and the Marathas and had to suffer humiliation, torture, and demands for money it could hardly meet and was also subjected to looting. So far the Marathas and Afghans had rarely come calling simultaneously in Delhi. So a clash had been averted. But the time was fast approaching when they would be there together and a bloody, fearsome clash was inevitable.

The situation was that a power vacuum existed in Delhi. The Mughals ruled only in name. Shujauddaulah was content in his rich kingdom of Awadh and at best desired to be a *vazir* of the Mughal empire, a position also coveted by Najibullah of Rohillas. Suraj Mal Jat would not have minded ruling Delhi but realised a more realistic ambition was to maximise the power south of Delhi in Braj Bhoomi, Agra and areas immediately south of Delhi. It was the Marathas and Afghans who would ultimately fight it out for control of Delhi and to hold the

Mughal emperor as the puppet. The Afghans were content controlling Punjab and moving into Delhi only to loot, castigate the helpless Mughal emperor and his equally unfortunate *vazir*. The Marathas were keen to dominate until Punjab and also regularly dun the Mughals for wealth. It was the clashing ambitions of the Marathas and Afghans in Delhi and Punjab that led to the decisive Third Battle of Panipat and changed the course of the history of Delhi.

The Marathas had begun to firm up an idea of Hindu Pad Padshahi by demanding the holy cities of Hindus controlled by Awadh. There was talk of the Peshwa Balaji Baji Rao placing his exceptionally handsome and talented son, Vishwas Rao on the throne of Delhi. But their efforts in this direction lacked any foresight, any plan and any concrete systematic work. The Marathas came to subjugate, demand *chouth*, put up forces to establish presence but never gave a serious, strategic thought to building administrative or military machinery to control the North. It was at best a tentative strategy to dominate and collect money, not to build the North as a firmly held extension of the empire.

The Afghans were only interested in domination and loot. Abdali's man in India was Najibullah. Abdali's latest invasion of India ended in 1757, the same year the British effectively snatched the rich territories of Bengal, Bihar and Orissa from the clutches of Siraj ud-Daulah. He left behind his son, Taimur Shah, and Sardar Jahan Khan in charge of Punjab at Lahore and withdrew. Into this vacuum appeared the Marathas with Raghunath Rao, the Peshwa's brother, vigourously leading the Peshwa's army along with the forces of Scindia and Holkar into Delhi, Doab and Punjab and all the way to Lahore routing the Afghan forces. The famous Maratha cry of *Attock pe Khatak* refers to this famous victory where the rampaging Maratha forces reached the fort of Attock in hot pursuit of the retreating Afghans. They left after installing Sabaji Scindia in Punjab, leaving Delhi in the hands of Dattaji Scindia, and putting Malhar Rao Holkar in the Malwa area for support. The Peshwa's army got busy in the South. Once again a major contest between the Abdali and a leading Maratha Peshwa general had been avoided. But it was not to be for long. The contest was inevitable, one of the bloodiest and toughest battles to be fought for Delhi.

Raghunath Rao retired from the North in mid-1758. Therefore, neither of the principal potential antagonists—Abdali or the Peshwa general—were there to contest on the same ground.

Abdali, on seeing the loss of Delhi and Punjab and the retreat of his forces before the Marathas, decided to return to the scene. He moved forward resolutely. First he entered Punjab and utterly routed the Maratha force under Sabaji Scindia, which anyway had no wherewithal to face the entire Afghan army under their redoubtable king. Sabaji fled towards Delhi. Dattaji Scindia, a brave and aggressive warrior, was then engaged in trying to overrun the Rohilla kingdom of Najibullah through a futile siege at Shukratal. Najibullah was an Abdali sympathiser. Dattaji was not successful in this siege and had to raise it anyway as soon as he heard of Abdali approaching. He rushed forward to support Sabaji along with his brother, Jankoji. Dattaji here displayed both wisdom and bravery. He kept behind a reserve force under Jankoji in case he himself lost and had to fall back on his reinforcements. He also sent back the heavy baggage and non-combatants. This is what saved the entire Scindia force from annihilation against Abdali. Therein lay Dattaji's military wisdom. His bravery lay in that he stuck to his guns, realised the Peshwa had given him the task of protecting Punjab and Delhi from the Afghans and did not shirk his responsibility from fear of the awesome menace Abdali posed. He moved forward and engaged Abdali's forces near Taraori only to be beaten and forced back to Delhi. He again kept the reserve force behind him and prepared to defend Delhi.

Abdali moved forward with Najib with whom he had affected a junction, and the Afghan army clashed with the Scindia army at Burari Ghat, north of Delhi. Dattaji fought with great vigour and bravery but was no match for Abdali. The Afghans had better numbers and firearms while the Marathas were equipped with swords, spears and arrows. It was an unequal and hopeless contest between a reasonably equipped Maratha chieftain and a first class Asiatic army of the Afghans and Rohillas. Dattaji was slain. His body was captured and an Afghan chief, Muhammad Qutb Shah, beheaded him, carrying the so-called trophy to Abdali. The Scindias retreated and Jankoji brought up his reserve in a futile bid to retrieve the day, only to be wounded and driven back, finally finding refuge in Kotputli. This is where the redoubtable and experienced Holkar chieftain, Malhar Rao Holkar, joined him.

The decision taken was to wage a guerilla war of harassment against Abdali rather than an open contest in the field where the Maratha sardars felt themselves at a disadvatange. Malhar Rao Holkar anyway preferred this form of warfare. However, after initial successes, Malhar Rao was surprised at Sikandrabad by Sardar Jahan Khan and forced to retreat, thoroughly beaten in early March 1760.

Abdali had done to the Marathas what the Marathas under Raghunath Rao had done to the Afghans under Taimur. An overwhelming force in each case had humiliated and driven out a comparatively weaker opponent. It was the turn of the Marathas to be driven out from areas they controlled just as earlier the Afghans had to retreat. The stage was now set for the big forces on either side to decide the contest—Abdali versus the Peshwa and this is precisely what happened on the fields of Panipat on 14 January 1761.

The Peshwa in the meantime had much to rejoice. There was a fierce contest between his army and that of the Nizam of Hyderabad and the Nizam was defeated by the Marathas under the generalship of Sadashiv Rao, also called Bhao, the cousin of Peshwa Balaji Baji Rao. Revenues, territories, forts and cities controlled by the Nizam fell like nine pins into the hands of the Peshwa and the Mughal power in Deccan was almost completely humbled. Sadashiv Rao Bhao was greatly honoured. He anyway was in administrative and financial control of the Peshwa's office and this victory proclaimed him as an invincible general.

Until now, the Peshwa's campaigns in India had been largely divided into two—the North under his own brother, Raghunath Rao, and the South under his cousin, Sadashiv Rao Bhao. The Peshwa always had a more comfortable relationship with his cousin rather than his brother and thought more highly of Sadashiv Rao Bhao's capabilities. However, he had entrusted the generalship of the North to his own brother, Raghunath. So when the time came to decide who should confront Abdali, force him out of North India and reclaim Maratha control over Delhi and Punjab, the choice automatically fell on Raghunath Rao.

However, there soon arose an issue that changed the scheme of things and perhaps the fate of the Marathas in Delhi. In the meeting where the plan was to be formalised there arose a bitter feud between Raghunath and Sadashiv, both rival claimants to the affections of Peshwa Balaji Baji Rao. Raghunath was formally asked to lead the campaign into the North against Abdali. However, while being entrusted with this command, he had to face some prickly comments from Sadashiv on what was perceived to be a failure of his earlier expedition. Raghunath had indeed driven out the Afghans from Delhi and Punjab in 1758 all the way to Attock on India's northwest border. But in the process, instead of gaining revenue and easing the debt burden of his brother the Peshwa, he brought in an additional debt of 80 lacs. Sadashiv wished Raghunath the very best but pointedly remarked about not repeating the mistakes of the past campaign in the North, flushed as he was with his own success in terms of revenue and territory against the Nizam in the South.

Raghunath objected to the language used and got terribly incensed. He got angry at what he perceived as a notable military success being belittled by Sadashiv in purely financial terms. He hit back saying there was a big difference between fighting in the North with its larger rivers, tougher terrain, hostile forces and further from the Maratha homeland than fighting in the South where rivers were narrower, terrain less hostile and nearer the Maratha homeland with help forthcoming at shorter notice. He took umbrage at Sadashiv Rao's insinuation that his efforts had been less than noteworthy. He felt that instead of being praised for a commendable effort which no Maratha general had achieved before, he was being made to feel small and a success termed as a failure. He angrily remarked that those who belittled his achievements and supposedly knew better, should then themselves take over and lead the campaign against Abdali. He left the meeting in a huff saying he was least interested in leading the Maratha army in the North against Abdali in the light of the unjustified remarks made against him by Sadashiv, and the Peshwa's failure to counter such remarks.

The choice therefore automatically fell on Sadashiv Rao or Bhao Saheb as he was called. He was popular and considered very sound both administratively and financially. Furthermore, he had proven military capabilities, albeit in the South and was felt ideally suited to lead the battle against the redoubtable Afghan king, Ahmad Shah Abdali. It was pertinent that he also enjoyed the complete confidence of Peshwa Balaji Baji Rao or Nana Saheb as he was called. The Peshwa therefore entrusted for the first time, the command of his north-bound army to Sadashiv Rao Bhao to drive Abdali out of India, leaving behind his own brother, the sulking Raghunath Rao. He also made his son, Vishwas Rao, the heir to the Peshwa throne, the nominal commander of the army but entrusted Vishwas to Bhao's care, hoping Vishwas would gain some highly credible military experience in the process.

In the light of what happened later in Panipat, this one change could well have been the key reason apart from several other major ones that led to the events of January 1761 at Panipat. Bhao had no experience of

North India and its war conditions, had little experience of dealing with the politics of the North, had never fought the Afghans and was moving into unfamiliar territory. Raghunath had fought in the North, knew the conditions, and also knew when to fight, when to withdraw and how to handle the powers in the North, where alignments achieved could swing fortunes either way. He would have been more circumspect, better in negotiation and military tactics when dealing with the rapidly varying situations and alignments in the North. So the Peshwa decision to make Bhao the head of the Northern expedition resulted in a man ill-versed in the conditions of the North taking on an enemy on an unfamiliar turf. In that sense, the seeds of disaster were set in the very inception of the campaign.

Bhao set out on his expedition at very short notice with an estimated total of 30,000 men, notable among them being the Huzurat, the elite imperial troops of the Peshwa and around 8,000 Telangi soldiers under Ibrahim Gardi, an artillery expert who had trained under the formidable French general, De Bussy. Apart from the handicap of not knowing the North, he was also handicapped for funds, having been just supplied two lacs by the Peshwa. He was supposed to make arrangements for this forthcoming decisive war on his own. Having taunted Raghunath Rao for having lost money in the earlier campaign in the North, he could hardly be seen asking for money. This was a basic mistake where financially Bhao had painted himself into a corner through his haughty taunt of Raghunath as lack of funds would hit him badly once alone in the North.

Bhao crossed the Chambal in June 1760 all the time in dire need of money and asking for it from Govind Ballal, a prominent Maratha sardar and support in the North.

Bhao's policy was to enlist allies to the Maratha cause, increase his strength in terms of men, arms and money so as to create a winning front against Abdali. Key to this was friendship with four important powers in the North—the Jats under Suraj Mal sitting south of Delhi; the Sikhs northwest of Delhi; Rajputs in Rajputana; and most importantly, the most resourceful and powerful ruler in the North—Shujauddaulah, Nawab of Awadh. A combination as powerful as this backed by Bhao's Maratha forces could easily have got the better of Abdali.

However, the Sikhs were too far in the North and talking to them and getting them on the Maratha side was not easy. The Rajputs had been too embittered by past Maratha depredations against them and preferred to stay neutral. Suraj Mal showed support as he had suffered a lot from the Afghan invader. However, the big blow was the switching of allegiance of Shujauddaulah to Abdali. Shujauddaulah would have been a great support to Bhao with his huge kingdom, money and army. Bhao, unused to the ways of the North, did not shower attention on Shuja that Abdali did. Abdali sent Najibullah himself to handle Shuja. Najib swore on the Koran, urged common cause under the banner of Islam on the Maratha infidels, and reminded Shuja of the past Maratha demands for taking over the holy Hindu cities in the Awadh kingdom, and through repeated entreaties and assurances, won Shuja over to Abdali's side. Therefore the third mistake of Bhao was his inexperience and inability to win key allies in the North. Abdali, cool as a cucumber, did the opposite. He had the resourceful Rohilla chief Najib, other Pathan chiefs in Rohilkhand, and now the extremely powerful Shuja on his side.

Bhao's original plan had been to cross the Yamuna, enter the Doab and force Shuja to side with him. Heavy rains forced him to stay on the other side of the Yamuna and he could not move into Awadh. Abdali forces and ambassadors moved there faster and won Shuja to Abdali's side. Finding any further approach to Shuja untenable, Bhao turned towards Delhi. He realised that just as it was impossible for him to enter the Doab east of the swollen Yamuna, it was equally impossible for Abdali to cross the Yamuna to the west and protect Delhi. Delhi was garrisoned by a weak Afghan garrison and surrendered to Bhao after a brief resistance in August 1760. This was taken as a major Maratha triumph ahead of the forthcoming big struggle with Abdali and the Marathas took great heart from the capture of Delhi.

Shuja proposed to intervene between Abdali and the Marathas and proposed to effect an agreement. His condition was vazirship of the Mughal empire. Suraj Mal, a great potential ally in the North, was not happy with Bhao's attitude, arrogance and lack of respect. Bhao should have realised that it was important to keep one ally on his side in the North, the warrior Jats, who would have been a formidable military and logistics support in the ensuing contest. However, unlike Abdali who handled Shuja so diplomatically, Bhao did not handle Suraj Mal's concerns in an effective manner. The failure in not being able to get Shuja on his side was compounded by the differences that developed between Bhao and Suraj Mal, the Jat Raja. Suraj Mal rode out of the

Maratha camp and Bhao lost his only remaining ally in the North. This was his fourth mistake. The absence of Suraj Mal from his side in the Battle of Panipat not only deprived the Bhao of a combative and well-equipped ally, it also denied him a base near Delhi which he could rely on for food and money. It was a massive blow to Bhao.

Another Maratha leader severely antagonised by Bhao was Malhar Rao Holkar. A seasoned veteran who had been a key instrument in Maratha successes in the North, Malhar Rao had a great connect with Najibullah on the Afghan side and could have effected a settlement. Malhar Rao also knew the North very well, and was, in fact the best among Maratha generals. He was not for giving a pitched battle with the Afghans but for continuous guerilla welfare. He would have wanted a strategy where the continuously harassed Afghans, missing their cooler homeland and oppressed by Maratha tactics and the hot climate, would go back with a seemingly honourable settlement. He was also for the Maratha army staying closer to their bases in Delhi and Gwalior and not venturing too far north. But from the very beginning he was treated with disdain by the Peshwa Brahmin leader and referred to as one coming from a family of goatherds. His voluminous knowledge of the North was ignored and he was not given the respect due. He was driven to being a sulking participant in the events that unfolded and his advice ignored. This was Bhao's fifth mistake.

Abdali tried to parley with Bhao. He was for a settlement where he would go back to Afghanistan, have control on the Punjab, and Najib rendered safe. However, after the capture of Delhi, Bhao, who had instructions to drive the Afghans from Punjab, felt he had already dealt a shattering blow to Abdali and sooner or later would settle terms at his own time. Therefore he did not give much weightage at that time to Abdali's overtures.

However, the capture of Delhi, though a blow to Abdali's prestige, was more of an annoyance and hardly a shattering blow. It is from this instance that the fortunes swung the Afghan's way. For Delhi had nothing to offer Bhao in terms of what he required most—money. The Mughals had fled and had no money to give. The North Indian chiefs were mostly aligned with the Afghans and were not going to do the Marathas any good. The only person who could have supported the Marathas had left in a huff—Suraj Mal. Bhao was alone and he sent piteous letters to the Peshwa asking for money and complaining that there was no money or grains to be had. His camp was pitched in the northwest of Delhi in Shalimar gardens and his men started fasting and animals dying. In desperation, he took the unpopular step of ripping off the silver ceiling of Diwan i Khas and realising nine lacs from it but this was only temporary succour. Abdali, on the other hand, while he could not cross in to give battle on the west, was well-supplied by Najib and Shuja and did not have the same problem.

Bhao desperately required money if he was to keep a viable force fighting fit. By September 1760, he was desperate. The idea then was mooted to capture the fortress at Kunjpura. Kunjpura was a fortress possessed by Afghan Nijabat Khan and contained massive grains and a horde of money for provisioning the Abdali army. Its capture would give Bhao the food grain he wanted and some money. Bhao issued forth with the vast Maratha army and surrounded Kunjpura. The Afghans were no match. A part of the Afghan army stayed foolishly outside the fort and was routed by the Marathas. They then turned back to enter the fort and find refuge only to see the Marathas hotly pursuing them, entering the fort alongside and capturing it in the face of desperate Afghan resistance. Abdussamad Khan was killed. Qutb Shah, who had beheaded a fallen Dattaji Scindia and was seen by the Marathas doing so, was similarly beheaded. Nijabat Khan died of his wounds. So the Bhao got temporary relief.

However, this was one move that also got him into a position that took him completely away from his home base. It enabled Abdali to cut him off as the Bhao had moved further north away from Delhi and Abdali could now get into position between him and Delhi, Gwalior and Agra. Having captured Kunjpura in the third week of October, Bhao should have immediately turned back to Delhi with his booty. Instead he stayed back to celebrate Dushehra and then undertake religious ceremonies at Kurukshetra. Malhar Rao Holkar was quite upset about this. Two factors could have made Bhao do so. One was to move into Punjab and tie up with Sikhs to form a joint front against Abdali in Punjab. The other was the swollen state of the Yamuna. Bhao did not think Abdali could cross Yamuna from the east and block his way back.

To his utter horror, he learnt while near Kurukshetra, that Abdali had crossed the Yamuna at Baghpat and was proceeding north to confront him, destroying Maratha *thana*s on the way. The Bhao was now trapped up north, away from any base or succour near Delhi, no allies, unsustainable money or grains, and surrounded by hostile forces. The hunter had become the hunted. This was Bhao's biggest mistake and would prove to be fatal to Maratha fortunes. It showed his lack of understanding of the battle environment.

Abdali's move to cross the unfordable Yamuna and move to the west of it was forced by the Bhao's capture of Kunjpura. That a treasure and vast amounts of food grain had fallen into Maratha hands was magnified as a defeat by the killing of large number of Afghan soldiers and notable captains. Abdali had made a bold and decisive move to confront the Marathas.

Bhao had captured Kunjpura by 17 October 1760 and then celebrated Dushehra there. He then decided to move northwards to Kurukshetra. Either he was oblivious to the danger of his path southwards being blocked by Abdali or he felt that it was impossible for Abdali to cross the swollen Yamuna. Either way, given the fact that he wasted time feasting in Kunjpura and did not deem it expedient to return to his base in Delhi at the earliest and that he turned further north meant that either he felt Abdali could not cross the Yamuna or he wanted to team up with the Sikhs in the North to form a joint front against the Afghans. This strategy would prove to be the undoing of the Marathas as a desperate Abdali went up and down the Yamuna until he found a fordable position at Baghpat and on 26 October crossed over to the western side to confront the Bhao.

The Bhao spent seven days at Kunjpura oblivious to the Afghan efforts to cross over to confront him. He started for Kurukshetra on 25 October, just a day before Abdali made his crossing. He immediately turned back and reached further south to the city of Panipat. The Maratha and Afghan forces found themselves facing each other separated by a distance of five to seven miles at the city of Panipat. The Afghans had reached there rolling up any Maratha resistance found so far on the western bank and having a sharp tussle with the Maratha vanguard near Panipat before driving it into the main body of Marathas. Here the two armies waited, at last face to face on the first of November. The stage was set for a fierce battle for Delhi, the legendary Third Battle of Panipat.

The other big problem for Bhao was that he had a large body of non-combatants in his army—women, old people, camp followers and suppliers, a strength much bigger than his fighting army. Bhao carried all these non-combatants with him all over, to Kunjpura, Kurukshetra and now Panipat. This extra number of people required huge quantities of food and also protection. It severely stretched Bhao's resources and also made his movements cumbersome and lacking flexibility. Every move he made had to consider how to carry and protect his non-combatants, especially women. He could not risk even a fast breakthrough to Delhi because of this cumbersome burden. He should not have ignored the advice of Malhar Rao of leaving these people in Gwalior and moving forward only with fighting men, equipment and material. A reason given for the large body of followers was that many of them came north to do a pilgrimage of the holy cities. The very objective of fighting a tough war with a seasoned Afghan army and its commander seems to have been diluted with a questionable twin objective of pilgrimage jeopardising the primary objective of defeating the Afghans.

Each side then hunkered down for the battle, digging deep trenches and felling trees to both hold up the earthworks thrown up as well serve as obstacles to an enemy onrush. Each side felt it had an advantage and could defeat the other by driving it to starvation.

The Marathas were the more aggressive, initially coming forth, attacking enemy positions and patrols and carrying of cattle and horses. An initial Afghan strategy of not countering such moves aggressively led the Marathas to believe the enemy was demoralised. This could hardly have been the case for Abdali could not have so adventurously forded the Yamuna and ridden up so fast to confront the Bhao.

The Bhao was not lacking in initiative. He however lacked allies. The only person he could bank upon was Gobind Bundele. With a view to cutting off Afghan supplies coming to them from Rohilla territories in Upper Doab, he asked Gobind to enter that region, cut off supplies and harass territories. He hoped to handle the twin objectives of cutting off Afghan supplies and reducing his soldiery by getting Rohillas to move back to defend their territories.

Meantime, the skirmishing and clashes between both sides began to take on a serious intensity. On 19 November, Gardi troops from the Maratha camp tried a night attack on Afghan positions but were beaten back. On 22 November, the Afghan *vazir* went relatively lightly guarded a bit too near the right wing of the Marathas, was recognised as an important noble by the Scindia contingent and attacked. He could withdraw to safety only when reinforcements reached him. The Afghans suffered more than the Marathas in this engagement and could save their high-ranking chief only through desperate measures. This served to bolster Maratha morale and buoyed their spirits.

The most serious engagement before the final battle happened on 7 December when the Rohillas, exasperated by Maratha attacks and cannon firing, attacked the main Maratha camp and advanced upon the trenches displaying determined aggression and fine musketry, driving back the Marathas. The alarm spread throughout the Maratha camp and they launched a deadly counter-attack. The Maratha cavalry beat back the Rohillas but were countered by Rohilla gunfire. Ibrahim Gardi's Telingas then came up and routed the Rohillas, forcing a retreat. The Afghans were beaten back with heavy losses but on the Maratha side, the highly trusted and dependable lieutenant of Bhao, Balwant Rao Mehendele, was shot dead, severely impacting Bhao himself.

It is after this incident that things turned highly negative for the Marathas and in favour of the Afghans.

Abdali now upped the ante. He started closing all routes of supply to the Marathas and sending cavalry parties to surround the Maratha camp and preventing any finances or food from reaching them. Also, he sent 5,000 picked horsemen every night close to the Maratha camp and prevented them from issuing forth to harass the Afghans. Bhao had to buy food grain at very high prices leading him to bankruptcy.

Abdali now turned his attention to Gobind Bundele. Bundele had been threatening the dominions of Abdali allies in Doab and also cutting off supplies to Afghans. Abdali sent a force of 5,000 cavalry to counter him. This force attacked Bundele near Shahadara, routing Maratha forces, then attacked Ghaziabad and then surprised an unready Gobind Bundele in Jalalabad, routing his forces, killing him and cutting of his head. This head was later sent as a present to Bhao by Abdali. This was a very severe blow to Maratha fortunes because with this disappeared the last hope of Marathas in terms of harassing Afghans from the outside and supplying money and food to the Maratha army. Bhao was now completely isolated, faced shortage of foodgrains and finances and things rapidly became downhill for him hereafter. On the other hand, the Afghan army now had an uninterrupted supply of foodgrains. The Marathas henceforth would be a starving and weakening army in the face of a resurgent and well-supplied Afghan corps. Moreover, Bhao was now hemmed in from all sides with even Kunjpura up north recovered by the Afghans under Diler Khan.

The Marathas were to be sent a sum of over rupees four lacs by Naro Shankar from Delhi but a large part of this money got lost as the Maratha contingent carrying this money blundered into the Afghan camp, were recognised and cut up to a man. A few days later, a desperate body of non-combatant Marathas went in search of food, grass and wood in the dense jungles near Panipat. These people numbering close to 20,000 were discovered by Afghan cavalry and put to death. These were a series of crushing blows for the Maratha camp.

This succession of incidents severely demoralised the Maratha army. They had no money. And they were holed up in Panipat where there was no grain to be had. Their numbers were perishing both from conflicts with Afghans as well as from famine and cold. They were not well prepared to handle the cold of the North in December and January. They were surrounded on all sides by Afghans and were not able to break out. Bhao and his army were being driven to despair.

Bhao, who had until sometime back imagined he was in a superior position and refused to parley with Abdali, now began to send feelers for peace and a settlement. Abdali sensed blood. Bhao sent a message to Shujauddaulah giving him a carte blanche to negotiate peace. Abdali and his *vazir* were willing but Najib would not listen. He was mortally scared that were peace to happen, Abdali would return leaving him to the mercy of the Marathas who would wreak vengeance after Abdali had left for Afghanistan. He instigated Afghan captains to wage *jehad* and each Afghan cried for the blood of infidels. Abdali decided to ignore Bhao's offer for peace and now the tide was irrevocably against settlement and in favour of battle.

The Maratha position became so desperate that on 13 January, the Maratha generals and soldiers marched out to Bhao's tent and demanded a hearing. They felt it was impossible to stay in their current condition anymore and it was more honourable to wage a last ditch desperate struggle for either victory or defeat. They demanded that the Marathas go into battle and decide the issue as carrying on in the current condition was no more bearable. Bhao himself realised that the time had come and issued orders for battle next day.

So a desperate, worn out and famished Maratha army, with no friends around got ready for battle. The last remaining grain was distributed for the last meal before battle and the Maratha army came out forming for battle an hour before day break. They took the next three hours to settle into battle positions.

In the meantime, Bhao made a last minute piteous appeal for peace sending a letter to Shuja saying the cup was full to the brim and for Shuja to let him know if anything was possible for peace because after this there was no turning back. The letter had the opposite effect as Shuja rightly guessed it as a Maratha intent to give battle the next day. He hastened forth to inform Abdali who immediately rode out, confirmed the news through several reports and gave orders to get ready for battle. The Afghans too marched out for taking up battle positions and the stage was set for the Third Battle of Panipat to be fought on 14 January 1761.

When the main armies faced each other, the Afghans and their allies outnumbered the Marathas by a ratio of four to three. There would be 60,000 Afghans facing a 45,000 strong Maratha army. Marathas numbers were what had set out originally from their homeland and augmented by allies but had only faced reduction in manpower once they set out from Delhi on the fateful march to Kunjpura and then Panipat.

Abdali had not only been augmented by Najib Khan and other Rohilla Sardars but also by Shuja and a fresh contingent of 8,000 superbly mounted fresh heavy cavalry led by Atai Khan from Afghanistan.

The Marathas had the Huzurat or the household elite troops of Peshwa in the centre commanded by Bhao and the Peshwa's exceedingly handsome son, Vishwas Rao. They numbered close to 15,000. On the extreme left were the disciplined Telangi musketeers, numbering close to 9,000 under Ibrahim Khan Gardi. In between were troops commanded by Damaji Gaekwad and Vithal Sehdeo. To Bhao's right were Antaji Mankeshwar, Pilaji Jadhav, Shamsher Bahadur and Yashwant Pawar with close to 7,000 troops. On the right flank, the main body of troops was commanded by Jankoji Scindia, about 7,000 in number and the extreme right was captained by Malhar Rao Holkar with 3,000 troops.

A total approximating 45,000 troops made up the main Maratha army, weary, hungry and quite demoralised in the cold winter morning of Panipat. In final desperation, hemmed in by hostile forces, facing the well fed Afghan army, there was a sense of doom and gloom in the Maratha force accompanied by an intense desire to do or die in the battle. The Marathas had however a potent weapon in their heavy artillery that they distributed across the front.

THIRD BATTLE OF PANIPAT
MARATHAS
RIGHT
RIGHT CENTRE
CENTRE
LEFT CENTRE
LEFT
MALHAR RAO HOLKAR
JANKOJI SCINDIA
SADASHIV RAO BHAO / VISHVAS RAO
DAMAJI GAIKWAD / VITHAL SEHDEO
IBRAHIM GARDI
LEFT
LEFT CENTRE
CENTRE
RIGHT CENTRE
RIGHT
NAJIBULLAH
SHUJAUDDAULA
SHAH WALI KHAN
HAFIZ RAHMAT KHAN / DHUNDI KHAN
BARKHURDAR KHAN
RESERVE
AHMAD SHAH ABDALI
AFGHANS

Opposing these was the Afghan army led by the redoubtable Ahmad Shah Abdali supplemented by his Indian allies from Rohilkhand and Awadh. On the right extreme was Barkhurdar Khan with 3,000 troops, in a position so as to envelop and outflank the Maratha left flank. On the inner right were the Rohillas under Hafiz Rahmat Khan and Dundi Khan, about 15,000 in number. So the Afghans on the right clearly outnumbered a disciplined Gardi-led Maratha force on the Maratha left. In the centre was Shah Wali Khan with 15,000 chosen Afghans commanding the centre. Shah Wazir was to bear the brunt of the Maratha attack. Inner left was the Awadh Nawab Shujauddaulah, leading 3,000 troops. Further left again was Najibullah with his Rohillas, a force of 15,000 troops, the most inveterate enemy of the Marathas. On the extreme left was Shah Pasand Khan who led 5,000 troops, again in an enveloping position to outflank the Marathas. The Afghans had comparatively lighter artillery in front, they had *zambaruk*s manned two to a camel, about 2,000 in number, that were to play a decisive and deadly role in the battle, owing to their mobility and marksmanship. Abdali was behind his main centre in a red tent with a bodyguard of 3,000.

Clearly, while the Afghan centre was matched by the Maratha centre, it was on the left and right flanks that the Afghans outnumbered the Marathas and moreover, as was the wont in Islamic armies, some of the best troops were kept in the reserve, to be launched later in battle as fresh, hardy troops on an exhausted enemy.

The Marathas began the battle three hours after setting out and one hour waiting for dust to settle down with their heavy artillery launching cannonade. This proved to be least effective as it was badly aimed and too long in range. Abdali had positioned his army closer to the Marathas and therefore the impact of heavy artillery played no positive role in terms of destruction for the Marathas. The cannonade sailed harmlessly over the heads of the Afghans. Bhao had disdained the Holkar advice for light and mobile harassing guerilla warfare putting much faith in his heavy artillery and infantry. He wanted to face Abdali and decimate his army in a pitched battle. And here he used his heavy artillery with no proper planning and by his lack of thinking, neutralised a huge advantage he had relied on so far.

Once the cannonade had ended with little effect, the Marathas beat back an ineffective cavalry attack from the Afghans. Then the main Maratha attack began. Ibrahim Khan Gardi went up to the Bhao, made a *salaam*, assured him of how his troops would be true to the salt of Bhao, went back to his troops and leading with a flag in one hand and musket in the other, charged the Afghan right. It was an obstinate struggle that ensued between the Afghan right and Maratha left, where the trained Telangi musketeers of Gardi went in right earnest after the Rohillas. The European trained musketeers proved more than a match for the Rohillas and slew close to 9,000 of them. The Rohilla army retreated in dismay and Hafiz Rahmat and Dundi Khan tried in vain to rally them around. Gardi attacked the Rohillas with seven battalions, wisely pushing two of his battalions to the extreme left to counter the flanking position of Barkhurdar Khan and also attacking and neutralising him. The battle raged on. However, to their credit, though taking a bad beating, the Rohillas grimly held on. What possibly saved them was their larger number and capacity to take larger casualties combined with an impetuous charge by Gaekwad and Vithal Sehdeo which possibly came in between Gardi's sepoys and Rohillas, thereby hampering Gardi fire and enabling the Rohillas to regroup and recharge. Be that as it may, this struggle raged on and at the end of it there were no victors on either side. The Afghan right was badly damaged and almost put out of battle. Hafiz Rahmat Khan was seen going around in a palki crying that all was lost. However, owing to his smaller numbers, Ibrahim Gardi also suffered huge losses and damage close to 80 percent. The Gardi force became almost non-operative. So the Afghan right and Maratha left sort of neutralised each other. There was one crucial difference. The Afghans had reserves to push back to reinforce their right. The Marathas had none owing to inferior numbers and the strategy of throwing all their resources in one pitched conflict.

Almost simultaneously to the conflict on his left flank, the Bhao now launched his main attack. He, along with Vishwas Rao, the Peshwa's son, launched the Huzurat, the elite troops of the Peshwa along with allied Maratha chiefs in a mighty attack upon the Afghan centre that was being led by the Shah Wazir of the Afghans. 15,000 Maratha troops, renting the Hindu war cry of "Har Har Mahadev" and waving their swords and spears, charged tumultuously into the Afghan centre braving the Afghan light artillery and *zambaruk*s. They dashed through the Afghan centre and grappled in a deadly hand to hand conflict with their Afghan enemies. The Maratha reputation for fighting a mobile battle, withdrawing when getting the worst of it, attacking when in dominance, was set at rest by the bravery of these elite troops which waged a do or die battle with their Afghan foes. The Maratha onslaught had a terrible impact on the Afghans who were not prepared for it. The Afghan centre was smashed and the Afghans ran in all directions before the Maratha impetuosity. The Shah Wazir was seen sitting on the ground, crying and screaming, calling upon his soldiers not to flee as Kabul was far away, beating the ground in complete frustration and throwing dust into his hair and face. In vain he called upon Shujauddaulah on his left to help him. But the Awadh Nawab refused to budge, thinking he might receive the same fate at the hands of the Marathas that the Shah Wazir's troops had met.

This was the scenario in this famous battle at 1:00 p.m. The Marathas had smashed the Afghan right and centre. The Rohillas were badly slaughtered and the Afghan centre had just about caved in. The Marathas were right on top at this stage. At this point of time, neither the Maratha right led by Scindia and Holkar, nor the Afghan left led largely by Najib, had come to grips with each other. The Scindia and Holkar troops had not fared too well in recent times against the Afghans and thereby kept a policy of not entering the conflict. Moreover, Holkar appeared an unwilling man dragged into a battle position he heartily disagreed with. It seemed that the Bhao's strategy of cutting through the Afghans by committing his best troops to a frontal assault would carry the day.

However, there was much more to happen. The Marathas had committed their best troops into a do or die conflict. Their right was low on morale. They had no reserves. And Bhao himself was not in the best of spirits. On the other hand the Afghans still had very good troops in reserve. Also their commander was of a different mettle, cool and calculating, not likely to give in under pressure and one who had seen battles from Iran to India. It was the presence of reserves and Abdali's splendid leadership here that changed the course of battle.

Abdali received the news around 1:00 p.m. that his right and centre had been smashed by the Marathas and the day was in danger of being lost. He was told that Afghan soldiers were fleeing the battle scene towards the rear and the main Afghan army was in utter rout. It was here that Abdali took a decision befitting a great commander. He ordered his bodyguards and reserves to find every man running away from battle and either kill or beat him so as to turn him back to battle. Thousands of men were found hiding and fleeing from battle but were turned back by the Afghan bodyguard into battle. A rout was turned into a reinforcing army. If

Abdali had lost heart at this stage, the Afghans would have retreated and been routed. The circumstances could easily have become a defeat for a less able commander. However, Abdali was made of sterner stuff and it was by his iron command that a retreat was prevented. Abdali turned back 7,000 such men and added his own bodyguard and reserve to create a reinforcing force of 13,000 which re-entered the battle.

The Marathas had no such reserve. Nor was it planned for as all had been staked on the initial onslaught. These 13,000 men entered and recharged the Marathas, who were by now spent and exhausted, more so by the two months of famished existence before the battle. 3,000 out of the Afghan troops reinforced the Afghan right and the Rohillas were reinforced. The decimated Maratha left flank had hardly any strength to counter this. 10,000 of the Afghan troops re-entered the combat zone in the centre and recharged the Maratha centre, which was losing strength fast. Abdali's instructions were for the reinforced Afghan force to repeatedly charge the Maratha forces in the centre and simultaneously for the Afghans replenished on the right to attack from the flank. These attacks were body blows that the fast depleting Maratha forces were not in a position to handle and they reeled under the onslaught. At the same time, Afghans on camels with *zambaruk*s fired their swivels into the Maratha army, causing havoc. The Marathas were soon retreating and being badly beaten. To magnify the damage, Abdali asked his slave soldiers to charge in batches, galloping in and discharging their firearms, then galloping out to recharge. This resulted in further manslaughter. The Marathas started retreating and losing numbers fast.

All this time, the Maratha right and Afghan left had stood in front of each other, not venturing into battle. Finally, Najib moved forward. He was cautious. His men went forward, threw up a protective earthen work and then advanced. Then the rest of his army followed. This manoeuvre was repeated until Najib Khan came face to face with the Marathas under Jankoji. He then discharged firearms into the Marathas who could not counter this and started getting mauled. The contest became uneven, and the Maratha right started getting slaughtered. This was while the Maratha left had been decimated and the centre was badly giving way under the Afghan countercharge. The entire Maratha force was being worsted in the wings as well as in the centre.

Bhao would have counted a lot on the Maratha right to force battle but unlike Abdali, he had not been judicious in placing his troops. His right, commanded by Scindia and Holkar, should have been bolstered by other troops as the Scindia and Holkar armies had little stomach for a fight with the Afghans.

Jankoji was young and counted a lot on support from Holkar. But Holkar, from the very beginning, had been treated with disdain by the Bhao. He had repeatedly urged against a pitched confrontation with the Afghans as he felt the Marathas had little chance in such a battle. He was always for running a mobile guerilla battle hoping to tire Afghans out and getting them to leave India because they could not face the Indian summer. He also had been against the move by Bhao to commit himself so much further north away from the home bases of Delhi and Gwalior. He had been horrified at the treatment meted out by Bhao to Suraj Mal and was dismayed by the Jat Raja leaving the Maratha camp. The presence of the Jats on this fateful day in the Maratha camp would have made a big difference. He was an unwilling commander in a battle scenario where he had predicted defeat and belonged to the school of Maratha thought that believed in living to fight another day. He vanished from the scene when he saw the Maratha fortunes taking a turn for the worse. Jankoji turned around to find the elderly man he relied upon nowhere in sight and also Scindia troops deserting with Holkar. Jankoji, though never flinching from battle, had hardly an army left to fight with.

Another explanation given for the Holkar army retreat from battle is that Bhao had instructed Holkar to take protective charge of Maratha women and non-combatants and take them to safety if the battle started going against the Marathas. Therefore Holkar may have had instructions to retreat and save Maratha non-combatants rather than stay if the tide of battle turned against the Maratha army.

In the meantime, terrible disaster continued to befall the Maratha army in the centre. At close to 2:00 p.m., Vishwas Rao, who had distinguished himself with great bravery in the thick of battle, was shot fatally. This amazingly handsome youth, who had been entrusted into the care of Bhao by his weeping mother before departure, had perished on the battlefield of Panipat. This news hit the Bhao like a bolt from the blue. He had Vishwas Rao brought to him and placed on his *howdah*. In utter misery, he gazed at his nephew. He must have felt the deepest sense of despair, grief and shame at this stage.

He had boldly set out from the Deccan, scorning the previous efforts of Raghunath Rao and promising to eradicate Abdali from India. Not only was he facing utter defeat in battle but the heir to the throne of the Peshwas, one who had been entrusted to his care, lay dead before him. In his own eyes he had no face left to show at the Peshwa court in Pune. This is where the Bhao completely cracked and showed his inferiority to Abdali as a commander. This is where he decided to fight to his death like a true soldier but completely forgot to manage his retreating army like a general, unlike Abdali.

Abdali, when faced with the rout and retreat of his army in the left and centre and an immobilised right, never lost heart. With steely determination, he pushed back his cowering and retreating Afghan troops to battle and stiffened them with reserves. He fought back with great tenacity and determination. He turned the tide of battle. True, Bhao had no reserves to fall back on. But he had his artillery. He had commanders like Gardi, Jankoji, Mahadji and others still there to fight. Maratha soldiers were present in numbers and he could have tried to retreat in an orderly manner to a more defensible position.

However, on seeing his nephew dead, he completely lost heart. He leapt onto his Arab steed from his elephant and charged into the thick of battle, seeking death. He forgot he had an army to command which would need to be taken to a position of relative safety. In an instant the Maratha army was left commander-less. News spread thick and fast of Vishwas Rao's death, of the Bhao disappearing into the rampaging Afghan host and of the Holkar troops vanishing from the battle scene. The Marathas started running from the battlefield, depleting their ranks.

Bhao still had his core troops around him. Into this merged the Gardi troops remaining in the left and Jankoji's retreating troops from the right. A core formed around Bhao in the centre increasingly being strangulated by the Afghans. The Afghan centre and Rohilla right and left enveloped the Marathas in a bear hug. Shah Pasand Khan from the left and Barkhurdar Khan from the right enveloped the Marathas further.

The Bhao was still not done. A man reputed to do 1,200 Surya Namaskars a day; he was not going to give in easily to death, even though he was seeking it. He had three horses shot under him. Again and again he regrouped his forces and recharged the Afghans with great bravery. However, the Maratha strength was depleting fast and each succeeding charge became weaker. Finally, only a handful of Marathas were left and Bhao was seen limping in the battlefield with a spear. He was accosted by a group of five Afghans. Attracted by his bright jewellery, they demanded surrender. The Bhao had little else but death on his mind. He refused and attacked the Afghan group wounding a few. However, his fate was sealed. He was wounded by his attackers and his head cut and carried off.

The rest of the Maratha army vanished and ran for its life. They were hunted by the Afghans for miles, captured and butchered. The neighbouring villages also had their hands full, looting and killing the retreating Marathas. The Maratha non-combatants were similarly found and killed. Panipat, where the running Marathas hid to save themselves, was ransacked, searched and all Marathas found hiding were butchered. Bhao and Vishwas Rao were already dead. Ibrahim Khan Gardi was captured and later done to death. Jankoji Scindia was captured, held for ransom by Barkhurdar Khan but later being under the danger of exposure, done to death. Mahadji Scindia, later to become the Master of Hindustan or Patil Sahib, barely escaped with his life. Yashwant Rao Pawar and Antaji Mankeshwar perished. Damaji Gaekwad and Malhar Rao escaped.

But the flower of the Maratha army perished. So too did thousands of non-combatants. Parvati Bai, wife of Bhao, escaped to Jat country and was respectfully and safely conveyed to Pune. Abdali fought and won the battle of titans against Bhao. Maratha presence disappeared from North India for a decade while Abdali went back to Afghanistan. The Peshwa heard the news, was heartbroken and retreated to Pune, to die almost six months later.

The battle had been fought to fill the power vacuum created in the heart of India, Delhi. With the Marathas perishing and Afghans going back, no great power came to the centre and North India remained bereft of a stable, centralising force. The Marathas did step in later but not in a manner sustainable enough to hold back a situation tailor-made for a disciplined and crafty nation like Britain to step in and rule India for 150 years. The Maratha return later depended more on the genius of one man called Mahadji Scindia, rather than on a united and strong Maratha confederacy under the Peshwa. Over to Britannica. This is what a power vacuum in the centre does, it creates a situation where national independence becomes completely jeopardised and then lost. The Maratha attempt to create a strong and central authority in Delhi failed and Delhi was to see a continuous reversal of fortunes, a power vacuum of sorts paving the way for foreign European rule.

This is what was achieved by Indians in the third and last battle at

Panipat, a battle lost that resulted in the defeat of the Marathas in the battle for Delhi and ultimately for the control of North India.

CHAPTER XV

Battle of Delhi

A FEW BATTLES HAVE BEEN CALLED BATTLES OF DELHI, LIKE THE battle between Hemu and Tardi Beg or the battles fought in or around Delhi between factions in the Mughal court. However, a battle that has been singularly called the Battle of Delhi and directly resulted in replacement of one major power, the Marathas, by another, the British, is the battle fought on 11 September 1803. This battle was fought between the forces of Daulat Rao Scindia led by Louis Burquoin and the British forces led by Lord Lake.

By the end of the eighteenth century, it was clear that the struggle for India would be between two powers, the Maratha Confederacy and the British East India Company. India did not have, during the eighteenth century, a strong central monarchy controlling centrally the economic and military resources of India. All the Grand Mughals were dead, powers that the British could not have dared to antagonise. After the death of Hyder Ali, and owing to the allegiance of the Nizam of Hyderabad as well as the short sighted policies of the Peshwa court, the British overcame and defeated Tipu Sultan, thus obliterating the kingdom of Mysore as a major power. The Jats were never again the same in the North after Suraj Mal. The Sikhs were just about emerging as a major power under Ranjit Singh and were positioned more to the northwest and not into playing a role in defining who would rule India. The kingdom of Oudh was now under British subjugation thanks to successive defeats suffered after 1760 by Shujauddaulah. The Rohillas had been finished off by the Marathas and Rajputs and were no longer a major military power. The contest was now between the Marathas and the British.

The Marathas had the Peshwa in the centre but it was a weak leadership with hardly any military or economic prowess. The leadership in the

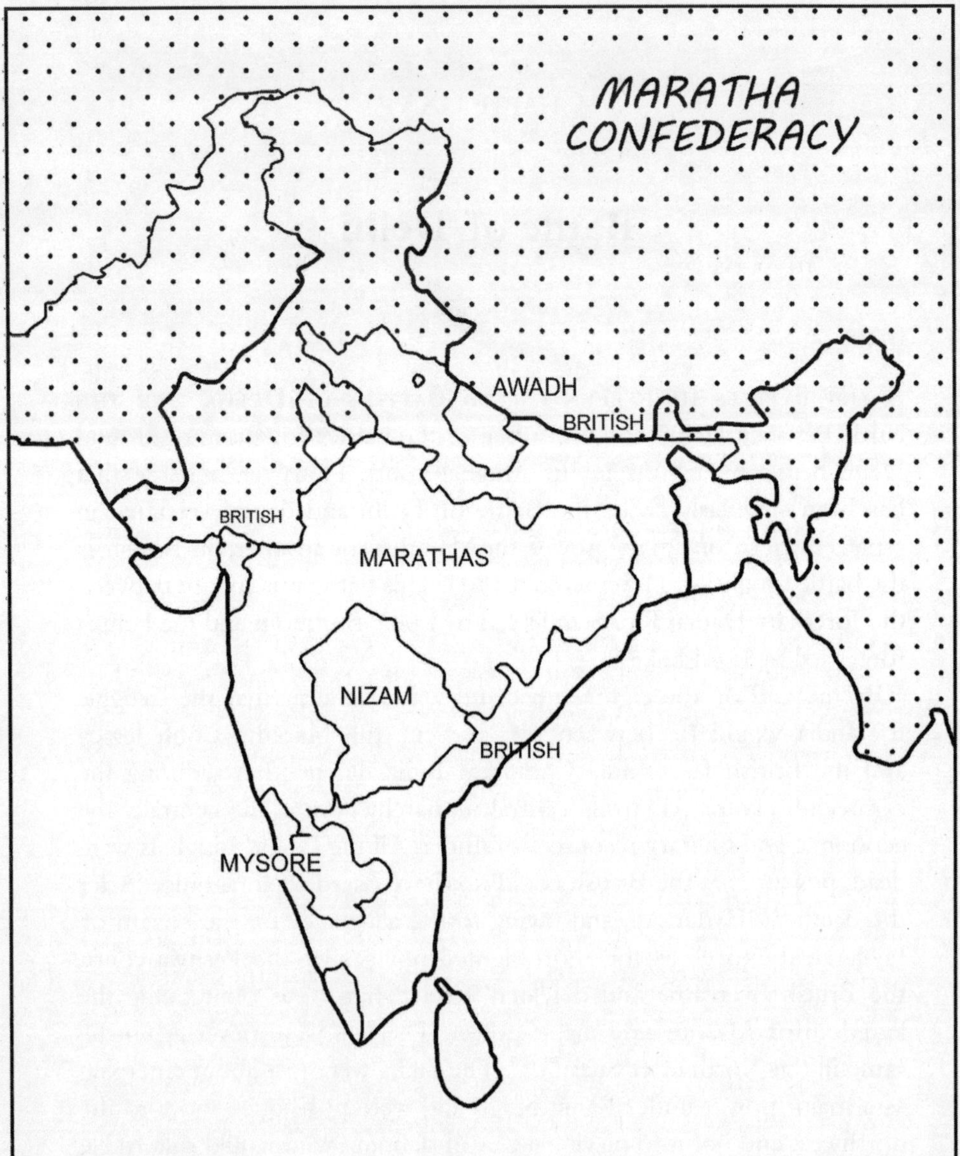
MARATHA
CONFEDERACY
AWADH
BRITISH
BRITISH
MARATHAS
NIZAM
BRITISH
MYSORE

Maratha Confederacy lay now with the Scindias under Daulat Rao who probably possessed the finest artillery and infantry combination in India. The other pillar of Maratha power was the Holkar dynasty under Yashwant Rao Holkar who possessed the finest cavalry available to an Indian power. A third pillar was the Bhonsles from Nagpur.

Unfortunately for the Indian nation, this confederacy was being driven apart by internal quarrels and wars. The Indians had not learned their lesson from the times of Mohammed Ghori, when the Gahadvalas fought the Chauhans who fought the Chaulukya Rajputs. All these Indian powers were defeated one by one by Muslim armies. We had not learnt from what happened at the time of the Tughlaqs. The Marathas were to meet the same fate in quite a similar manner, one by one.

Mahadji Scindia is undoubtedly one of the finest military leaders produced by India. He not only inflicted defeats on the British in the first Anglo-Maratha war, subjecting them to humiliating terms of surrender, but was a bulwark for Indian independence in North and Central India. With him there, there was no hope for the British to even entertain thoughts of conquering North and Central India. The British remained confined to Awadh and there was repeated talk of Scindia leading an invasion of Awadh as well as Bengal to free these parts of British yoke.

However, Mahadji Scindia had been long in the fray since 1750s; a veteran of wars fought with Afghans, Rajputs, Jats, Rohillas and the British, and was nearing the end of his life. He died near Pune, some say under suspicious circumstances. This led to a very young Daulat Rao Scindia, a youth in his teens, with little or no military experience as well as callow in politics, to take over. He could never be the same deterrent threat to the British that Mahadji was. He was a leader the British could take on.

At the same time, Scindia virtually dominated the Maratha Confederacy with his infantry and artillery, all European trained and led. He dictated terms at Pune although his own power centres lay in Gwalior and Ujjain apart from control of Doab in North India. At this time, Scindia and Peshwa were close and opposed to Holkars. This internecine struggle led to initial military setbacks for Holkars and the death of the Holkar dynasty sons like Malhar Rao and Vithoji at the hands of the Scindia and Peshwa combine. This led to a serious rupture in the Maratha Confederacy, to which so far the British were patient spectators. There is anyway little point in interfering to weaken the enemy, when it is hell bent upon self-destruction. It is a trend that continues to this day in India when we cannot decide whether it is the enemy's soldiers or jehadis who kill Indian soldiers with impunity. It is of little consequence they are from an enemy country as long as brilliant debating points are scored by supposedly astute politicians.

The setbacks suffered by the Holkars threw up a brilliant leader in adversity, Yashwant Rao Holkar. Until the death of his brothers, he was considered insignificant and strange. Once the Holkar dynasty got badly threatened by the Scindias, Yashwant Rao rose to prominence and struck back. A man of military genius, a born leader in warfare who led his attacking cavalry personally, Holkar defeated the Scindias repeatedly and finally at the Battle of Hadapsar leading to the Maratha capital at Pune being rendered defenceless. The Peshwa fled in utter terror despite reassurances from Yashwant Rao Holkar and went further and further away. What followed was an event that ensured India would ultimately be conquered by the British. Peshwa Baji Rao II sought refuge with the British and signed the Treaty of Bassein. This made the British the protectors of the Peshwa and incumbent upon the Scindias and Holkars to recognise Baji Rao II as Peshwa. The powerful Marathas counted this as a major threat and insult and challenged the British. This led to the second Anglo-Maratha war.

On one hand were the British with professionally led armies and outstanding leaders like Arthur Wellesley (later famous as the Duke of Wellington who defeated Napoleon at Waterloo) and Lord Lake, each of whom created a Grand Army in the South and North respectively. Ranged against them were Scindia and Bhonsle as well as Holkar. However, to the utter delight of the British, Scindia and Holkar were at each other's throats, a disunity one continues to see even in today's mutually recriminatory politics.

When war loomed large, Scindia did propose to Holkar a unified stand against the British and his *vakil*s did spend a long time at the Holkar court arguing for unity to take on the British. However, the wounds of earlier rupture were too strong in the mind of Holkar and this internal conflict was too big for a combined Maratha front against the British. They failed to recognise the fact that the British had always defeated Indian powers one by one—Siraj ud-Daulah at Plassey, Shujauddaulah at Buxar, Tipu Sultan at Seringapatam. If only these two formidable powers had united, as individually they gave a very tough time to the

British in the following war, the history of India may not have been one of 150 years of British rule, but of a powerful nation ruled by domestic powers. It was not to be and each of them, Scindia and Holkar, fought the British one by one. They fought well and bitterly but so did Prithviraj Chauhan and Jaichand Gahadvala against Mohammed Ghori. The end result was the same. The Indians lost to the invaders, busy as we were in our extremely important internal conflicts, too myopic to see how the foreign power is ready to usurp control of the country. Scindia lost, so did Holkar. They tried to get together again several times but it never materialised and the British ruled India.

Lord Lake was assigned the task of reducing Maratha possessions in the North and for the purpose created a Grand Army for the North. Opposing him were Maratha garrisons spread across the North in Koel, Aligarh, Agra, Delhi and other outposts. The Marathas boasted of an infantry trained by European mercenaries backed by very strong artillery. In normal circumstances, they would have been quite confident of handling the invading British army. But those were the days of Mahadji Scindia, a general seasoned by years of warfare who had seen victories and defeat, advances and retreats, and learnt from both. Quite easily the most formidable military personage in India, he died in somewhat mysterious circumstances near Pune and was replaced by his young adopted son, Daulat Rao, who had neither the military nor the political experience. He had fallen foul of the wives of Mahadji Scindia too.

However, his biggest problem was that the very sources which gave strength to Mahadji's army were going to become his biggest weaknesses. These were the legendary figures in the Scindia army—Perron, Pedron, Fleury, Burquoin, and Lucan, among a host of others. They had trained the Scindia army. However, their continued and committed leadership was central to its success. They had not only trained the army in European fashion, they were also its leaders. It was essential for the Maratha army to have these leaders to lead this army in battle for victory.

The problem started here. There was a deep schism between the European and Indian elements in the Scindia army. The Indians felt that the foreigners would not stand by the Maratha army when the inevitable conflict happened with a European power like the British. The Indians felt that these foreign military experts would ditch the Scindia army and switch over to the British. This was not far from the truth. The important European leaders were in touch with the British army. They were negotiating for surrender and switching over leading to a safe passage. Their urge to do so was further exacerbated by the fact that they felt the Indian leadership in the Maratha army did not trust them and were out to get them. In fact, it was known that most European officers of the Scindia army had expressed reservations about fighting the British and were keener to either avoid the war or surrender to the British.

Daulat Rao was urged by his Indian sardars to destroy this foreign element but he was helpless. He did not know what to believe—the repeated assurances of his foreign generals or the urgings of his Indian generals. He was caught in a bind and ultimately had to trust his mercenary European generals.

This proved to be disastrous. Driven both by the desire to not fight the British and also by a desire to seek safety and carry out all the money made in India, they were in direct touch with the British. The terms were surrender at appropriate times and safe passage. This was the ultimate betrayal of the Scindia army. This was to be the major cause of the Maratha defeat and must surely rank as one of the greatest betrayals in Indian history leading to a successful foreign conquest.

The commander-in-chief of the Scindia army was Perron, a successor to the legendary De Boigne. In Mahadji Scindia's time, he would not have dared to even think of refusing to fight the British. But he was regularly in touch with Lake and negotiating terms of surrender. He fought a half-hearted battle at Koel and then withdrew. His protégé, Pedron, was in contact with the British. He was in charge of a prominent Maratha fortress at Aligarh, considered very difficult to conquer. Again the betrayal of foreign mercenaries paved the way for British success. Pedron openly advocated surrender of the Maratha garrison to the British. To their immense credit, the Maratha chiefs under Pedron resisted, imprisoned him and prepared for resistance. Imagine the morale and weakness of an army whose chief openly advocates surrender, having sold out to the British. Led by less experienced chiefs, let down by men who trained and led them, their chances of success diminished.

More was to follow. Lucan, another Scindia army officer, defected. He not only gave invaluable information to the army of Lake but also led them into Aligarh fort, obligingly showing them the secret way to winning it. The Marathas lost Aligarh and Pedron surrendered to a grateful British. Perron, the man on whom Daulat Rao depended the most, surrendered soon after and also gave the British invaluable information on how to defeat the Maratha army. A Maratha army fought the British ditched by their trainers and leaders, betrayed by their commander-in-chief and was now solely dependent on its Indian leaders for success. Fleury made a successful raid on the British cantonment at Shikohabad, obligingly let the surrendered garrison leave with their lives, unlike the British who shot surrendered Marathas in cold blood. He, too, surrendered soon afterwards.This was, in fact, to be the pattern: Fight a half-hearted battle, be in contact with the British and then surrender. The Maratha garrisons started surrendering and withdrawing—Khurja, Sikandrabad and so on. The victorious Grand Army of Lake was on its way to Delhi. Delhi was the capital, the seat of the Mughal emperor, Shah Alam. The Maratha garrison there was led by Louis Burquoin, a Frenchman.

Lake advanced crossing the Hindon River. Burquoin advanced across the Yamuna by way of the Old Fort to give battle. The two armies closed in on each other. The field of battle could either be described as Patparganj or Dadri. Today the Noida Golf Course stands there, close to where the Delhi Metro whizzes past. The British hoped to defeat the Marathas and capture the person of Shah Alam and become the masters of Hindustan, replacing the Scindias. The winner of the Battle of Delhi would control the affairs of Hindustan in the name of the helpless and captive Mughal emperor. The stage was set for the famous and sanguinary Battle of Delhi.

Lake's army started its approach to Delhi very early on the morning of 11 September and kept marching until 10:00 a.m. The Marathas had moved across the Yamuna with heavy artillery and Sikh cavalry to support. The Marathas had a total force of about 20,000 including 6,000 cavalry. The British strength was estimated at 4,500 men. The British army moved across an area which had heavy grass cover of a tall variety. due to which visibility was low. However, the British army saw the Maratha cavalry approaching and their 27th Light Dragoons and 2nd and 3rd Bengal NC were ordered out to move forward. However, the Marathas had a trick up their sleeve. The Maratha horse started retiring and the British forces moved forward into the trap. The Marathas had concealed their artillery cleverly and in a formation that created an arch in front of the British army. The moment the Marathas sensed that the British had moved sufficiently into the trap, they opened their artillery with a vengeance on the unsuspecting British.

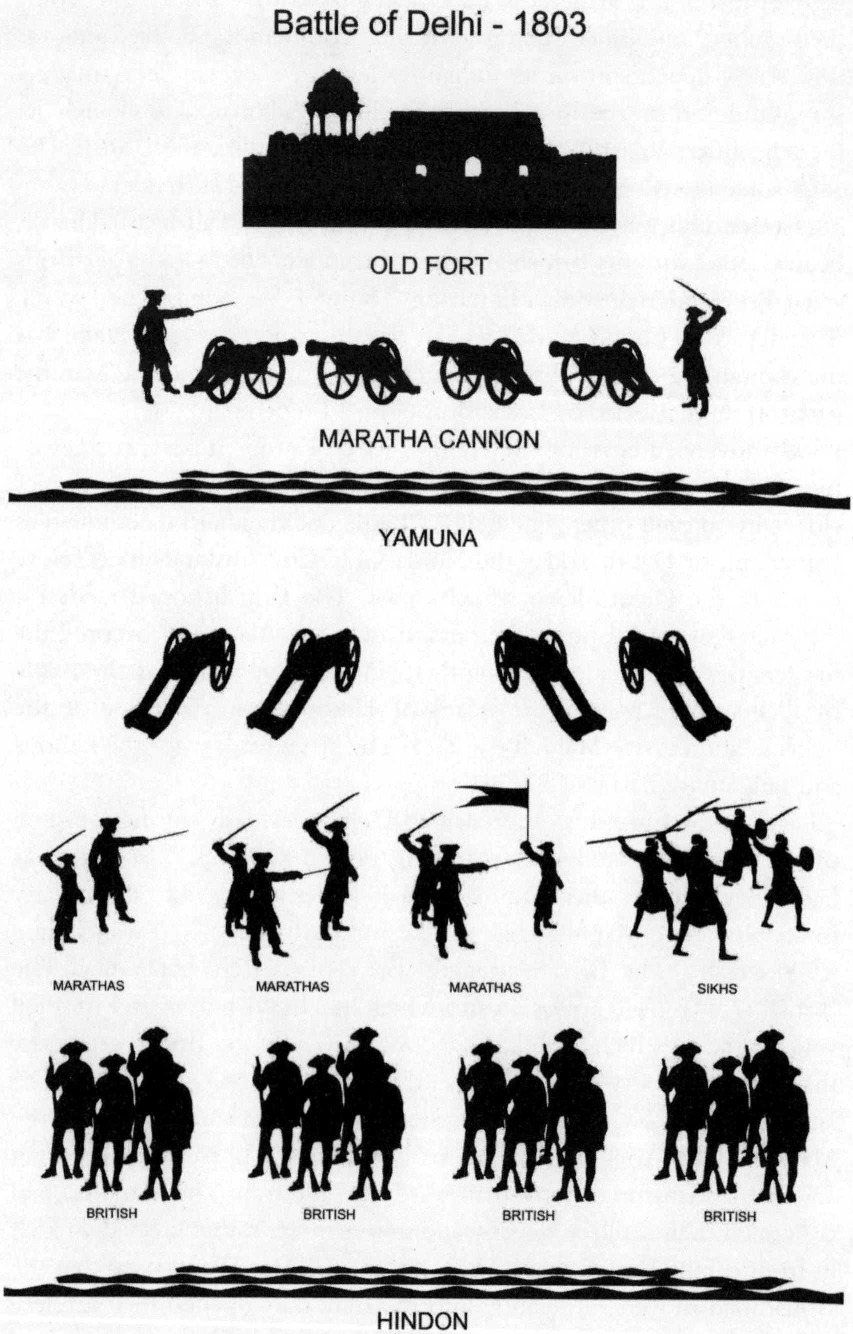
Battle of Delhi - 1803
OLD FORT
MARATHA CANNON
YAMUNA
MARATHAS
MARATHAS
MARATHAS
SIKHS
BRITISH
BRITISH
BRITISH
BRITISH
HINDON

The British soldiers and horses started getting shot and sliced due to the Maratha artillery attack. The Marathas had brought very heavy artillery and accompanying ammunition and seemed determined for victory. Such heavy artillery would be difficult to pull back across the river in case of a lost battle requiring retreat to safety. It seems the Maratha army had gambled on a win all situation.

The loss on the British side was considerable. They could hardly counter with any kind of artillery or musket fire. Lake had two horses shot under him, one of them being offered to him by his son. British officers also started succumbing to the heat, not just the artillery salvos. It seems the Marathas had trapped the British army well and could press on for victory.

It was here that Lake showed his tremendous abilities as a field commander of outstanding qualities. Not losing his nerve, he embarked on a manoeuvre that proved to be decisive. He got his cavalry to start retreating backwards slowly. In the meantime, his infantry, screened by the cavalry and therefore not visible to the Marathas, was asked to move forward.

The Marathas, seeing the British cavalry retreat, presumed that Lake was retreating. Now it was their turn to commit the same mistake that the British had made earlier. The Maratha infantry moved forward along with light artillery to destroy the retreating army by pouring fire and attacking it. To their utter shock the British cavalry split into two, wheeled right and left and turned back on the Marathas, ready for a counter-attack. The Marathas were in for a shock and totally unprepared. The British infantry moved forward in the face of Maratha artillery fire and spewed fire on the Marathas. The Maratha army had no general on their side to retrieve the situation and retreated in disorder with the British infantry in pursuit. The British cavalry also attacked in cohesion. The Marathas broke and ran back in disorder.

The Marathas ran back to the river Yamuna in complete disarray and disorder with no general to take charge as Lake had done during the British retreat, stopping the rot in the process. The Marathas jumped into the river to swim to safety on the other side. However, the British poured fire into the river through their infantry, cavalry and gallopers and a very large number of casualties were more due to the British attack on a disorderly retreat.

The Maratha artillery posted on the Yamuna bank fired back and prevented further Maratha casualties but the day was lost. A large amount of Maratha artillery and ammunition fell into the hands of the British. British army casualties were estimated to be between 500 to 600 but the Maratha casualties would have been anywhere between five to eight times that number.

What followed was highly predictable and shows the low level of commitment to Scindia of the foreign mercenary officer corps. Burquoin, Gessin, Guerinnier, Del Perron and Jean Pierre surrendered. Lake entered the Red Fort in grand style and was received by the Mughal emperor with great warmth. He had merely exchanged one protector, Scindia, for another, the British. The British later moved on to defeat other Maratha forces both in South and North India as Assaye and Laswari happened. But Delhi was lost, and a disorganised and non-cohesive Maratha Confederacy was beaten. The British would rule India as a nation for 144 years.

Chapter XVI

Siege of Delhi, 1857

After the British defeated the Marathas in Delhi in 1803 and seized control of the imperial capital, the Mughal emperor became a puppet in their hands. The emperor was Shah Alam and he was followed by his son, Akbar Shah. A mere shadow of his predecessor, Akbar the Great, who has been one of the greatest monarchs to have ruled India in recorded history, Akbar Shah was again without any powers and had a peaceful sojourn under British benevolence. He was succeeded by Bahadur Shah II who was destined to be the last Mughal emperor who sat on the throne of Delhi, though by then it was merely a throne in name, not in power.

Much changed in India between 1803 and 1857. By the end of the eighteenth century the British had seized Bengal, Bihar and Orissa. Oudh was more or less in their hands. They had the Nizam as their ally and therefore Hyderabad was also practically in the British net. They had to contend with a formidable foe in Hyder Ali of Mysore who they could not defeat and conquer. His equally formidable son, Tipu Sultan, humbled the British military power on many an occasion but an alliance of the British, Marathas and Nizam worsted him, forcing tough conditions for peace. This was followed by the decimation of the Mysore kingdom, the death of Tipu at the siege of Seringapatam and the British conquest of Mysore.

The year 1803 was a landmark one for British arms in India as the British defeated the mighty Maratha Confederacy in a series of landmark battles—Aligarh, Delhi, Laswari, Assaye and Argaum to name a few. The Scindias capitulated and the British had removed their most formidable obstacle in India surprisingly easily. This left Holkar to fight the British.

Yashwant Rao Holkar did a marvellous job notching several remarkable wins and almost capturing Delhi back from the British. But he paid the price for not recognising the ultimate threat that the British posed to the existence of any independent and powerful kingdom. He refused to align at the right time with Scindia against the British and eventually had to fight them single-handed. A British defeat at Bharatpur at the hands of a Jat-Maratha combine was a significant event but eventually Holkar was alone in fighting the British and accepted their offer of peace. The Marathas were now a shadow of their original self and the third Anglo-Maratha war of 1818 was between a masterful new ruler of India, Great Britain, and an emaciated Maratha Confederacy. The subsequent Maratha defeat left only Sindh and Punjab to evade the British dragnet. Sindh was soon taken over without a fight and only the mighty Maharaja Ranjit Singh stood between the British and complete domination of India.

Ranjit Singh was a formidable military ruler and could have given the British a very hard time. However, neither he nor the British were interested in taking each other on. The British anyway had the policy of attacking Indian kingdoms not when they were at their strongest but at their weakest. Ranjit Singh was therefore to be left alone while other Indian powers were tackled. Ranjit Singh, on his side felt that though he may defeat the British initially, the ultimate success would belong to the seafaring power and it was best not to take them on.

However, the moment he died, the powerful Sikh kingdom fell into disarray, affording the British an opportunity to intervene. The resultant Anglo-Sikh war saw many a bitter battle being fought—Mudki, Ferozeshehr, Sobraon, Chillianwala, and Gujrat to name some of them. Among these, Chillianwala was a significant battle as the Sikhs worsted the British forcing a retreat. If it had not been for treacherous generals and a Lahore Durbar at loggerheads with the Khalsa, the Sikhs might well have won and sparked a huge military resurgence in India against the British. The formidable British came close to defeat in some of these battles and had to beat an ignominious retreat from Chillianwala. But eventually British military power triumphed and the Sikhs lay down their arms after the battle at Gujrat.

The British power now had conquered the whole of India. It governed directly or through friendly Indian rulers who acknowledged British paramountcy. The British quickly consolidated.

Tipu Sultan's descendents were exiled to Kolkata from Mysore. Dalip Singh went to Great Britain itself. The Mughal emperor was a virtually captive in Delhi. Peshwa Baji Rao II, again a shadow of his illustrious

INDIA
in 1857
KASHMIR
PUNJAB
DELHI
NEPAL
GWALIOR
CAWNPORE
RAJPUTANA
BENGAL
CALCUTTA
NIZAM
MADRAS
BRITISH

namesake Baji Rao, one of the greatest military leaders India has produced, was exiled to Bithur near Kanpur. The Scindias and Holkars were subservient to the British. So indeed was the whole of India.

This enabled the British to consolidate. They started knitting India into an administrative whole. They also brought in British education and technology. They became the rulers. But in the process, they changed from being traders to becoming conquerors to ultimately arrogant rulers. And the bitter truth is that they achieved this with a highly trained Indian army called the sepoys over a nation where mutual infighting was more important than jointly fighting major external threats.

As rulers, the British developed an attitude of insolent superiority towards Indians who were called niggers and natives. The Doctrine of Lapse was brought in by Lord Dalhousie that proclaimed that any Indian kingdom under British paramountcy where the dying king produced no heir lapsed to British rule. A subservient nation had no option but to accept this tyranny and there arose a category of Indian rulers who had to give up their kingdoms to the British, stoking immense resentment. Peshwa Baji Rao had not produced an heir and adopted Nana Saheb Dhondhopant. The Peshwa received a pension and the British refused to recognise Nana Saheb as deserving of that pension after the demise of the Peshwa. The Kingdom of Jhansi was usurped as the British refused to recognise Gangadhar Rao's adopted son as a legitimate heir. The British also informed the Mughal emperor that he was to be the last on the throne. They had decided he make his next in line a prince and exile him out of Delhi to a distant estate.

The net result was a simmering undercurrent of resentment against British high-handedness. There arose a situation with a potential to coalesce forces that were capable of coming together to oust the British. These were the powerful zamindars, local kings and chieftains who had their own grouses against the British.

Although they had antagonised the Indian ruling races, the British failed to realise that they had won India on the back of an army largely composed of Indian soldiers, the sepoys. Mostly Purbias, and composed of the Rajputs and Brahmins, these soldiers had fought for the British from India to Afghanistan to Burma to China. They were immensely loyal. They were largely recruited from the lands of Oudh. But of late they had started perceiving themselves to be mistreated by their colonial masters. This manifested itself in lack of pay hikes, almost no opportunities for growth above junior ranks and an aloofness the newer officers in the British army showed towards the Indian sepoy as opposed to the friendliness of the earlier officers.

Into this simmering discontent of fire was thrown the kerosene of suspicion where the sepoy got hit by two blows. One was the abrupt removal of Wajid Ali Shah from the throne of Oudh and his exile to Kolkata. Most soldiers of the British Indian army were from Oudh and had a liking and respect for Wajid Ali Shah. This unjustified removal stunned them. But the bigger blow was the threat the sepoy perceived from the suspected attempt by the British to change his religion. This was something no sepoy was ever going to tolerate.

The sepoys suspected that through wily moves like missionaries proselytising, or the alleged mixing of impure material in flour and forcing sepoys to give up native customs, the British were trying to change their religion to Christianity. The latest innovation the British proposed was a new rifle and a new cartridge. This cartridge required the sepoys to bite off on one end and then put the material in the barrel of the rifle for firing. A rumour arose that the end to be bitten contained material laced with cow or pork fat. Biting the first was anathema to the Hindus and the second unacceptable to the Muslims.

The sepoys protested. The British officers were adamant that the cartridge was to be used and all rumours regarding use of pork or beef were falsehoods. Across the country, a simmering discontent arose among the sepoys and in parade grounds the sepoys first expressed apprehension and then refusal to use the cartridge. This forced the British to take disciplinary action. The parade grounds and firing practice sessions became grounds of discontent and a rumour spread among the British Indian army like wildfire.

Into this simmering firewood, the Indian rulers who had felt themselves deprived and unfairly treated by the British threw their own contribution. Prominent among them may have been Nana Saheb and his wily *diwan*, Azimullah Khan. They could have been the centerpiece of a loosely knitted conspiracy team that may have helped stoke the fire of discontent among the sepoys. In fact, the role played by Azimullah Khan in the 1857 War of Independence is highly underrated. Mysterious *chapattis* began moving between Indian towns and villages as well as lotus flowers among sepoy battalions. Some unknown message was being passed in a subtle way but it obviously signified some ominous change about to happen. Historians over the years have tried to interpret these happenings in different ways but suffice to say, these carried a message of revolt among the sepoys and Indian masses against the British masters.

An initial incident was a well-known event in Barrackpore in Bengal, where a sepoy called Mangal Pandey rebelled against the use of cartridges, became violently uncontrollable, thereby injuring a couple of British officers who tried to control him. He ultimately shot himself, though surviving the ordeal. He was captured and hung along with another sepoy, Ishwari Pandey, who had not taken action against him in time. This incident did not at the time lead to immediate further incidents. But the fire had been lit. The rumours became stronger and the British never realised that they were in the middle of a burning cauldron of intense hate from sepoys, local populace, erstwhile rulers, zamindars and firebrand religionists.

The explosion happened on 10 May 1857, when the sepoys rebelled in Meerut, very near to Delhi after some of their fellow sepoys refused to bite the cartridges and were humiliated and imprisoned. Fires broke out in the British sectors, the sepoys looted the magazine, freed their fettered comrades and went on a spree of killing any Britisher or Christian, military or civilian, they could see. Then, as if on a pre-agreed or maybe impetuous but unanimous decision, they all turned their horses and feet towards the imperial capital of Mughal India, Delhi, setting the stage for the final violent battle for Delhi.

At the Mughal court was the octogenarian Mughal king of Delhi, Bahadur Shah Zafar, a poet, a dilettante, a man of words, not action. He was passing the remaining years of his life on British subsistence and posed no threat to anyone. He had no pretensions of any false power and knew that he was an emperor in name only and could not have even remotely visualised any attempts to revive the long lost empire of the Mughals. His eldest son was Mirza Mughal. His favourite wife was Zeenat Mahal who had a favourite son in Mirza Jawan Bakht. Mirza Mughal was in the line to succeed. However, Zeenat, and under her influence Bahadur Shah, wanted Mirza Jawan Bakht to succeed. The British, on the other hand, had their own idea about what to do next. They were determined that Bahadur Shah would be the last Mughal on the throne of Delhi and his successor would be relegated to a princely status to an estate somewhere, thereby ending the Mughal dynasty on the throne of Delhi.

Into this complex position rode in the mutinous sepoys from Meerut over the bridge of boats into the hallowed Red Fort or Lal Qila. Zafar, having just finished his breakfast, saw a cloud of dust approaching the bridge of boats and crossing the Yamuna. He also saw a fire and smoke in the distance. He ordered the man in charge of the fort, Captain Douglas, to inquire into these happenings. The sepoys from Meerut gathered under the Red Fort and told Bahadur Shah that they had rebelled, killed the British at Meerut and had come to meet the king. Captain Douglas argued for them to turn back but the sepoys trotted off in another direction to find an entry into the fort. The king ordered Captain Douglas to close all the gates and deny the sepoys entry which the latter hastened to do. However, disturbances arose in the city and fire and smoke were seen from the European Quarters in Daryaganj.

The sepoys soon murdered Captain Douglas, Simon Fraser, Padre Jennings and went about killing all Britishers and Christians. The palace staff also rose with them and soon the British were scurrying for cover and safety. The Red Fort became an abode of the sepoys and they gathered in the Diwan-i-Khas, clamouring to see the king, who refused to meet them, and who instead asked them to go back as he had no desire to associate himself with them. He was apparently satisfied with his existence at the mercy of the British and saw no gain aligning himself with what he considered mutinous sepoys.

The king, however, found himself besieged by the sepoys who told him of the reasons for their revolt and their decision to come to Delhi and seek the leadership of the king against the British. Zafar tried in vain to resist but ultimately he gave up, blessed the sepoys and assumed their leadership. He was initially an unwilling leader of an army determined to fight the British.

Between the Red Fort and Kashmiri Gate was a British magazine and Lieutenant Willoughby and his colleagues found themselves besieged by the sepoys and attackers for the control of the magazine. Willoughby, rather than give up, blew up the magazine. In the process some of the attackers and defendants were killed but ammunition was denied to the besiegers. Willoughby and his friends escaped and the British found refuge in a tower called the Flagstaff Tower, only to find themselves in great danger as more and more sepoys deserted them. Finally the British quit the tower and went further way from Delhi to Karnal to find refuge.

In the meantime, more and more sepoys descended on Delhi and an army of sepoys, backed by local population, started coalescing around an initially reluctant but increasingly malleable Bahadur Shah Zafar, creating a force large enough to drive the British out of Delhi, proclaiming the aged emperor, Bahadur Shah Zafar, back on the throne as the Emperor of Hindustan. This cry echoed around Delhi and the rest of North and Central India, where regiments of sepoys deserted the British, massacring those Britishers they could find. These regiments, as if at a signal, made their way to Kanpur, Lucknow, Jhansi and other towns, asking for local leaders like Nana Saheb, Begum Hazrat Mahal and Rani of Jhansi to lead them against the British, help drive the accursed *firangi*s out of India, under the overall leadership of the Mughal emperor, Bahadur Shah Zafar. It was strange how after years of emaciated existence, a Mughal empire was being reborn and how a rebellious force largely of Hindu sepoys looked for India's freedom from colonial rule under a Muslim potentate. Even more amazing was the hallowed grip the central seat of the Mughal emperor had on the minds of Indians across the country, even after a hundred years had passed of this seat losing all authority and power.

However, the British managed to telegraph to their centres in Punjab of the sepoy outbreak and the message reached the British commander-in- chief, General Anson, at Shimla. Firstly refusing to believe it, he dithered. Then finally he was persuaded that the rebellion indeed had happened and was aroused from his dazed existence. He headed towards the plains and reached Ambala to gather what was called the British Field Force to move towards Delhi in an attempt to reclaim it. Delhi, to the British, was all-important and reclaiming Delhi was central to reclaiming India.

It was thirteen days later that the British Field Force started marching from Ambala to Delhi on 24 May 1857, only for its commander, General Anson, to die of cholera on 27 May. John Nicholson in Peshawar also managed to get a mobile force going towards Delhi to reinforce the British effort to retake the imperial city. The British realised that to win back India they had to win the battle for Delhi.

The British had realised that the so-called sepoy mutiny had not remained confined to a sepoy rebellion but had indeed become a War of Independence where several power centers of Indian resistance had emerged to defy and expunge the British from India under the local Indian rulers backed by a heterogeneous army of sepoys, local soldiers and citizenry. It was now not a mutiny, but an armed struggle launched by a conglomeration comprising erstwhile Indian kings and queens, local rulers, zamindars, religious leaders, their local armies, members of general public and the mutinous sepoys. Even if there was a lack of central leadership and control, there was a central coalescing figure called Bahadur Shah Zafar. The mere nature of the widespread conflagration across Central and Northern India made it an all out War of Independence against an oppressive foreign ruler, the British.

The British realised all too well the need to recapture Delhi to demolish the epicentre of the outbreak and they did not underestimate the importance of recapturing this critical city, if they were to regain control of India, a control they were fast losing. The battle for Delhi was to become central to the battle for India after 54 years.

A notable figure among the British was William Hodson, considered a black sheep, who collected irregular cavalry composed of Sikhs and started generating resources to assist the British cause. He recruited a spy, a one-eyed person called Rajab Ali and sent him into Delhi to establish connects with Bahadur Shah's queen, Zeenat Mahal, Hakim Ahsanullah Khan, Munshi Jiwan Lal and others. Hodson, with the aid of Rajab Ali, established a spy network in the city of Delhi and started getting regular reports of the Indian position, the state of affairs in Bahadur Shah's court and the deposition of sepoys. More importantly, he gained an adherent to the British cause in Zeenat Mahal, who detested the sepoys and also had a collaborator in Hakim Ahsanullah, an opening which would give the British inestimable advantage against the Indian army inside Delhi. Once again, internal dissensions and the strange Indian ability to align to a foreign power against their own countrymen would prove to be India's undoing.

General Henry Barnard, in the meantime, took over from General Anson and started marching towards Delhi with a force of 600 cavalry, 2,400 infantry and 50 artillery pieces.

In parallel, the Mughal court became active again. Certain Mughal princes, with no military experience, assumed leadership positions among them Mirza Mughal, Zafar's eldest son; Mirza Khizr Sultan, another son; and Mirza Abu Bakr, a grandson. Mirza Jawan Bakht was kept away by Zeenat Mahal, who wanted to ingratiate herself with the British and hoped to get the throne, once the sepoys had been expelled, for Jawan Bakht.

Mirza Mughal was appointed commander-in-chief with unanimous consent. He had no military experience but contributed with industry and endeavour in the days to follow. Zeenat Mahal all along felt that the sepoys had completely endangered the position of the imperial family and expected the British to win in the end. So she kept in touch with them and has been accused of actively conniving to ensure a British win, hoping that would make them agree to her son Mirza Jawan Bakht becoming the heir to Zafar.

While the palace politics was playing out, there occurred a ghastly incident in the Red Fort. The sepoys accused the king and Hakim Ahsanullah of shielding fifty-two British prisoners in the fort. These prisoners were dragged out and in spite of severe protestations from the king, they were done to death and their bodies thrown into the river on the 16 May 1857. This, and other such incidents throughout the war of 1857, inflamed British opinion and led to ghastly reprisals from the British when they started recovering and winning again.

By end of May, General Archdale Wilson set out from Meerut with a force of 2,000 infantry, some cavalry and guns to rendezvous with the Delhi Field Force on its way from Ambala. The meeting was to happen at Alipore. Simultaneously, a decision was taken by the Mughal court to attack Meerut from where the first mutinous sepoys had come and evict the British from there so as to reduce the threat to Delhi. In principal, it was a good decision. The Indians were being proactive. A force was sent under Mirza Abu Bakr to take Meerut. These two forces, one British coming from Meerut to Delhi and the other Indian going from Delhi to Meerut, met at River Hindon.

This was the beginning of the battle for Delhi as this battle continued sporadically and then on a high scale until September 1857. It was a long drawn out battle, which until the very end, was in balance. What decided the fate of the first battle was what decided the fate of the last in September 1857. This was the very different quality of leadership possessed by each side.

The British had battle-hardened and capable military leaders who had led large bodies of armies successfully in battle. On the Indian side and anywhere in India, there were no generals left. Low level commanders from the ranks of Indian sepoys and utterly inexperienced Mughal princes led the Indians to battle. The sepoys fought well and their artillery did great damage to the British. They contested hotly with the

British at the Hindon crossing. There was a bitter struggle. The British charged with bayonets at the Battle of Hindon and drove the sepoys back although they fought vigourously.

Neither side could claim victory until a shell exploded near Mirza Abu Bakr, the Mughal prince ostensibly commanding the Indian forces. He was overcome with fear, got on to a horse and promptly bolted from the battlefield, deserting both his army and the battle. The retreat of their "general" had an extremely demoralising impact on the Indian army who were used to being led in battle by intrepid British officers. The Indian soldiers also retreated in disorder, leaving victory into the hands of the British. Resolute generalship from the Indian side could have forced the British back and depleted the British morale intent on retaking Delhi. It could have prevented a confluence of the British force from Meerut with that from Ambala. The opposite happened whereas this Indian army could have forced the British back. The Indians fled in disorder and many of them drowned in the Yamuna. The interesting part is that the British were too badly damaged post-battle to pursue and move forward. This is how close and bitterly contested the battle was and could have gone the Indian way if they had been led by a good general.

It was finally on 7 June that General Wilson's force from Meerut managed to join General Bernard's force at Ambala and a British formation began to emerge on the outskirts of Delhi to give the Indian forces inside a battle for the imperial city.

However, a more serious battle ensued on 8 June. The Indian forces had planned a block opposing the arriving British forces at a place north of Delhi called Badli ki Serai. An artillery force had been mustered and infantry sent under Mirza Khizr Sultan to stop the British from approaching Delhi. Behind this force, the ridge in the north of Delhi had artillery mounted as a second line of defence.

The British moved forward under General Bernard and ran straight into the first line of defence. The sepoys' artillery and muskets blazed furiously as the Battle of Badli ki Serai commenced in the early hours of 8 June. The British army casualties were intense and men and animals fell heavily on their side. Yet they were a determined army hell bent on recapturing Delhi. In spite of the heavy casualties and onset of withering fire, they kept advancing. On coming close, they charged with bayonets and yet again an Indian army was not able to withstand a British bayonet charge. This was compounded by the fact that the sepoys had no determined leadership on their side and Mirza Khizr Sultan fled in the midst of battle causing his army to also flee following his example. Yet another "general" failed the Indian army. This flight led to a disorderly retreat due to which the second line of defence on the ridge also crumbled. The British now occupied the ridge and had control on Indian artillery. However, here they had to pause. Not only did they have no energy left but had also suffered losses too high to sustain any more advance. If only the Indians had stayed on to fight under a capable general, the fate of Badli ki Serai might have been different as also the outcome of the Battle of Hindon.

The Indian army now retreated behind the walls of the city of Delhi and an ongoing artillery duel commenced between the British and Indian gunners with the latter proving more successful. In the meantime, more and more disaffected sepoys marched into Delhi increasing the strength of the Indian army inside. Also pouring in were several jehadis from neighbouring towns with the avowed objective of defeating the British but also bringing in a religious Islamic fervour into the contest. This had the potential to damage the Hindu-Muslim unity exhibited so far in Delhi. The majority of sepoys fighting against the British were Hindu Purbias and in the process they were supporting a Muslim monarch's quest for regaining power. And here were jehadis pouring in for what they called an Islamic struggle. Only resolute action by Bahadur Shah Zafar prevented an internal communal conflagration for which he deserves full credit.

The British, although they had come to reconquer Delhi, found themselves soon becoming the besieged rather than the besiegers. The British force was small and so was their artillery. The sepoys were increasing strength daily and had better artillery. But unlike the British, they had no generals. They were led by commanders who had never led armies in battle. So every day they came out in large numbers and attacked the British positions on the ridge in a frontal assault lacking any kind of sensible military strategy or tactics. They were repeatedly trying to dislodge the British from what was Bara Hindu Rao and exhibited insane bravery in frontal attacks. However, these were unimaginative attacks and the sepoys got beaten back every day with large casualties. A more imaginative three-pronged attack was launched on the British position by the sepoys trying to surround them from all sides and was barely beaten back. Had these multi-directional attacks been sustained, sooner or later the British would have been forced to retreat, so weak were their numbers and so low their morale.

In the meantime, in the oppressive months of June and July, the combination of humidity and heat began to take a toll on the British. While the sepoy attacks went on, though unsuccessfully, the heat and the accompanying trying conditions on the ridge started killing the British army. They lost a second general when General Bernard died on 5 July and was succeeded by General Thomas Reed. Reed could not handle the rigours of the command entrusted to him either and soon retired to Shimla. He was succeeded by a fourth general, General Wilson. So it was not a very comfortable position for the British with one commander-in-chief after another going down. Where they were in a superior position to the Indian forces is that they always had experienced generals to replace the one dying or leaving. On the Indian side there were no personalities capable of commanding armies in a battle, nobody capable of any kind of strategy or winning tactics.

General Wilson was not the most dashing of commanders but definitely sagacious. He did not inspire bravado but went about systematically strengthening the British defensive position on the ridge, forbidding counter-attacks so as to reduce British casualties.

To make matters worse for the British, in early July, a large force of Indian sepoys arrived in Delhi from Bareilly. It consisted of a large body of infantry, cavalry and significant artillery. It had brought with it money to serve the Indian army. But most importantly it brought with it Bakht Khan, the nearest thing the Indian army got to a leader capable of leading them against the British in the last Battle of Delhi. Bakht Khan was a well-built *subedar*, who was distinguished by his large moustache, and carried experience of the Afghan wars. He was a formidable warrior and was to be the fiercest opponent the British faced in the Battle of Delhi. His arrival was a turning point for the Indian army inside Delhi. In fact, very little recognition has been given by the Indian nation to this valiant soldier who proved to be a bitter opponent of the British, and his name, along with that of Azimullah Khan, should go down in golden letters in the struggle for independence in 1857.

Bakht Khan was appointed commander-in-chief of all Indian forces inside Delhi, replacing Mirza Mughal whose leadership or lack of it concerning the battles of Hindon and Badli Ki Serai had not inspired confidence. Bakht Khan soon tried to restore order and announced strict measures against looting and indiscipline. He then launched continuous attacks against the British driving them to despair. On 9 July he almost overran British positions on the ridge through a three-pronged attack led in person but his lack of generalship experience prevented him from realising how near he had come to exterminating the menace threatening Delhi.

However, as fighting progressed, even Bakht Khan's efforts proved futile in dislodging the British from the ridge. There was, given the lack of military experience inside Delhi, insufficient appreciation of how much damage had been caused by Bakht Khan to the British. Due to lack of generalship and the sepoys being led by very junior level officers, there was a clear lack of strategy. Only frontal attacks were mounted on the British to dislodge them from the ridge. While fighting was severe and the sepoys demonstrated exemplary bravery, these attacks were repulsed by the British. If only the Indian army had repeatedly attacked from the rear and that too simultaneous to a frontal attack, the chances of a British defeat were high. However, there was no general of sufficient military experience to appreciate this and the result was continuous losses for the sepoys, although British strength too depleted. There was a clamour for faster results in the Mughal court which was obviously not in line with the situational reality. This resulted in Bakht Khan being replaced inside a month again by the man he had dislodged earlier, Mirza Mughal, as the commander-in-chief.

There was, in the meantime, at the time of Eid, a possibility of a major conflagration between the Muslim and Hindu components of the Indian army on the issue of killing of cows by the Muslims at festival time. Zafar, realising the tremendous potential of harm, immediately forbade killing of cows and thus prevented a major catastrophe. It was a very judicious and noble step taken by him.

However, Bahadur Shah Zafar was not made of the sterner stuff meant for leading armies in war. As July progressed to August, he felt that he was siding with a hopeless cause. Not made for any rigorous military struggle, he started losing heart and sending feelers to the British just as his wife, Zeenat Mahal, was doing. Therefore, the Indian cause became a lost cause as the leadership at the very top was compromised and was seeking a way out with help from the British. Zafar, in the process, proved to be a weak swaying reed in the wind. Under pressure from the sepoys, he went over to their side. Once he saw the British prevailing, he opened discussions with them.

As the Mughal leadership of Bahadur Shah and Zeenat Mahal became consigned to working out a deal with the British, the food shortage in the city grew worse, as did money and water shortage. The sepoys grew desperate and the depredations on Delhi citizenry increased. The British were now more confident at the Ridge. The only thing that kept the Indian army going was the continuous arrival of fresh sepoy contingents who were made to attack the ridge as fresh troops came in and joined the struggle against the British. A heavy contingent also came from Neemuch to help the Indian cause.

In the meantime, a major event occurred on 14 August 1857, when General John Nicholson came to supplement the British force with a mix of British, Punjabi Muslim and Sikh troops and artillery. He immediately set about infusing vigour and greater aggressive purpose to the British cause and got into a massive tangle with the British overall commander, General Wilson, asking for an immediate attack. He made his opinion of the defensive strategy clear to Wilson and was for an all-out attack. But Wilson would have none of it, instead preferring to strengthen the defensive positions and waiting for the large siege train to arrive before launching a decisive assault on Delhi.

The Indians now tried a different trick. They decided to move with a large force and artillery out of Delhi via Ajmeri Gate and feigned a move towards the west as if leaving Delhi. But instead of doing that, they planned to cross the Yamuna canal near Najafgarh and double back to strike the British in the rear near the ridge. Bakht Khan led the force of 9,000 but it immediately ran into heavy rain. It was 24 August and this force soon became disjointed, water ravaged and exhausted with hardly anything to eat. Moreover, there were two major factions within this force, the Bakht Khan contingent and the Neemuch contingent, each detesting the other. Lack of unity among Indians again came to the fore and presaged doom for them.

The British watched this column move out. Either they had been told by their spies of this plan or they could second guess Bakht Khan. Nicholson was ordered, with 2,500 men comprising British and Indians equally, to confront this force. General Wilson also encouraged him to go ahead as he was not quite enamoured of Nicholson's aggressive ways. Nicholson anyway had been itching to do so and moved his force mercilessly on 25 August in the rain.

The Indian force by now had become disjointed, with the Neemuch contingent in front near Najafgarh and Bakht Khan near Palam. The Neemuch contingent was resting exhausted when Nicholson came upon them. He positioned his artillery to fire into them, causing havoc. His men advanced with bayonets and caught the Neemuch contingent in a hopeless position, making them suffer grievous losses. They were saved from complete annihilation by the arrival of the Nasirabad contingent that gave covering fire. A spiteful Bakht Khan stayed behind at Palam, preferring to see the Neemuch contingent roasted and soon gleefully received the retired and beaten Neemuch army. Once again the sepoy cause failed and the British returned victorious. Bakht Khan suffered much approbation at the court of Delhi for letting the cause down and rightly so.

By the first week of September, the eight mile long British siege train arrived consisting of miles of carts carrying ammunition and sixty Howitzers. The stage was set for the attack on Delhi.

The British set up their artillery and went to work, work they had long and patiently been waiting for. Their sixty-strong artillery battery opened hell on the walls of Delhi in an attempt to open breaches. The Indian army realised inside that the time had come for the final reckoning, the final battle for Delhi. In fact, the final battle to be fought for Delhi in Delhi had begun in real earnest. The rebels fired back from their artillery and there was heavy damage to both sides.

The impending British assault, however, did one thing which the four preceding months had failed to produce. It brought together unity in the Indian ranks as all geared up to fight back and were determined not to let the British conquer the city. There were preparations made to strengthen internal defences and the Indian soldiers geared up on the walls, gates and houses with cannons and guns to repulse the invaders. This was something that the British did not expect, used as they had become to Indian armies being defeated by them. The Indians, rather than give up or become demoralised by their failures so far, decided to buckle down for a determined fight.

The British started advancing at 3:00 a.m. on 14 September 1857 and were ready and in position by dawn. They advanced in four columns on the city and were met by a hail of fire from artillery and guns. The Indian defenders inside were determined to repulse them and inflicted heavy losses. Both sides were equally determined and the British kept going forward in spite of heavy losses, trying to make their way through the breaches they had made in the city walls. A desperate party of sappers kept going until they finally succeeded in laying charges and igniting them under the famous Kashmiri Gate. This is one gate where this battle has been captured most by subsequent artistes and typically symbolises the 1857 War of Independence.

The gate having been blown and the breaches having been entered, the British, despite heavy casualties inflicted by the Indian army, rushed into the city, their target being the Red Fort. A column went towards Skinners Haveli opposite St. James Church. Another went towards the Jama Masjid via Chandni Chowk. Another made its way from Bara Hindu Rao.

This was the situation until 7:00 a.m. The British had imagined that the Indians inside would flee once the British had gained entry into the city. However, they were in for a surprise. The Indian army inside had done its homework well and had planted themselves in houses, walls, lanes and openings from where they struck back fiercely. Gunfire and grapeshot racked the British. Hundreds fell dead just in the short distance between Kashmiri Gate and Skinners Haveli. The British were forced to halt. Nicholson who was trying to reach the Lahori Gate from Kashmiri Gate tried to rally his troops in exasperation. He valiantly charged down a lane but was shot mortally, ultimately to die from his wounds.

At the same time, a British column that had made its way via Chandni Chowk to Jama Masjid, found themselves attacked by a multitude of jehadis armed with swords, axes and other weapons. The jehadis had been waiting for this moment and they unleashed their entire pent up fury on the British, causing heavy damage and forcing them back up Chandni Chowk. Bakht Khan and Neemuch troops, for once acting in unison, counter-attacked the column coming in from Bara Hindu Rao side and drove them back to the pavilion.

This kind of resistance was most unexpected for the British. They had been forced back from Jama Masjid, beaten back at Bara Hindu Rao and were stopped dead in their tracks just after Kashmiri Gate.

The British were forced to rethink, halt their advance, and regroup, making Skinners Haveli their headquarters, just a short walking distance from where they had entered from Kashmiri Gate. One who has been a part of that area would know how short the distance is and therefore how little was the progress made by the British towards Red Fort. They were being resisted furiously, their casualties were heavy and they were being counter-attacked and in danger of encirclement. Wilson, the British commanding general, contemplated retreat but was compelled not to do so by his junior officers.

If the Indian army had counter-attacked with force and planning, they could have beaten back the depressed British from Delhi and the British might have even retreated to Karnal, losing the Battle of Delhi. However, there was little coordination on the Indian side. The king, Zafar, whom they looked up to for leadership, was by now a depressed and negative figure worried to death about what the victorious British would do to him. His queen had opened successful negotiations with the British officer, Hodson. Zafar was desperately trying to get a pardon from the British and was completely prepared to ditch the brave army he had pompously led a few weeks back. So the Indian army was being led by rulers prepared to betray them completely. It was hardly a situation that could lead to any success or victory.

The big victorious push from the Indians was never to be. The Indians did beg the king to lead them in an attack on the invading British and a huge multitude gathered outside the Red Fort urging Bahadur Shah Zafar to lead them in battle. He came out but, terrified of British bullets, retreated.

Soon a feeling of doom and gloom overcame the Indian army and people started leaving the city via Ajmeri Gate. Citizens and soldiers started departing. Bakht Khan left and so did the Neemuch contingent. The Indian resistance collapsed and the British started advancing.

The British captured the Red Fort by 20 September, almost a week after they had entered the city via Kashmiri Gate, a bare two kilometers away. Such was the bitter opposition they had faced from a leaderless army. Zafar made his way finally to Humayun's tomb, the Mughal necropolis.

The British took over the city and indulged in mass slaughter and plunder. Led by Hodson, they finally captured Zafar, Zeenat Mahal and Mirza Jawan Bakht from Humayun's tomb. Little would Humayun have ever imagined that the proud and powerful Mughal dynasty he was setting up would ultimately come to ruin inside his own tomb.

The princes Mirza Mughal, Abu Bakr and Khizr Sultan were captured and shot dead by Hodson after being stripped naked near what is aptly called the Khooni Darwaza or the Bloody Gate. Zafar was tried and

Khairul Manzil, built by Maham Anga, Akbar's foster mother.
(Photograph copyright © Rajeev Katyal, 2016)

Babar inspecting the Gwalior Fort.

National Museum - New Delhi Collection (Acc no: 50.336/340)

Akbar wearing a golden striped safa with plume.
National Museum - New Delhi Collection (Acc no: 52.39)

The Mughal emperor, Jahangir, holding a picture of the Madonna.
National Museum - New Delhi Collection (Acc no: 58.58/31)

Empress Nurjahan, wife of the Mughal emperor, Jahangir.
National Museum - New Delhi Collection (Acc no: 60.1720)

Emperor Shahjahan on a royal elephant.
National Museum - New Delhi Collection (Acc no: 63.1730)

Dara Shikoh with his beloved Rana Dil.

National Museum - New Delhi Collection (Acc no: 58.27/16)

Murad Baksh, the youngest son of Emperor Shahjahan.
National Museum - New Delhi Collection (Acc no: 56.59/46)

Bhao Singh receiving the sword of honour from Muazzam, son of Aurangzeb.
National Museum - New Delhi Collection (Acc no: 50.14/23)

Raja Sawai Jaisingh of Jaipur.

National Museum - New Delhi Collection (Acc no: 51.71/220)

Awadh Sultan Asaf-ud-daulah in a garden.
National Museum - New Delhi Collection (Acc no: 58.58/37)

The court of Mughal emperor, Shah Alam II.
National Museum - New Delhi Collection (Acc no: 76.559)

Kashmiri Gate—site of the attack by the British to reclaim Delhi in 1857.
(Photograph copyright © Rajeev Katyal, 2016)

Maharaja Ranjit Singh.
National Museum - New Delhi Collection (Acc no: 72.313)

Plaque showing fallen British soldiery in the attack on Kashmiri Gate in 1857.
(Photograph copyright © Rajeev Katyal, 2016)

St. James Church, where the British rested after taking Kashmiri Gate.
(Photograph copyright © Rajeev Katyal, 2016)

Noida Golf Course—site of the Battle of Delhi, 1803.
(Photograph copyright © Rajeev Katyal, 2016)

sent to captivity in Rangoon, to die far away from India, lamenting the situation.

Bakht Khan, after having pleaded unsuccessfully with the king, Bahadur Shah, to accompany him in his escape from Delhi, vanished from the city to try and fight another day.

The final Battle of Delhi of 1857 was over. The British won and the Indians lost. Delhi was to be reclaimed by the Indians from the British ninety years later in 1947 through a non-violent struggle. The battles of Delhi since then have been electoral and hopefully will continue to be so.

Chapter XVII

Highs and Lows of Indian Unity

We have seen how an imperial capital has always been the central focus for the existence of India's empires from the beginning of what has been recorded in history or what are called our epics. The Battle of Mahabharata was a battle for Indraprastha. The clash between the eleven *akshauhini*s of the Kauravas and the seven akshauhinis of the Pandavas took place for the control of Indraprastha, and left the Pandavas victorious.

The first historically recorded Indian empire, though not necessarily the first Indian empire in history, had Pataliputra as its capital. The Mauryas assumed control of India. At that time, India as a country existed not only from south to north, surrounded by the sea and the Himalayas as natural barriers, but existed from east to west across a much wider swathe of area. This expanse from east to west would reach the Indus and then cross into what is called modern day Afghanistan. The Mauryan empire came into existence because India was divided into independent kingdoms and republics. Each valued its independence zealously but failed to recognise that unity was essential when it came to tackling a foreign menace which was dangerously intent on conquering India. Then these very broken up independent states of India would neither serve to save India nor survive on their own. Alexander proved it by his quick victories that he achieved the moment he entered the Indian frontiers in modern day Afghanistan and marched towards the Jhelum. A determined Porus was defeated but made the Greeks realise the dangers of encroaching further into India where much larger and more resourceful armies awaited them. Hence the Greeks withdrew from the Beas River.

However, a well-organised central resistance with the strong Magadha kingdom as the nucleus could have defeated Alexander. Unfortunately a pleasure-loving Dhananand never got around to thinking thus and neither did the independent states. Therefore a central resistance to the invading Greeks that Chanakya implored the Nandas to organise was not to happen. An invader came hurtling into India and defeated Porus, Massaga and Mallois and several other kingdoms. India was scarred and the kingdoms to the west realised the vulnerability.

Chankaya and Chandragupta Maurya had the national vision to realise that this weakness could spell catastrophe for India in the future and set about their task of creating a united India. Kingdoms and republics were annexed or subjugated using a variety of techniques, some military and others political, just as Sardar Patel did from 1947 to 1950. A unified empire started emerging and finally Dhananand was overthrown and executed. Pataliputra passed into the hands of Chandragupta Maurya. It took some time to consolidate things but ultimately a strong, centralised Indian empire took shape with Pataliputra as its capital. It stretched across the Indus from the east and then into Central and South India.

Again a formidable threat emerged in the form of the Alexandrian general, Seleucus Nikator, the inheritor of the eastern part of Alexander's empire. He marched forward with a formidable army hoping to repeat, and if possible exceed, the successes of Alexander. However, a different India awaited him with a strong and capable central leadership combine of Chandragupta Maurya and Chanakya. A strategy was chalked out and the invader was met, defeated and repulsed. Seleucus not only could not gain territories but had to part with territories of his own, as the arrangements concluded after the conflict showed.

This is the difference a unified India under a decisive and strong leadership could make to the outcome of a conflict with the most powerful military machine then known to the world. All the military techniques—be it mounted archers, the Greek phalanx and heavy cavalry proved futile against a well-prepared and well-defended India combined under a strong and centrally controlled empire. Chandragupta Maurya's military genius and the political astuteness of Chanakya proved more than a match for the invading Greeks.

This central Indian empire remained strong under Chandragupta's successors Bindusara and Ashok. No foreign invader dared to attack India. However, it could have been towards the end of Ashok's rule or maybe during the time of his successors that invasions and internal dissensions served to disrupt the unity of India. Maybe it was the pacifist path taken by Ashok under Buddhism or maybe it was the weakness of his successors, but a well-organised and militarily strong India ceased to exist. The result was a repeat, but this time successful, ingress of the Greeks.

Unity deserted India and returned only in the form of the Gupta empire, considered by many to be the Golden Age of India. Chandragupta Vikramaditya consolidated a strong India and his conquests and achievements are highlighted in the famous iron pillar near the Qutub Minar. India became a strong and united country with strong rulers like Chandragupta and Samudragupta. The latter, with his many military achievements and own personal accomplishments, is considered to be India's Napoleon and also possibly one of the most accomplished monarchs ever to rule India.

During the Gupta times, a very aggressive and dangerous threat emerged in the form of the Huns. They were not only a threat to India but also to Rome, an empire they humbled on many an occasion.

From time to time, a people or a nation tends to discover unity, develop a strong military capability under an ambitious leader or develop as a strong and aggressive nation under a system of governance. This nation then tends to develop energy and a strong inclination to dictate its wishes to the rest of the world, mostly in military, and sometimes in economic, terms. While the rest of the world is declining or is static or is not as powerful, this particular nation become an irresistible force and is difficult to control. Its power and control spreads to large parts of the world, destroying whatever comes in the way.

It happened to the Persians in the middle of the millennia before Christ and then to the Greeks under Alexander. The Greeks became a mighty military machine and conquered large parts of the civilised world, be it Persia, Egypt and the borders of India. These military victories translated into a cultural triumph as Greek philosophy, art and culture was adopted by or assimilated into conquered territories so much so that the mother culture of Europe is considered to be Greek. After the Greeks, it was the turn of Rome, then the Huns, then Arabs, followed by Turks, the European powers, largely Great Britain and France. The twentieth century was largely an American century and now it could be the turn of China.

In the beginning of the first millennia post-Christ, it was the Romans who were all-powerful. The Huns discovered energy and military power and raided large parts of the civilised world, including Rome and India. In India they had to contend with a strong Indian empire led by the Guptas with a strong military leader in Skandagupta. After initial reverses, Skanda triumphed and defeated the Huns. Once again the emphatic need for a strong, united India was observed. However, what was also seen was that the invading enemy never gave up, so strong was its internal energy and military ambition. The Guptas became weaker and the Huns kept coming, sounding the death knell of the Gupta empire and a strong India.

Harsha came back to rule large parts of North India and the second half of the millennia between AD 500 and AD 1000 saw a tripartite struggle between the Palas in the East, the Pratiharas in the North and West and the Rashtrakutas in the South for supremacy in India. It was also the time when the centrality of the Indian empire shifted westwards from the east to the city of Kanauj. The control of Kanauj indicated paramount sovereignty. The Palas, Pratiharas and Rashtrakutas emerged winners at different times. Fortunately for India, the threat from external sources had deflated by this time and this internecine struggle left India unscarred from foreign invasions.

However, it was not to be delayed any further. The Arabs acquired centrality, military strength, a new religion and a desire to conquer and rule the earth. They overran Arabia, the Middle East, captured parts of Spain and entered France. They destroyed the mighty Persian empire in a series of battles and then turned their eyes towards India. India had strong kingdoms and the Pratiharas became their chief foes with King Bhoja maintaining a strong army to deal with the *mlechha*s (barbarians).

However, complete central unity was elusive and the western frontier of India was weak. King Dahir ruled Sindh and was a powerful military ruler. He encountered multiple Arab expeditions by land and sea and defeated them. However, a more determined Arab assault under Mohammed Bin Qasim, a seventeen-year-old boy wonder and a military genius, could not be contained and the result was the defeat and death of Dahir. In AD 712, the control of Sindh passed on to the forces of Islam. The Arabs reached as far as Multan and then turned their gaze issuing threats and ultimatums to the kingdoms of North and Central India. Fortunately for India, these kingdoms were still powerful to counter the Arab threat.

Major defeats were inflicted upon the invading Arabs by the Pratiharas, historians mentioning Nagabhatta Pratihara inflicting a particularly decisive one. There is mention of a continuous struggle between AD 800 and AD 1000 between Islamic armies and the new defenders of India, the Rajputs, who had by now emerged in North and West India as the new martial and ruling arm of India. The control of North, West and Central India passed on to the Rajputs. They defeated the invading Muslim armies in a series of battles called the Battles of Rajasthan.

However, the Turks became the new all-powerful military and proselytising arm of Islam. Under Mahmud Ghazni, they found a remarkable military leader, the first soldier of his age. He defeated and caused the death of Jaipal, the ruler of Northwest India from Punjab to Kabul. Mahmud, having once breached the Indian wall of defence in Northwest India, came in and found a woefully weak and disunited India. Let alone a strong central Indian empire, there were not even powerful kingdoms to oppose him. Seventeen invasions followed, leading to deaths of Indians, destruction of kingdoms and desecration of temples, the sack of Somnath being particularly well-documented.

The period between AD 1000 and AD 1020 must surely rank as the worst in Indian history when it comes to defending India against an invader bent upon massacre, loot, rape, plunder and destruction of its religious and cultural symbols. Unity, if not worked hard on to maintain, leads to fissiparous tendencies and the inclination to implode inwards, inviting foreign loot and rule. Only the kingdoms of Kashmir and that of Central India under Vidyadhar stood firm.

After Ghazni's attacks had finished, the Rajputs took control and created large kingdoms for themselves. But a strong central Indian empire under the Rajputs failed to merge. The Chaulukyas of Gujarat fought the Chauhans of Delhi who fought the Gahadvalas of Kanauj and so on and so forth, in merry abandon. There was no one to focus like Chandragupta did after the Greeks departed under Alexander. The result was an ambitious general called Mohammed Shahabuddin Ghori who took advantage of this internal fragmentation, shrugged aside a couple of initial defeats and proceeded to decimate the Rajput kingdoms one by one—first dealing with Prithviraj Chauhan of Delhi and Ajmer and then with Jaichand of Kanauj.

India's back was broken and Islamic rule established itself. North India became an Islamic Sultanate, soon to breach the Vindhyas and enter the hitherto insulated Deccan. The Muslims, however, had different ideas and realised the importance of creating strong central empires, militarily capable of defending their newly won empires and expanding further. They established Delhi as the seat of power as it gave them both a platform to expand further into India and also to defend further ingress from the northwest.

These Muslim Sultanates were not always successful. However, under a succession of ruling dynasties like the Mamluks, Khiljis, Tughlaqs, Sayyids and then the Lodhis, they created strong empires, which, at their peak, not only gave them expanded territories but helped repulse invaders from the northwest like the Mongols. In between there were defeats such as the invasion of the Turks under Tamerlane to conquer the Tughlaqs. However, these Turkish and then Afghan kingdoms came to be realised as Indian kingdoms and these people came to be recognised both in India and outside as Indian empires.

A weak Lodhi empire led to the successful invasion of Mughals and the establishment of another Golden Age for India that lasted under six strong Mughal emperors from Babar to Aurangzeb. The Persians, Uzbegs, British and Portuguese all came in, made sporadic military efforts but realised they were up against a strong monolith called the Mughal empire, one of the grandest the world has seen. Therefore these foreign forces confined themselves to cultural, trade and diplomatic efforts. The punishment meted to British forces by Shaista Khan, an uncle and general of Aurangzeb, is documented by Jadunath Sarkar.

It was the weakening of the strong central rule in the Mughal empire after Aurangzeb that led to first the Persians and then the Afghans followed by the British to come in and conquer parts of India. Nadir Shah found a weak Mohammed Shah Rangila easy to handle and that particular military defeat led to semi-independent kingdoms in Bengal, Awadh and Hyderabad. India as a centrally ruled single entity was finished for a couple of centuries, leading to death and destruction, first at the hands of the Persians and then of the Afghans under Abdali.

India, in the eighteenth century, became a prey for external forces. The British came in from the east and south and the Afghans came in from the northwest. Internally, the Maratha Confederacy consolidated large parts of India. Other powers were Hyder Ali in Mysore, Alivardy Khan in Bengal, Nizam in Hyderabad, Awadh in North India and Rohillas and Jats in the Northwest with the Sikhs gathering momentum. However, not one of the forces, though each by itself was very powerful, had the ability to create a centrally ruled Indian empire. The Marathas had the capability but somehow split fissiparously rather than integrate into a cohesive whole. If they had integrated, India's history might have been very different.

Fortunately the Afghans saw themselves more as plunderers rather than settlers in India, which they could well have been, given the strong nexus between Abdali's Afghans and the Rohilla chiefs of North India. They came, conquered, but did not stay.

This enabled the British to keep chipping in at the parts rather than having to contend with a whole. And this is what they did. First came the turn of Bengal after the death of Alivardy Khan. The British won by political strategem rather than through military superiority at Plassey, and Siraj ud-Daulah was killed. The Mughal empire centred in Delhi was a mere shadow of its earlier strength and had no power to help its nawab in Bengal. Bengal, Bihar and Orissa came under effective British control. The rest of India was not even involved in this struggle. The Marathas were interested until Orissa with the Bhonsles conflicting with Bengal. The Marathas under the Peshwa, Holkar and Scindia were either fighting with Mysore or the nizam, or raiding Rajputs or Delhi occasionally. They had not even evinced any interest in what the British were doing in Bengal. They looked only at Abdali as their serious contender for paramountcy in North India and had no time for a Western power and its advances into India.

The big event immediately after Plassey in 1757 was the Third Battle of Panipat and the Maratha rout at the hands of Abdali who also left immediately for Kabul. India now saw a power vacuum. There were the British who were present in Mumbai and Chennai in a much localised capacity but had suddenly created a territory for themselves in East India. Yet no one took notice of them as serious power contenders. The Afghans were always a threat but as periodic invaders. The Marathas were emerging as the ones to fill in as an all-India power. Hyder Ali and the nizam were confined to the South, and Jats, Sikhs and Rohillas as well as Awadh to the North.

The Maratha defeat at Panipat put paid to their all-India ambitions for the time being. They pulled back to the south and west in sheer consternation and then into a series of internecine squabbles in the Peshwa household that further held back their re-emergence in power equations. Delhi and its imperial environs were bereft of a power that could start laying a claim to imperial hegemony. This was definitely a position where one power could aim to come in and start creating conditions for an all-India take over.

The British consolidated first as they found themselves in a confrontational situation with a major North Indian power called Awadh. Shujauddaulah aligned himself with Nawab Mir Qasim of Bengal and Emperor Shah Alam and tried to throw the British out of Bengal in order to restore that province to the Mughal empire. He fought a series of battles and fought them bitterly and well. He had the rich resources of Awadh and a considerable army. But he was up against a very professionally equipped British enemy with British and Indian battalions drilled to very high levels of efficiency. He also paid the price for his very foolish decision to align with Abdali against the Marathas in the Third Battle of Panipat. Not only did he ensure the Marathas suffered from lack of food but also were defeated and made to retreat. Abdali had his loot and left. But when it came to fighting the British, Shujauddaulah had no support. The Marathas were by now in utter disarray after the defeat at Panipat and had left the North for the time being. Abdali had also left. So he had to fight the British alone. Not only was he defeated comprehensively, he had to accept British overlordship and financial demands. The Battles of Buxar and Kora were big defeats for Nawab Shujauddaulah of Awadh. Awadh was lost by the Mughals to the British. The British came further into India. The emergence of a strong Indian central power to fight foreign foes was placed in further jeopardy.

However, all was not lost. Hyder Ali, who inflicted many defeats on the British in the first Anglo-Mysore war, was still strong in Mysore. He should have attacked and captured Madras (now Chennai) and driven the British out. For some reason he preferred to enter into a treaty with a foe that always had evil intentions.

Then came the first Anglo-Maratha war as by now the Marathas seemed to have sorted out their internal problems and Mahadji Scindia and Tukoji Holkar had emerged as competent military leaders. The result was a defeat for the invading British in the Western Ghats and an abject surrender. This was followed by a humiliating retreat forced on the British force led by Colonel Goddard who came to take revenge and restore the British position in West India. Then Mahadji forced the British to a stalemate in Central India. The British realised they had a formidable power to contend with in Mahadji Scindia and therefore called their imperial expansion to a halt in India, faced as they were with two formidable military foes in Mysore and the Marathas. This is also an input to those who regard the British as a perennially successful military power in India. They should realise that the British suffered several humiliating defeats by competently-led Indian armies and if only India had been united or been largely united under a strong power; it would never have passed under foreign rule.

The British bided their time and played the Indian powers, one against the other. They also waited for the formidable Indian rulers who were also good generals, to die. In the absence of a strong central authority that could have realised what the British were up to, the various Indian powers were intent on fighting their internal battles rather than the long-term vision of resisting foreign intervention.

In the 1770s and 1780s, the British were confined to East India and half of what is called Uttar Pradesh today. They had armies and well-defended garrisons in Madras and Bombay. The Marathas had parts of West India, Central India, parts of Doab, Rajasthan, Gujarat and Delhi and its imperial environs under their rule. Mahadji was called the Master of Hindustan. Hyder Ali was a formidable adversary for the British ruling a powerful kingdom in Mysore while the Nizam was inching towards becoming a British ally at Hyderabad. Jats and Sikhs were powerful in the Braj region and Punjab respectively.

At this point of time, the number one power in India was the Maratha Confederacy with the levers of power having shifted to Mahadji Scindia. It was here that things started unravelling for the Marathas and in favour of the British. The British had in place a three-pronged system consisting of presidencies and armies in Mumbai, Chennai and Kolkata to make a bid for India. They also had the backing of a strong government and industrial power in Great Britain.

Hyder Ali died in 1782, most probably of cancer, and the British, much to their relief, got rid of a formidable foe. The Indian system was dependent on the capabilities of a ruler and the highs and lows of Indian kingdoms rested on this single person. Tipu Sultan succeeded him. He was as good a general and an inveterate foe of the British. He fought and defeated British armies on several occasions. He is one of those Indian rulers with multiple victories against British armies and he imprisoned British officers. He was an outstanding general. However, the British war effort found to their great delight allies in the Marathas and the nizam.

Much to Mahadji Scindia's disgust in the North, the Maratha armies of the Peshwa in the South and West aligned with the British and soon defeated Tipu.

It was one of the most ridiculous decisions the Marathas could have made because getting rid of Tipu meant the British would now come after the Marathas. Mahadji Scindia kept imploring the Peshwa to aid Tipu rather than the British but in vain. By the time the Marathas realised their folly, the British attacked Seringapatam, captured it and killed Tipu in 1799. So now the British, in addition to Bengal, Bihar, Orissa and Awadh, had Mysore in their kitty.

It was perfect British strategy. Wait for an experienced Alivardy Khan to die and go after the young and inexperienced Siraj ud-Daulah to capture Bihar, Bengal and Orissa. Then they waited for Hyder Ali to die and went after Tipu. Tipu was a great general but not a great diplomat. He could not neutralise Maratha support to the British and lost his life and the war. Almost in parallel, Mahadji Scindia died and in the process was removed the greatest obstacle the British had in gaining paramountcy in India.

There was a power vacuum in India in the central overriding power and the struggle was between the British and the Marathas. Although the British tasted humiliating defeats in the first Anglo-Mysore and first Anglo-Maratha wars, they patiently bided their time.

As time passed, it became a matter of struggle between a British effort based more on a parliamentary system and well-organised military and industrial infrastructure versus an Indian system where the strength of the state depended upon the genius of the individual ruler. As long as Alivardy Khan was around, the British never thought of imposing their wishes or going to war. Once Siraj ud-Daulah came in, being raw and inexperienced he was easy meat for British political and military strategy.

The same was the case of Mysore. Hyder Ali was more than a match for the British. His son, Tipu, no less capable militarily, could not handle the British as well as his father, and finally succumbed to defeat. Then the British turned their attention to the Marathas. Tipu died after Mahadji as the British patiently finished off Tipu first. Then they turned their attention to the Marathas who had for some strange reason found it more politic to back the British against Tipu.

The Marathas under Mahadji had been a different kettle of fish. He had not only led them to victory over the British in the first Anglo-

Maratha war but his aggressive and energetic military leadership made it clear to them that they could not hope to advance into the Indo-Gangetic Doab or Central India. Mahadji also became a focal point for Maratha struggle against the British as he could draw upon the resources of Holkar, Peshwa and Bhonsle. James Grant Duff, the noted historian of the Marathas, has called him the Master of Hindustan, easily the most formidable political and military personality among Indians in the eighteenth century.

But his death proved a cruel blow to Maratha fortunes. Not even the death of the great Shivaji had impacted them so badly. His successor was a raw and inexperienced teenager, Daulat Rao Scindia. He had hardly any military or political experience save a very impressive European officers-led army left behind by Mahadji. Maratha unity, or whatever there was of it, crumbled overnight.

The Scindias and Holkars fought against each other. The Peshwa was caught in a pincer in between. In utter consternation, he fled to the British. The Treaty of Bassein was signed. The most significant event that imposed British rule in India followed. The British decided to go to war with the Marathas and vice versa. The British, meticulous planners as always, got a Grand Army in the South ready to fight under Arthur Wellesley, later the famous Duke of Wellington and conqueror of Napoleon Bonaparte. They got a Grand Army ready in the North under Lord Lake.

The Marathas also got ready but to fight one another, something Indians have been notorious for since ancient times. The Marathas decided to fight the British by fighting against each other first. So Scindia and Holkar fought each other to the utter delight of an amused British foe.

Holkar defeated Scindia and they became enemies for life. So when the second Anglo-Maratha war was to be fought, the British fought the Marathas one by one. It was not like the first war, where Holkar and Scindia fought and defeated them in the Western Ghats, Nana Sahib Phadnavis's army sent by the Peshwa made a mess of his British foes and Scindia fought them to a standstill in Central and North India.

A more incredible example of lack of unity, a combined failure to realise the folly of an enemy taking advantage of your division is not to be found. Scindia and Holkar could not join hands against the British. Daulat Rao Scindia had experienced infantry, good leaders and fierce artillery. Yashwant Rao Holkar had the best cavalry in India. He was a great general. But he could not forget his previous humiliation at the hands of Scindia or the fact that Scindia was responsible for finishing off his brothers. Off went Scindia to fight the British alone with some support from Bhonsle. Scindia's European-trained armies fought well but were betrayed by their European generals. Scindia lost the war.

Soon it was the turn of Holkar. He fought well but was alone. He got some support from the Jats. He and the Jats defeated Lord Lake in the Battle of Bharatpur. Holkar won many notable victories against the British. But he was alone. He went to Ranjit Singh for support but common cause could not be found. The turn of the Sikh kingdom came much later but the seeds were sown when the Marathas and Sikhs could not combine against the British.

Holkar signed a treaty, and the British having captured Delhi became masters of Hindustan, replacing the Scindias. Subsequent victories against the Marathas and Sikhs were a foregone conclusion. The final battle to control Delhi and India was lost by all Indian kingdoms—Awadh in Buxar; Scindia in Assaye, Laswari and Delhi; Holkar in the environs of Delhi; Sikhs in Sobraon, Ferozeshehr and Gujrat; and Jats in Bharatpur.

The war of 1857 was an energetic and powerful attempt to rid the country of its foreign yoke. It had lesser chances of success against the then most organised and formidable military and industrial power in the world. It was a belated though brave and energetic attempt by Indians to forge a unity under a Mughal monarch again and throw off a foreign invasion and foreign rule. It is amazing what a powerful grip the concept of a Mughal emperor ruling from Delhi had on the minds of all Indians. Forgotten was the religion of this personage. A Mughal emperor was the embodiment in the minds of Indians of a unifying central authority from Delhi (or Dilli) capable of leading a strong united India. No matter if the Mughal emperors had ceased being strong central rulers almost a hundred years back. In 1857, when India wanted freedom and unity, it turned to that hallowed symbol from history to lead it.

But India did not have quite the resources to defeat the foreigners. It did not have trained armies apart from the sepoys who had earlier served their British masters. It had hardly any generals capable of leading them in battle. It had a few intrepid leaders in the Rani of Jhansi, Tatya Tope, Bakht Khan, Azimullah, Nana Saheb, Begum Hazrat Mahal, Kunwar

Jagdish Singh and others, but this was insufficient to achieve their objectives.

It took ninety more years to win freedom and a unified India. Not for a moment should we forget that this freedom and unity cannot be taken for granted. It needs to be preserved carefully.

Chapter XVIII

Lessons from History

It is often said that those who do not learn from history, are condemned to repeat it. It is seen throughout this book that it is especially true of India.

Ambhi of Taxila, and Porus, were sworn enemies. Ambhi facilitated Alexander in overcoming Porus. Magadha sat back and watched Alexander decimate India's border kingdoms until he left owing to the good fortune of India.

The complete absence of a strong central unity in India enabled the Arabs to conquer Sindh. Mahmud Ghazni ravaged a divided and enfeebled India at will seventeen times. A people who are unable to organise themselves into a well-governed, centralised entity, fall easy prey to an adversary that might economically and culturally be no match, but militarily is well-organised to take advantage.

Prithviraj Chauhan and Jaichand had cause to quarrel and hence cause to fight Shahabuddin Ghori separately. They also lost their kingdoms and lives separately in due course. Internal conflict for them was more important than combining to take on an extremely dangerous external invader. The South was insulated and hardly prepared to take on this threat in the form of Allaudin Khilji and Ghiyasuddin Tughlaq. India became an Islamic Sultanate from north to south.

These Islamic conquerors took on an Indian hue and became recognised as Indians. However, internal squabbles put paid to their strengths. The Tughlaqs were beaten by Taimur Lang. A week Ibrahim Lodhi was defeated by Babar, ravaged as Lodhis were by conflicts with the Rajputs, Bengal and Gujarat.

The Mughals were strong for 200 years but the internal decay led to weaker and weaker rulers, resulting in massive decrease of military and economic strengths. The result was their decimation at the hands of the

Marathas, Afghans and other Indian kingdoms.

A strong centrally governed entity was a possibility under the Maratha Confederacy. However, they lacked the unity and foresight. The result was a disaster in the early nineteenth century and India became enslaved under the British.

Such lack of unity and foresight is peculiar to India. It happens in cycles and keeps happening—be it Rajputs, Lodhis, Mughals or Marathas. It happens frequently and the results are long term and disastrous—be it Greek invasions, Muslim invasions, Afghan invasions or British invasions. The Indian power—be it the Mauryas, Rajputs, Tughlaqs, Lodhis, Mughals, and Marathas ultimately gives in. India has faced long periods of foreign rule. It impacts its self-confidence, its place in the hierarchy of nations, economic strength, its culture, religion and social mores and customs. The 1857 revolution was an expression of anger by Indians from various strata of society against how the British had mercilessly changed the ruling equations, social customs, economic practices and demonstrated insensitivity to religious feelings.

Large scale religious conversions, destruction of places of worship, imposition of and enslavement to a foreign culture and language, complete overthrow and humiliation of political rulers followed. Massacre, rape, plunder, destruction were inevitable. The ultimate humiliation was enslavement under foreign rule.

What has caused this to happen repeatedly in the past? There have been reasons at different points of time, some common and some peculiar to the times. One is a tendency to think sub-nationally rather than nationally. Individual desires of a state, region or people tend to overshadow the feeling of Indian-ness. Delhi and Ajmer fought Kanauj more successfully than they did Ghori. Rana Sangha fought Lodhi better than he did the Mughals. Holkar defeated Scindias but not the British. It seems as if it was more important for Indians to fight internally rather than an external foe that was far more dangerous as he was ultimately going to finish of all Indian entities fighting each other. As long as the central ruling entity existed and was strong enough to ward off these internal conflicts as were the Mauryas, Guptas, Pratiharas, Khiljis, Mughals and Marathas, India remained free. The moment the central forces became weak, these sub-national entities became unmanageable. The nation became splintered and was unable to take on external aggression as has been described often in this book.

Today India exists as a strong, centrally-governed entity under a parliamentary system. It has states and union territories. Whenever there has been a movement to split a part of the country away, it has been dealt with successfully in either a political or a military manner. This has been the fate of secessionist movements—be it in the Northeast or Kashmir or the Khalistan movement or any other movement. However, the very fact that such movements have come to the fore means this tendency to think in sub-nationalistic terms continues. Today, the central authority is strong enough to handle it and hopefully it shall always remain so.

But there has to be a continuous emphasis to strengthen the nationalistic rather than the sub-nationalistic thought in this country. Institutions that strengthen the nationalistic agenda, be they in the field of security, governance, management, culture, sports or politics, need continuous strengthening. The ability of the security forces to handle such emergencies is critical. So also is that of the political process to help sub-nationalistic movements get expression within the constitutional framework. It is important to strengthen those cultural and economic movements that integrate the country so that continuous pride in an Indian nation keeps increasing.

Today, parties that can govern India as single central entities are on the wane. The power is going towards more regional and state level parties. Or to parties that are not regional in thinking but definitely in strength. Coalitions are the order of the day rather than strong central parties governing India. Only recently has a national party barely managed to cross 50% majority in Parliament and it is considered quite an achievement.

Coalition governments in India have run successfully over the last three terms of five years each but in the process decisions that could have been taken in the interest of the country have suffered—be it how to handle the Naxalite movement or to vote appropriately on the Sri Lanka issue. A minister gets into a particular cabinet position and takes all decisions favouring his or her state. Economic decisions that can take the country forward hang fire.

The fault lies with these central parties who tend to look at short-term government formation rather than long-term issues like spreading their presence in all areas of India, developing cadre, handling both local and central issues effectively. They need to identify with local issues much better. These parties have leaders who have more presence on television than on the ground. These parties need to spread their effort more on the ground. They need leaders who can identify with and represent local issues or else they will continue to yield ground to regionally or state level strong parties. Chances of strong central parties dim while those of regional parties go up, strengthening the case for coalition rather than central party rule. This in the long run may mean strengthening of forces that compromise with national security or economic interests. Lack of central control or authority, as we have seen, has weakened India in the past.

Another issue is the sheer scale of corruption that has pervaded the entire country. It has reached every level of governmental and political functioning. The highest authorities have been accused of it. Scams of huge proportions pervade the country. Coruption has pervaded sports and the much venerated defence forces. The common man cannot get his work done easily without greasing palms. In this pervasive atmosphere of corruption, the onward march of the economy has taken a hit as decisions that lead to economic progress get delayed and money that should be spent on building infrastructure and manufacturing may not be getting utilised the way it is meant to be. Even defence procurement has taken a big hit. This can impact the growth and strengthening of India both economically and militarily, leading to weakening in terms of its international position and its defence preparedness. A scam-ridden defence procurement area has given rise to even the Air Force having reduced squadron strengths. History has shown that lack of defence preparedness has led to successive defeats in the past—be it the Mughals or Tughlaqs or Rajputs. Allaudin Khilji, Akbar and Mahadji Scindia are rare examples in Indian history of defensive strength. Historians have repeatedly referred to the measures taken by Allaudin Khilji to thwart and disrupt Mongol invasions; Akbar extending the Indian empire beyond the Indus; and Mahadji Scindia successfully taking on the British.

Moreover, a country's defence preparedness and international stature depends a lot on its economic strength. India's status multiplied when we discovered we are no longer only an agricultural country but one of the ten most industrialised nations in the world in the 1970s. Our pride went up manifold. It was the result of years of hard work and investments post-independence, the foundation of which was laid by Pandit Nehru.

Our international stature got a big boost from our software industry and people began to look at India differently in the 1990s. Continuous growth of over 7% in the 1990s and early part of the first decade of the twenty-first century made us a destination for FDI and made us close to being an economic star. All this wanes if corruption hits the country. Economic decisions do not get taken and wheels of progress grind slowly. Corruption may have its root causes in the way our society operates but has become brazen top down and it encourages many others to adopt similar corrupt practices. Only leadership dedicated to clean governance and an India where corruption is minimised can get the country rid of this cancer.

The third problem we have as a country is our defensive mindset. We have hardly ever invaded any other country, rare examples being Chola naval incursions over the seas and the 1971 war of Bangladesh. Perhaps it has to do with the fact that as a country we are like a sub-continent and thus different parts of it have at times come together under an empire or at times split into mutually recriminatory units with little care for the rest of the world. We have been too preoccupied with ourselves. Perhaps this country was fertile and full of riches and therefore too self-contained within its boundaries for it to go pursuing riches outside its boundaries. There was little reason to go shopping overseas. Or perhaps the physical isolation induced by the Himalayas, Hindu Kush and the surrounding seas precluded thoughts of going into ventures abroad.

Consequently, we have always been a prey to invasions. Be it the Persians, Greeks, Sakas, Huns, Arabs, Turks, Mughals or British. We have always waited for the offensive from others. An emaciated India has lost to invaders. The invader has kept coming and whenever we have been strong we have won and lost when we were weak. The invader has always waited for this weakness to emerge which happens when, after long central rule, weaknesses emerge. Thus we wait to be conquered. We fought most of the decisive battles of history close to the imperial capital of Delhi and lost them and lost our empires and independence. We have waited for the invader to keep coming and concentrated on defence. The effectiveness of this defence has waxed and waned with time. It is this defensive mindset that has done us in.

Prithviraj Chauhan woke up to Ghori when the empires of the two became adjacent to each other in Punjab. He did little to prevent that from happening. A proactive approach to meeting this threat away from the capital, not even allowing it to emerge, would have helped. On the other hand, Allaudin Khilji reacted differently when he was invaded by the Mongols. Not only were they mercilessly treated but the Sultan realised that they would keep coming. So he strengthened his army, built frontier fortresses well-replenished and then sent punitive forces into enemy country to destroy their confidence and capability, eliminating their threat forever.

Chandragupta Maurya had a proactive policy built on a solid spy network and formidable forces. He is said to have met Seleucus near the Indus and comprehensively defeated him there. Jalaluddin Mohammed Akbar not only conquered large parts of India, he drove across the Northwest, crossed the Hindu Kush and captured Kabul. The defence of the frontier was pushed further away from the capital and it was only almost 200 years later that a Nadir Shah breached it, aided no doubt by a pusillanimous and weak Mughal emperor, Mohammed Shah Rangila, who had no clue what to do.

Mahadji Scindia not only defeated and made a large British Force surrender in the Western Ghats; he drove to the frontiers of British Indian territory in North India and fought them to a stalemate. The British realised they had reached the limits of their expansion in India for the time being.

Today, we keep strengthening our defences against terrorist groups who merrily come and bomb our economic capital Mumbai, raid our Parliament, set up terrorist networks and bomb our cities, question our sovereignty and appear a helplessly divided country of one billion people terrorised into defensive postures. A diplomatic and armed offensive is far from our minds. It is the same old Panipat mindset. Akbar, Scindia, Rajaraja Chola, Allaudin Khilji and Indira Gandhi are examples of Indian rulers who dared to defy the status quo and changed history in the process. Examples we can follow.

A fourth area one needs to touch upon is the strange phenomenon Indians have of letting others tell us what our history is. We were never great writers of history and what we had of our ancient history was largely swept away in fire and destruction over centuries of invasions. But we suffer from some strange notions which are inexplicable, to say the least.

For example, a lot of Indians firmly believe that there was never ever a country called India and the British united and integrated us. This comes from another notion many carry that a country like India could only exist in its current version of a landed territory ruled by a democratic parliamentary brand of government. There is a mistaken belief that India as a unified entity was gifted to us by a benevolent British nation.

India has existed as a nation from ancient times ruled by monarchs. And frankly so have other nations—be it Great Britain, China, Egypt among others. Parliamentary democracy ruling a country is a recent phenomenon in history, only a few hundred years old. All nations have been ruled and have existed as nations ruled by omnipotent monarchs. Ancient texts of India mention Chakravarthin rulers who ruled as Universal Monarchs—Mandhata, Sagar, Janamejaya and Bharat to name a few. These universal monarchs have been mentioned as having conquered large parts of Bharatvarsha and maybe lands beyond, and enjoyed universal sovereignty, welding the country into one. The earliest historically recorded empire in Indian history is the Maurya empire set up by Chandragupta Maurya in the fourth century BC. It was carried forward by his successors and then Guptas and Harshavardhana. After him, the Pratiharas, Rashtrakutas and Palas had in turn ruled over large parts of India, formidable almost pan-Indian empires.

This tradition was later carried on by the Mauryas, Guptas, Muslim Sultans and Mughals. The British only repeated what the earlier monarchs achieved over the past centuries. Since ancient times, India on numerous occasions has been one country ruled by universal monarchs.

The history of China and its timelines have curiously been like India's. It expanded as one huge empire, then lost unity, then expanded again. The regions of Xijiang have been as often out of Chinese grip as they have been in it. It has depended upon the strength of the central Chinese empire. Tibet has been only a recent acquisition for China and that too tenuous at best until the Chinese invaded it in 1950s.

On the 50th anniversary of our independence from the British, we were desperately explaining to journalists of that country whether we are a failure or success as a country. What parameters decide success or failure of a country? If you do not write your own history but let others tell you whether you had a civilisation or not, how advanced it was or not, whether you were a country or not, then you are condemned to a status where not only the world but you yourself would question your integrity. So we sit patiently and explain to the world why Kashmir cannot be independent or given to Pakistan and how it is a part of India. It is the same with Arunachal Pradesh vis a vis China. This is because deep in our minds we seem to doubt whether we have a right to continue as a nation since we think we were not one historically. An emaciated neighbour, considered a failed state world over, can question our national integrity while we rush to reassure them of theirs.

And because of such notions, we ourselves depict our history as mythology. We would be ready to believe any fable from the West as true but what is quoted as history in our own religious texts is mythology for us. Even today, Indians continue to call Saraswati a mythical river. What the ancient texts described as "Naditamme Ambitamme" with geographical positioning, has in all probability been proven to exist by geological, satellite and various other scientific methods by not only Indians but foreigners, the Americans being notable among them.

If the finding of the ancient Saraswati river bed is true, then a lot that has been described in our ancient texts about the people and times may be correct. And it is Saraswati too and not only Indus that could have been the cradle of India's ancient civilisation from where ancient Indian empires would have blossomed out under Chakravarthins. Events written in our texts described as having happened around it from Vedic to Mahabharata times could be correct.

Any other country would have jumped at the chance and launched massive archaeological excavations to understand the timelines and remains of our ancient civilisation, but we have hardly made a move. A nation that does not move vigourously to establish its historical credentials, its ancient lineage, its civilisations, its empires, customs and culture would always doubt its existence as a perennially existing ancient nation and its contribution to the world. And therefore it would always have a defensive mindset. It would at times weaken and fail to defend its freedom and integrity.

Unfortunately, we also have this intense desire to believe that our internal quarrels are far more important than the threat from a neighbouring nation. For Ambhi it was more important to downgrade Porus and ally with Alexander. The quarrel between Prithviraj and Jaichand was far more important to them than the threat from Ghori. Ultimately both perished. The Mughals fought their intricate courtroom battles neglecting Kabul and let Nadir Shah in. The Marathas and Tipu fought each other and the British triumphed. Holkar fought Scindia and both were decimated by the British.

Even today, we fight internally on whether those who killed our soldiers are Pakistani soldiers or terrorists. How does it matter so long as they come from that side of the border? We squabble over a federal versus a central character of our nation and the Naxalite problem is eating into the country.

The need of the hour is to have an inclusive character to our country. We are not Hindus, Muslims, Sikhs, Christians. Our history has been very complex. Over centuries and millennia, various people have been added to our land mass and become Indians. But we have always been a country the world has coveted. We have always been India. We cannot have a one-sixth Muslim population and not carry it along with us. We also cannot have further division of the country and remain strong and united. We cannot allow fissiparous tendencies to exist. Once such a process begins, it might accelerate. We have a Naxalite problem because large numbers of our countrymen have been denied inclusive growth.

To sum up, we need to watch out for factors that inhibit the rise of a strong centrally-governed India that grows economically, educationally, militarily, and culturally in an inclusive manner. History has shown that whenever we have been governed centrally in a strong manner we have prospered. Factors that hold us back are our lack of sense of our own history, our tendency to think sub-nationally, our inclination to focus more on internecine squabbles than the foreign threat, our lack of defence preparedness, our defensive mindset, corruption, our inability to carry all sections of society along and the lack of willingness to strengthen factors that enhance our unity.

If we handle these factors, we will emerge as the leading nation of the world. Otherwise history will repeat itself.

Appendix

Chronology of Key Events

712	Mohammed Bin Qasim defeats Raja Dahir of Sindh and establishes Muslim rule foothold in India
1000-1027	Invasions of Sultan Mahmud of Ghazni that ravaged India
1178	Sultan Mohammed Ghori defeated by King Mularaja II of Gujarat
1190-91	King Prithviraj Chauhan defeats Sultan Mohammed Ghori at Tarain in the battle for Delhi
1192	Sultan Mohammed Ghori defeats King Prithviraj Chauhan at Tarain at another battle for Delhi
1193	Sultan Mohammed Ghori defeats and kills King Jaichand of Kanauj at the Battle of Chandwar, effectively decimating Hindu resistance in the Ganga-Yamuna plains
1206-1287	Slave dynasty Sultanate in Delhi
1290	Jalaluddin Khilji captures the throne of Delhi
1296	Allauddin Khilji ascends to the Delhi Sultanate throne in 1296 after disposing off Jalaluddin Khilji
1297-1308	Sultan Allaudin Khilji defeats repeat Mongol invasions on Delhi at successive battles for Delhi
1320	Sultan Ghiyasuddin Tughlaq ascends the throne of Delhi as the Tughlaq dynasty replaces the Khiljis

1398	Taimur Lang defeats Sultan Mahmud Shah Tughlaq's forces in the Battle of Delhi, setting the stage for the worst ever sack and massacre of Delhi
1450	Sultan Bahlol Lodhi ascends the throne of Delhi, putting the famous Lodhi dynasty in power
1526	Babar, the king at Kabul, defeats Sultan Ibrahim Lodhi at Panipat at the critical Battle of Delhi, establishing the Mughal empire
1556	Hemu defeats Tardi Beg, the Mughal general, at Tughlaqabad to capture Delhi and ascend the throne as King Hemchandra Vikramaditya
1556	Mughal forces commanded by Ali Quli and Bairam Khan defeat and kill Hemu's forces at the Second Battle of Panipat, a battle for Delhi that effectively re-establishes the Mughal empire in India for over 200 years more
1658	Battle of Samugarh where Aurangzeb defeats Dara Shikoh and settles who would next rule India from Delhi
1707	A critical Battle for Delhi is fought at Jajau after the death of Aurangzeb where Muazzam defeats and kills Azam Tara and is enthroned at Delhi as King Bahadur Shah I
1712	Jahandar Shah defeats Azimushshan at Lahore and wins the battle for Delhi to succeed Bahadur Shah,a worthless Emperor, with whom begins the decline in the prestige of the Mughal emperor
1713	Farrukh Siyar defeats Jahandar Shah and captures Delhi to become the next Mughal emperor. After this, the Mughal emperor becomes a puppet of *vazirs*, a major inflexion point for the Mughal empire.
1719	Mohammed Shah (Rangila) ascends the throne of Delhi. His rule is marked by neglect of administration and frontier defences
1739	Nadir Shah invades through the Northwestern

	frontier and descends on Delhi. He defeats and captures the Mughal emperor, Mohammed Shah, at Karnal and comes to Delhi. He conducts a brutal and unparalleled loot of Delhi, impoverishing the Mughal empire. He carries away the Kohinoor and the Peacock Throne to Persia
1757	Lord Clive defeats Nawab Siraj ud-daulah at Plassey, establishing a large British foothold in East India, an event considered by many to be the foundation of a British Empire in India
1761	Ahmad Shah Abdali defeats Maratha forces led by Sadashiv Bhao camped at Panipat in the battle for Delhi, decimating Maratha ambitions for a decade
1764	The British army led by Hector Munro defeats Nawab Shujauddaulah of Oudh and his allies at the famous Battle of Buxar, giving the British ingress into the Gangetic heartland beyond East India, setting the stage for their later confrontation with the Marathas for paramount power in India
1779	Maratha forces under General Mahadji Scindia defeat and force a British surrender
1794	Death of Mahadji Scindia, ending a major roadblock in the path of the British to capture India
1799	Defeat and death of Tipu Sultan of Mysore at the hands of Arthur Wellesley, later to become famous as the Duke of Wellington
1803	British forces led by Lord Lake defeat Maratha forces led by General Louis Burquoin, displacing Marathas with the British as the protectors of the Mughal emperor, Shah Alam
1857	India's First War of Independence starts with the troops outbreak at Meerut in May, preceded by the Mangal Pandey incident in March at Barrackpore
May 1857	Sepoys from Meerut enter the Red Fort, kill

	the British and install the Mughal emperor back in power
September 1857	The British recapture Delhi in a one-week battle for Delhi after storming the Kashmiri Gate bastion
1859	Tatya Tope captured and executed by the British

Bibliography

Ahmed, Syed Sami, *The End of Muslim Rule in India*, Justice Kayani Memorial Law Society, 1997.

Bhargava, M.L., *Hemu and His Times (Afghans vs. Mughals)*, Reliance Publishing House, 1991.

———, *Saga of 1857: Success and Failures*, Reliance Publishing House, 1992.

Chenoy, Shama Mitra, *Shahjahanabad: A City of Delhi, 1638–1857*, Munshiram Manoharlal Publishers Pvt. Ltd., 1998.

Cooper, Randolf G. S., *The Anglo Maratha Campaigns and the Contest for India*, Cambridge University Press, 2005.

Dalrymple, William, *The Last Mughal: The Fall of a Dynasty, Delhi, 1857*, Viking, Penguin Books Ltd., 2006.

Dalvi, Brig. J.P., *Himalayan Blunder*, Natraj Publishers, 2010.

Danielou, Alain, *A Brief History of India*, Inner Traditions India Home Office, 2003.

David, Saul, *The Indian Mutiny, 1857*, Viking Penguin Group, 2002.

Dowson, John, *A Classical Dictionary of Hindu Mythology and Religion, Geography, History and Literature*, Rupa & Co., 1989.

Duff, James Grant, *History of the Mahrattas*, Low Price Publications.

Dutta, Pushan Kumar, *Relics of the Lesser Mughals: A Retrospect*, UBS Publishers Distributors Pvt. Ltd., 2005.

Eraly, Abraham, *The Last Spring: The Lives and Times of the Great Mughals,* Published in Viking by Penguin Books India (P) Ltd., 1997.

Hansen, Waldemar, *The Peacock Throne: The Drama of Mogul India,* Motilal Banarsidass, 1986.

Hearn, Gordon Risley, *The Seven Cities of Delhi*, S.B.W Publishers, 1997.

Hibbert, Christopher, *The Great Mutiny: India 1857*, Penguin, 2000.

Inamdar, Nagnath, *Pratighaat*, Bhartiya Gyanpeeth, 2006.

Irvine, William, *Later Mughals*, Munshiram Manoharlal Publishers Pvt. Ltd., 1996.

Keay, John, *China: A History*, Harper Press, 2008.

Keay, Julia, *Farzana: The Tempestuous Life and Times of Begum Sumru*, HarperCollins Publishers India, 2013.

Khushalani, Gobind, *Chachanamah Retold: An Account of the Arab Conquest of Sindh*, Promilla & Co. Publishers, 2006.

Kumar, Suphal, *Delhi: City of Yoginis*, Pilgrims Publishing, 2006.

Majumdar, R.C., *Ancient India*, Motilal Banarsidass, 2015.

Malleson, Colonel G.B., *The Decisive Battles of India: From 1746 to 1849 Inclusive*, Low Price Publications.

Manucci, Niccolao, *A Pepys of Mogul India (1653- 1708)*, Srishti Publishers & Distributors, 1999.

Maxwell, Neville, *India's China War*, Natraj Publishers, 1970.

Misra, Amaresh, Mangal Pandey: The True History of an Indian Revolutionary, Rupa & Co., 2005.

Mukherjee, Rudrangshu, *Mangal Pandey: Brave Martyr or Accidental Hero?*, Penguin Books India, 2005.

Mukherji Dr. Radha Kumud, *Hindu Civilization*, Bharatiya Vidya Bhavan.

Nath, Major General Rajendra, PVSM, *Military Leadership in India*, Lancers Books, 1990.

Nirmal, Anjali, *The Decisive Battles of Indian History*, Pointer Publishers, 1999.

Palsokar, Col. R. D., *Baji Rao: An Outstanding Cavalry General*, Reliance Publishing House, 1995.

Patil, Vishwas, *Panipat*, Bharatiya Gyanpeeth.

Paul, E. Jaiwant, *Rani of Jhansi Lakshmi Bai*, Lotus Collection Roli Books (P) Ltd., 1997.

Peck, Lucy, *Delhi: A Thousand Years of Building*, The Lotus Collection, Roli Books Pvt. Ltd., 2005.

Qanungo, Prof. K.R., *A History of the Jats*, Originals, 2003.

Rathbone, Julian, *The Mutiny: A Novel*, Little Brown, 2007.

Rawlinson, H.G., *An Account of the Last Battle of Panipat and of the Events Leading to it* (Casi Rajs Pandit), Humphrey Milford Oxford University Press, 1926.

Raychaudhuri, Hemchandra, *Political History of Ancient India*, Oxford University Press, 1997.

Robinson, Francis, *The Mughal Emperors and the Islamic Dynasties of India, Iran and Central Asia*, Thames & Hudson Ltd., 2007.

Sandhu, Major General Gurcharan Singh, *A Military History of Medieval India,* Vision Books Pvt. Ltd., 2003.

———, *A Military History of Ancient India*, Vision Books Pvt. Ltd., 2000.

Sarkar, Jadunath, *The Fall of the Mughal Empire*, Orient Blackswan Pvt. Ltd., 1991.

———, *A Short History of Aurangzib*, Orient Blackswan Pvt. Ltd., 2009.

Sen, Surendranath, *1857*, Published by the Director, Publications Division, Ministry of I & B, Government of India.

Sethi, R.S., *Forgotten Delhi from a Heritage Walker's Diary*, Vitasta Publishing Pvt. Ltd., 2009.

Sharma, L.P., *History of Medieval India, 1000–1740 AD*, Konark Publishers Pvt. Ltd., 1987.

Singh, Amarinder, *The Last Sunset: The Rise and Fall of the Lahore Durbar*, Lotus Collection, Roli Books Pvt. Ltd., 2010.

Singh, Khushwant, *Delhi: A Novel*, Penguin Books India, 1990.

Singh, Upinder, *Ancient Delhi*, Oxford University Press, 1999.

Spear Percival, Narayani Gupta, R.E. Frykenburg, *The Delhi Omnibus*, Oxford University Press, 2002.

———, *A History of India*, Vol. 2, Penguin Books, 1990.

Tope, Parag, *Tatya Tope's Operation Red Lotus*, Rupa & Co., 2010.

Versaikar, Vishnu Bhatt Godshe, *1857: The Real Story of the Great Uprising*, Mrinal Pande (Trans.), HarperCollins Publishers.

About the Author

Rajeev Katyal is an alumnus of IIM Kolkata, Delhi College of Engineering and St. Columba's High School. A veteran of the Human Resource Development industry, he has over thirty-one years' experience in the field of Education and Skill Development.

He has written, spoken and advised on various education and training forums. He is a member of the School Education Committees of both the Confederation of Indian Industry as well as the Federation of Indian Chamber of Commerce and Industry.

As Director Education at Microsoft, he led Microsoft initiatives in the Education sector of India, also interacting with leading Education bodies and authorities on policy and education initiatives. He has also led several Education and Training businesses at NIIT, travelling the length and breadth of India to implement large scale training programs. Today he leads a chain of schools in India and Japan called the Global Indian International Schools, virtually setting up and running schools from scratch to full functionality. Visiting 25 countries and setting up NIIT in 16 of them is an achievement he is proud of.

As a much travelled man across 30 countries and having covered the length and breadth of India, he has had a wide exposure but finds no place in the world more fascinating than his own country, India. A man fond of intense reading and internet surfing, he finds Indian history fascinating. He believes Indian history has to be written by Indians more than by outsiders. Only then will a body of knowledge on Indian history written from an Indian perspective will emerge that Indians can learn from. There is much to be discovered about India's past and what it can teach India today.

Rajeev is of the opinion that Indian history should be written in such a way that young Indians, history buffs and serious students of the subject find it readable and it changes their perspective of India and develops greater national pride.

Rajeev lives in Noida with his wife Preeti and two sons Arjun and Shiva.

About Indus Source Books

Indus Source Books is a niche, independent book publisher in Mumbai passionately committed to publishing good and relevant literature. We believe that books are one of the most important mediums of communication and we seek to bring out publications that help to serve the community and the world we live in.

At Indus Source Books, we celebrate the diverse spiritual traditions, culture, and history of the world and present it to our readers in a contemporary format that retains its essential flavour: "Indian Spirit, Universal Wisdom."

Visit our website www.indussource.com for more details.

Indus Source Books
PO Box 6194
Malabar Hill PO
Mumbai 400006
India
www.indussource.com
info@indussource.com